THE BRITISH EMPIRE AND COMMONWEALTH

D1290267

00658

The British Empire and Commonwealth

A SHORT HISTORY

Martin Kitchen
Professor of History
Simon Fraser University, British Columbia

St. Martin's Press
New York

THE BRITISH EMPIRE AND COMMONWEALTH
Copyright © Centre for Distance Education, Simon Fraser University
1994, 1996
All rights reserved. No part of this book may be used or reproduced
in any manner whatsoever without written permission except in the
case of brief quotations embodied in critical articles or reviews.
For information, address:

St. Martin's Press, Scholarly and Reference Division,
175 Fifth Avenue, New York, N.Y. 10010

First published in the United States of America in 1996

Printed in Great Britain

ISBN 0–312–16393–2 (cloth)
ISBN 0–312–16394–0 (paperback)

Library of Congress Cataloging-in-Publication Data
Kitchen, Martin.
The British empire and commonwealth : a short history / Martin
Kitchen.
p. cm.
Includes bibliographical references (p.   ) and index.
ISBN 0–312–16393–2 (cloth). — ISBN 0–312–16394–0 (pbk.)
1. Great Britain—Colonies—History.   2. Commonwealth countries-
–History.   3. Commonwealth of Nations—History.   4. Decolonization-
–History.   5. Imperialism—History.   I. Title.
DA16.K634   1996
325.341—dc20   96–25755
                                                              CIP

Contents

Acknowledgements

This book was written at the suggestion of Dr John Wighton, a most generous patron of Simon Fraser University. I am deeply grateful to him for providing the incentive to look again at the fascinating history of the British Empire and the Commonwealth. We share an enthusiasm for the Commonwealth even though our views on Britain's imperial past differ considerably.

Colin Yerbury removed many obstacles from my way with tact and understanding. Jane Fredeman removed a number of lurid adjectives and toned down some of my more provocative statements. David Barnhill made many helpful suggestions, and Martha McLaren was a sympathetic and wise critic. I am grateful to all of them and, needless to say, all errors and misjudgements are entirely my responsibility.

Martin Kitchen

The publishers wish to thank Oxford University Press for permission to reproduce two maps originally published in *The Oxford History of Britain* edited by Kenneth O. Morgan.

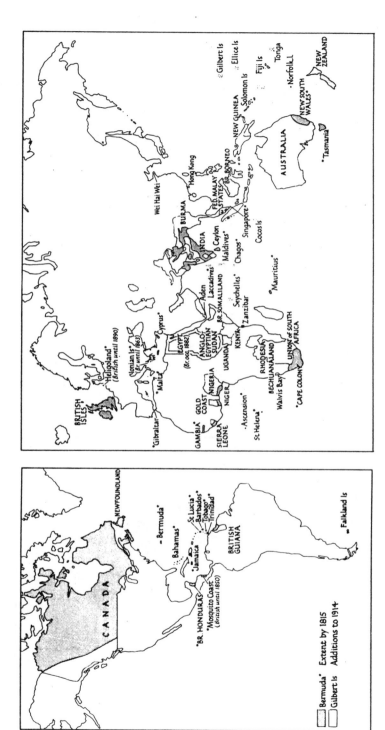

The Expansion of the British Empire 1815–1914

First map (right panel):

NEW ZEALAND
Tonga
Ellice Is
Gilbert Is
Fiji Is
Norfolk I.
Solomon Is
NEW GUINEA
NEW SOUTH WALES
AUSTRALIA
Tasmania
BR. BORNEO
Hong Kong
FED. MALAY STATES
Singapore
Cocos Is
Wei Hai Wei
BURMA
INDIA
Ceylon
Maldives
Chagos
Laccadives
Aden
BR. SOMALILAND
Seychelles
Zanzibar
Mauritius
Cyprus
Helgoland (British until 1890)
Ionian Is (Br. until 1863)
Malta
EGYPT (Br. occ. 1882)
ANGLO-EGYPTIAN SUDAN
KENYA
UGANDA
RHODESIA
BECHUANALAND
UNION of SOUTH AFRICA
Walvis Bay
CAPE COLONY
BRITISH ISLES
Gibraltar
GAMBIA
SIERRA LEONE
GOLD COAST
NIGERIA
NIGER
Ascension
St Helena

Second map (left panel):

NEWFOUNDLAND
CANADA
Bermuda
Bahamas
Jamaica
St Lucia
Barbados
Tobago
Trinidad
BRITISH GUIANA
BR. HONDURAS
Mosquito Coast (British until 1850)
Falkland Is

Bermuda — Extent by 1815
Gilbert Is — Additions to 1914

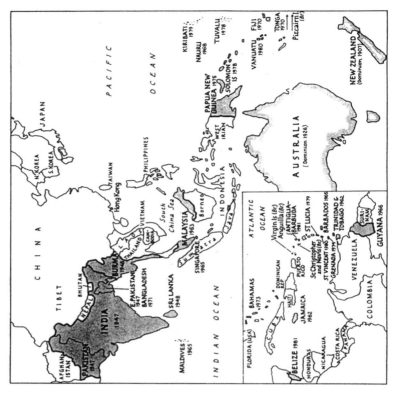

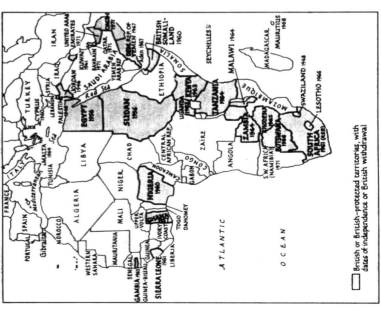

The Retreat from Empire 1947–1980

1 From the First to the Second Empire: 1400s to 1830s

Until the Treaty of Paris ended the Seven Years' War in 1763, Britain's colonies were chiefly in America and the Caribbean; afterwards, they were scattered worldwide. Though dividing the periods before and after 1763 into the "first" and "second" empires is both artificial and somewhat misleading, the terms do make a useful shorthand reference.

The first British Empire in America was not impressive, particularly compared to the great Spanish Empire. It was narrow strip stretching along the eastern seaboard from Halifax, Nova Scotia, to Savannah, Georgia. Exports were modest, and there was a desperate shortage of capital. The plantations in Jamaica, Barbados, and other, smaller Caribbean islands that produced sugar and tobacco were more prosperous, but they were not as advanced as the Spanish colonies of the early eighteenth century. In the southern colonies of Georgia, the Carolinas, and Virginia, there were similar plantations worked by African slaves. The British also prized New York, Maryland, Pennsylvania, New Jersey, and Delaware for their exports of tobacco, timber, and grain. By contrast, they increasingly regarded possession of Massachusetts, Connecticut, Rhode Island, and New Hampshire as a nuisance. These colonies produced little that was needed at home, raided the Newfoundland fishing grounds, traded with rival colonies, and even built their own ships rather than importing them at vast expense from Britain.

The differences between the plantation colonies of the south and the Caribbean and the settlement colonies to the north were dictated by geography, not by differences in political institutions. The British considered all the American colonies to be "dominions." This category was based on the ancient distinction between the "realm" of England, Wales, and later Scotland and the "dominions" of Ireland, the Isle of Man, and the Channel Islands. Dominions were dependencies of the Crown that had their own assemblies, legal systems, and finances. Parliament in Westminster, however, legislated for them, even though they were not represented in it.

In theory, the residents of the American colonies had a status equivalent to that of the Irish or Manx. The Crown delegated its powers in many of the colonies by making them into fiefdoms. Maryland, for example, was granted to Lord Baltimore by Charles I. Some colonies were founded by joint-stock companies, but most of them proved unprofitable and they were soon administered directly by the Crown. By the eighteenth century only Massachusetts, Connecticut, and Rhode

Island could claim "chartered governments," which gave them certain rights and privileges against the Crown and against Parliament. Other colonies, such as Virginia, which no longer enjoyed such rights, nevertheless resolutely claimed that they had not lost them.

Just as the plantation colonies were very similar to those of Spain and Portugal, the society of the settlement colonies closely resembled Britain's. There were an increasingly self-conscious middle class in the towns and sturdily independent farmers on the land. The Amerindians had been pushed back behind the Appalachians and later down the Ohio Valley, and the working class was made up of European immigrants, some of whom had come as indentured labourers. The various attempts to bring the colonies under the closer control of Westminster met with little success. Indeed, efforts to bring order into this patchwork of legal relationships failed, and the American colonists enjoyed a unique freedom from the interference of the metropolitan state. In some of the New England states the governor was elected, so the Crown, whose representative he was in theory, had no power at all. The colonies had representative assemblies and an upper house that was either appointed or elected and that acted as an executive council. Colonists could make and enforce their own laws, provided that they were given royal assent. Because the common law and court system guaranteed the colonists the same freedoms and protection as the British at home, they enjoyed more liberties than the colonists of any other nation. Since the assemblies controlled the purse strings, in some cases even determining whether the governor was to be paid or not, crown appointees had little power. Most of the colonies were thus virtually self-governing.

In Britain there was no clear idea about how to deal with this situation. The Crown was certainly responsible for the administration and defence of the colonies, but no minister or department of state was appointed to do so. The Board of Trade and Plantations, established in 1696, was designed to give advice to the Privy Council. It was not an executive body, and its president did not become a member of the Cabinet until 1768. No attempt was made to co-ordinate the efforts of other departments concerned with colonial affairs, such as the Admiralty or the War Office, the Treasury or the Commissioners of Customs, the Board of Trade or the Post Office. Parliament never turned its attention to drafting a colonial constitution; in fact, it seldom interfered in colonial affairs. Acts of Parliament did not apply to the colonies unless they were expressly included, not even the discriminatory laws against Roman Catholics and Dissenters, so they enjoyed far greater religious toleration abroad than in Britain. A Colonial Department was established in 1768, but it was abolished after the American Revolution to save money. That the colonies had been left pretty much to their own devices is the major reason why there was such a reaction in them when Parliament tried to assert its authority in 1763.

The British government hoped to bring the colonies together to form a powerful commercial empire in which each part would concentrate on doing what it could do best and contribute to the common good. Colonies were not expected to provide unwelcome competition. They were to produce goods that Britain could not, and they were given monopolies for such products. In return, Britain was to have guaranteed markets. Thus, sugar refining in the West Indies was frowned upon, as was the production of iron in New England. Trade between the colonies and other countries was also the subject of complaint, and there was a general feeling that the colonists showed a selfish disregard for British interests.

Under the navigation acts of the seventeenth century, all trade with the colonies had to be in British ships, and "enumerated" goods going to or from colonial ports had to be shipped through an English port regardless of their place of origin or destination. Only those goods that could not be produced in Britain were enumerated; those that were in direct competition with British goods or that could not be exported at a profit were excluded. Masters of vessels engaged in the colonial trade had to post substantial bonds, which they forfeited if they took their cargoes to foreign ports. On leaving colonial ports, they were obliged to pay "plantation duty," which amounted to a pre-payment of the duty paid on entry to a British port.

Industry in the colonies was limited to local needs. Textiles, for example, could not be exported, and the Hat Act of 1732 banned the export of hats from one colony to another. The Iron Act of 1750 encouraged the production of pig iron for the British market but forbade rolling mills and steel furnaces that might compete with British industry. In practice, these measures were not particularly onerous since the eighteenth-century colonies were in no position to compete with British industry. However, the advantages and disadvantages of the system were unequally distributed. Tobacco planters were excluded from profitable European markets, but sugar producers benefited from preferential tariffs. Consumers, both at home and in the colonies, had to foot the bill for colonial administration and defence by paying high prices. On balance, it seems that the colonists got the worst of the deal, but they realized that they had much to gain from being part of a large, prosperous market. In fact, the First Continental Congress specifically stated in the Declaration of Rights that they "cheerfully consent[ed]" to the navigation acts because they benefited all members of the Empire.

This tolerable state of affairs began to break down as a result of events in North America. Owing to the pressures of a rising population and increased immigration, the colonies began to search for new land across the Appalachians. Their movements led to conflicts with the Indians, to jurisdictional disputes between the colonies, and to confrontations with the French, who had built a line of

3

fortifications from New Orleans to the Great Lakes that hindered British expansion westwards. Between the weak British and French forces stood the powerful Iroquois federation, whose existence prevented the outbreak of a colonial war until 1741.

The wars against the French made it essential for the colonies to co-operate with one another and with the British military authorities. Furthermore, as the colonies pressed westwards, their land claims had somehow to be adjudicated. Either they had to work together to settle their differences, or Parliament would have to take charge. When the Albany Congress of 1754—which was convened in the hopes of achieving some form of colonial federation—failed, the British had to step in. But doing so was expensive. The cost of colonial wars, particularly the campaign in Canada, and the administration of the Indian tribes meant that the colonies could no longer expect to enjoy budgetary autonomy.

The process was gradual; it did not start suddenly in 1763. But to the American colonists it seemed like an abrupt break with the past with its "happy and liberal condition," and it served to fuel the discontent that led to the American Revolution.

Between the 1760s and 1830s Britain's Empire went through a period of transition from one made up largely of the self-governing colonies of America to a worldwide nineteenth-century one with politically dependent colonies. A number of factors caused this drastic change. The Americans achieved independence and forced the British to reconsider their attitude towards the Empire. Years of war against France led to massive British colonial gains. India was gradually subjected to British rule, bringing increasing numbers of Asians into the Empire. What remained of the American colonies, in Canada and the Caribbean, had to be reorganized.

The French ambition to link their possessions in Louisiana—centred on New Orleans—and their settlements in Canada by means of a line of forts along the Ohio to the Great Lakes presented the British with a serious challenge. In Canada, the French had settled around Québec and Montreal, but in addition to the settlers there were explorers, trappers, adventurers (the "coureurs du bois"), and, equally daring, Jesuit missionaries, who went to remarkable lengths to save Indian souls. The French made skilful use of the rivers and gained valuable experience in unconventional warfare in the course of their endless fights with the Indians. On Cape Breton Island they had built the fortress of Louisbourg, seen by the British as an insolent threat to their Atlantic shipping.

In 1745 Louisbourg was taken by Governor Shirley of Massachusetts in a bold action, but the British government made a serious mistake by not permitting him to continue his campaign to drive the French out of Canada. To make matters worse, Louisbourg was handed back to the French at the Treaty of Aix-la-Chapelle

(1748), which marked the end of the War of Austrian Succession. That the British got Madras in return was cold comfort for the American colonists. The French strengthened their defensive line, building such forts as Frontenac and Niagara on Lake Ontario, Presqu'île on Lake Erie, and, most important of all, Fort Duquesne on the Ohio. The French also won over many Indian tribes, for they had no desire to see the English colonists move westwards.

In 1754 George Washington took Fort Duquesne with the aim of making it possible for Virginians to cross the Ohio and for the Ohio Company to develop the valley, but the French soon recaptured it. Under General Braddock the British attempted to take the fort again, but they refused to listen to Washington's military advice. Marching in the open in close formation, they were easy prey for the French and Indians, who picked them off from the cover of rocks and trees. The Indians were greatly encouraged by this easy victory and began a series of bloodthirsty raids on British settlements. Meanwhile, the French sent the Marquis of Montcalm from France with heavy reinforcements to support the Indian attacks on the British frontier forts.

The British still had their powerful navy, and they were able to isolate the French forces in New France, but the situation was insecure. Prime Minister William Pitt, the elder, took over the responsibility for the war at a time when it was going very badly for the British from India to America. He provided a new sense of direction and purpose, and soon the British achieved a series of triumphant successes. A small force retook Fort Duquesne with little difficulty. General Abercromby and Lord Howe advanced up the Hudson from New York to Ticonderoga and Lake Champlain. A naval force approached Louisbourg. The attack on Ticonderoga was badly bungled, and Howe and most of his men were killed. However, Louisbourg fell to a British force led by General Amherst. His second-in-command was General James Wolfe, and Captain James Cook was in charge of navigation.

Wolfe was an unconventional general, and he was quick to realize that the British had much to learn from the French and the Indians about how to fight colonial wars. Although he was only thirty-three, he was given command of the attack on Québec in 1759. Cook navigated up the St. Lawrence without the aid of charts. Wolfe said: "Put me and my army on the Heights of Abraham and French America is ours"; but the problem of how to get west of the French citadel remained. An attempt along the north bank of the St. Lawrence and over the St. Charles River failed. Then, while the fleet continued to bombard the Beauport lines on the north bank, convincing Montcalm that they were about to launch another attack, Wolfe landed further down river, scaled the heights up a narrow path, and deployed his army on the plain. Montcalm was thus surprised and defeated. Both Wolfe and

5

Montcalm fell in the battle. The following year Amherst continued the campaign, taking Montreal. Thus, by 1760 the French Empire in North America had come to an abrupt end.

Once the American colonies became independent, the economic situation for the British in America was precarious. The Caribbean colonies continued much as before, but they had always depended on America for food and timber and as a market for their sugar. The British now feared that Caribbean trade would fall into the hands of the Americans and that they would lose the "long-haul" route to America, which they saw as an essential training route for the Royal Navy and a guaranteed source of income for the merchant marine. The British therefore decided to keep the Americans out of the Caribbean and continued to impose the navigation acts, which remained in force until the middle of the next century.

Elsewhere, the British did not fear the competition of foreign carriers. Provided they did not try to take over the trade between the colonies and Britain or intercolonial traffic, foreign ships were welcomed in British ports. British merchants sold goods to foreigners that they were unable to sell at home, where industries, such as Lancashire cotton, were protected. This relatively easy-going attitude was reflected in continuing lax colonial administration. Little attempt was made to bring the colonies under the close supervision of Whitehall, in spite of such measures as the India Act of 1784 or the creation of a colonial department within the Department of War and Colonies in 1801. Even in India the governors of Calcutta, Madras, and Bombay, although given broad policy directions to follow and subject to recall for failing to satisfy the home authorities, were essentially left to their own devices.

The story of the British in India had begun on 31 January 1600, when Queen Elizabeth I granted a charter to the East India Company. Although its prospects did not at first look very promising, it was soon making vast profits. At least until the middle of the eighteenth century, the Company was a fairly traditional commercial operation. It was run by a court of twenty-four directors, who elected the chairman and his deputy. The directors were in turn elected by the Court of Proprietors, which consisted of stockholders with investments of more than £500. Shareholders had every reason to be satisfied with the Company's performance. In the late seventeenth century, dividends averaged 22 per cent, and although they declined to about 8 per cent by the middle of the eighteenth century, these were extremely impressive returns by the standards of the day.

Some of the decline in dividends resulted from the increasing restrictions imposed on imports from India in order to protect the British textile industry. The

Company compensated for some of the loss of these markets by importing tea from China, and the tea was paid for, at least in part, by the export to China of goods from India that could no longer be sent to England.

The period from the 1740s to the 1820s saw the scattered seaboard possessions of the British East India Company expanded and consolidated into a powerful imperial state, divided, for administrative purposes, into three "Presidencies" with their capitals at the major trading ports of Calcutta, Bombay, and Madras. The involvement of the EIC in the economic and political life of India began with its participation as customer, supplier of specie, and maritime carrier in Indian trade and banking and through partnerships between company officials and Indian merchants. This involvement increased rapidly from the 1740s, when trade rivalry between France and Britain in India was ignited into a military conflict by war between the two states in Europe. Necessity and experience improved the Company's military capacity to a point at which its potential as an ally was recognized by Indian rulers and merchant groups. By 1765, participation in the economic and military affairs of eastern India had brought the Company political control of Bengal. British subjection of the major Indian powers in the south and west of the sub-continent, which originated again in the official and unofficial involvement of company agents in Indian economic matters, was largely achieved during the governor generalships of Marquis Wellesley (1798–1805) and the Marquis of Hastings (1812–1823) by means of a combination of diplomatic manoeuvres and expensive military campaigns.

The French and then the British began to intervene with their relatively well-trained, well-equipped, and—most important—regularly paid Indian troops in the dynastic conflicts of Indian rulers in the 1740s, the object being to obtain extra trading privileges by supporting the successful candidate for the throne. Robert Clive, a young East India Company clerk who had come to India in 1744, seized the opportunity provided by Anglo-French rivalry in the Carnatic to advance his career and, exchanging his pen for a sword, soon proved himself a soldier of genius. Clive's victory at the battle of Arcot (1751), the capital of the Carnatic, was a turning point for British fortunes. He marched from Madras with two hundred English soldiers, three hundred sepoys, and eight officers, four of whom were civilians temporarily seconded to the expedition. Arcot was garrisoned by twelve hundred men belonging to the French-backed ruler of the Carnatic, Chanda Sahib, who abandoned the fort on Clive's arrival but beseiged the British force once they were inside. It was late August 1751. These five hundred men and eight officers held out for two and a half months, but there were only two hundred men capable of active service to repel the final assault by Chanda Sahib on 14 November. Chanda Sahib's force now

7

outnumbered the British by nearly ten to one. The defence, however, was successful, and the following day the beseiging army marched away. It has been claimed that either Chanda Sahib himself or his troops had been bribed to raise the seige, but the apparent victory was significant not so much for the capture of the capital of the Carnatic or the set-back it imposed on the French, but rather for the prestige acquired by the British in doing so. From then on Indians began to see the British Company as a power to be reckoned with and, therefore, a power to be dealt with and propitiated. For the next two hundred years, until the granting of independence to India in 1947, the British presence in India depended on her ability to attract the co-operation of Indian groups and individuals and also, to a great extent, on her ability to convey the impression that British power was invincible.

In June 1756, the new young ruler of Bengal, Siraj-ud-daula, resenting increased British control over the trade and wealth of Calcutta and, particularly, the fortifications they had built in anticipation of hostilities with the French, marched on Calcutta with a large army. The British panicked, and led by the governor, Roger Drake, most officials fled to the ships at anchor in the river, abandoning about two hundred men and women in the town, which was easily taken by Siraj. One hundred and forty-six British prisoners were taken, and all but twenty-three died of heat, suffocation, or untended wounds when they were locked up for the night in one small room: "the Black Hole of Calcutta." It was not delberate cruelty on the part of Siraj: he had merely ordered the prisoners to be confined, but the British demanded retribution, and Clive was sent from Madras to exact it.

In 1757 Calcutta was retaken, the French were driven out of their trading base at Chandernagore because it was regarded as being dangerously close to Calcutta, and a group of Hindu bankers persuaded the not-too-reluctant British in Bengal to join them in removing Siraj from the throne and replacing him with an elderly general, Mir Jafar. Siraj was ambitious and resented the limitations on his power implicit in the privileges of foreign traders as well as their domination of the Bengal economy. Unfortunately for him, however, the most powerful local businessmen identified their interest with those of the East India Company. As a contemporary observer put it, the ultimate achievement of Siraj-ud-daula, who managed to alienate nearly everyone who might had supported him, was to make even Frenchmen hope that the English would defeat him. With the support of Clive, Mir Jafar defeated him at the battle of Plassey. The Company was now very much the power behind the throne and saw itself as a kingmaker. When Mir Jafar proved less amenable to company control than had been anticipated, he was forced to abdicate, and his son-in-law, Mir Kassim, was set up as ruler. The British were rewarded by Kassim with the right to collect and keep the land revenue of three Bengali provinces, but the combination of political power and economic opportunity led to corruption. Mir Kassim resisted the unfair advantages British traders now engineered for themselves in regard to customs dues and protested the coercive methods they used to acquire goods from Indian producers. He was deposed by company officials in Calcutta and then defeated at the battle of Baksar. The Company now controlled the whole of Bengal.

Clive had returned to Britain in 1760 with a gift of £234,000 from Mir Jafar. He was elected to the House of Commons and elevated to the Irish peerage. In 1765, however, he was persuaded by the directors of the East India Company in London, alarmed at the rapacious and irresponsible behaviour of their servants in Bengal, to return to India to "cleanse the Augean stables." Armed with quite extensive discretionary power, Clive had some success in reforming the worst practices of company officials. But he was there for too short a period to have a permanent effect, and by the 1770s, rising anxiety over the state of the Company's finances as well as public and government disgust at the corruption, led in 1773 to government intervention in the affairs of the Company.

During the first half of the eighteenth century, the East India Company was a prosperous and respectable commercial and financial corporation—both the biggest and most complicated trading organization in the country and, together with the Bank of England, the centre of a financial market that was to dominate international, as well as domestic, finance well into the nineteenth century. It had important links with the political as well as the financial world of London: there were always a few members of Parliament with company interests and a few directors who were also M.P.'s, attracted by the prospect of government contracts and other profitable rewards for their support of the government, and for much of the eighteenth century the Company was an essential contributor of long-term loans to the British government. During the 1760s and 1770s, however, despite access to the revenue of the whole of Bengal, the Company's administrative and defence costs began to outweigh its profits. At the same time some enterprising company servants were returning to Britain as "nabobs"—men with vast Indian fortunes gained in dubious ways, who were able to buy the extensive land-holdings in Britain that gave access to political power. In 1772, the year before the Company was obliged to apply for the renewal of its charter, it found itself forced to ask the government for a loan of a million pounds to stave off bankruptcy. The government set up committees of inquiry into company affairs whose reports were highly critical, and the following year, although the Company's charter was renewed, the government also passed a Regulating Act, which attempted to bring some order into Indian affairs.

Warren Hastings, a man from a poor Tory family who had risen through the company ranks to become governor of Bengal, was appointed governor general of Bengal with some authority over the activities of the subordinate presidencies of Madras and Bombay. He was given the casting vote over a council of four men, appointed in Britain, not India, and a new Supreme Court of Justice was set up in Calcutta, which would administer English law to British citizens; it had been impossible to bring English delinquents before the existing Muslim or Hindu courts. Indians continued to be tried under Muslim or Hindu law. Hastings had a deep admiration for Indian culture, he was a good administrator, and during his first two years of office he introduced a new order and harmony in to the Company's affairs. His commercial reforms were quite successful; his attempts to organize the revenue collection less so, but his main problems were caused by his relationship with the members of his Council, one of whom, Philip Francis, thought he should be the governor general rather than Hastings. Their differences made it impossible to establish any consistency in internal policy and divided the company service, both in Bengal and Britain, into factions. In 1780, the Company's retention of its possessions in southern and western India began to seem doubtful; the Bombay presidency's army had surrendered to a Maratha force in 1779, and in 1780 two Madras armies were defeated by Haidar Ali of Mysore, whose armies proceeded to ravage the Presidency up to the walls of Madras itself. Although decisive action by Hastings saved Bombay and Madras for the East India Company at this time, concern in Britain was mounting over the Company's arbitrary government and continued insolvency as well as its military ineptitude, and two special House of Commons committees were established, headed by Edmund Burke and Henry Dundas, to investigate charges of tyranny and corruption in Bengal and the incompetent conduct of foreign policy and war. In 1784, the India Act, giving the Crown greater control over British Indian affairs, was passed by the administration of the younger William Pitt.

In 1785, Hastings returned to England to face attacks in the House of Commons led by Burke. Four controversial incidents led to his impeachment before British Parliament. First, he sent, in opposition to company policy, a brigade of company "sepoys" (Indian Soldiers) to aid his ally, the wazir of Oudh, against an attack from neighbouring Rohilkhand by Afghan warriors who were settled in that region. Second, when accused of bribery by the members of his Council, he responded by charging his enemies' chief witness, Nand Kumar, with forgery. Kumar was tried, found guilty, and executed—a legal but excessively harsh punishment. Third, short of money for government purposes, his insistent demand for excessive taxes from the Raja of Benares goaded Chait Singh into rebellion, which led to the seizure of his lands. These were bestowed on Chait Singh's nephew, who was obliged to pay the Company a greatly increased tribute in return. Fourth, for the same reason, Hastings exerted pressure on the Begums of Oudh, the mother and grandmother of the Nawab. Hastings's enemies labelled this arbitrary despotism, and in February 1788, Hastings was brought to trial before the British Parliament. Edmund Burke wound himself into a rhetorical fury in an opening speech that ended with an all-purpose charge: "in the name of human nature itself, in the name of both sexes, in the name of every age, in name of every rank, I impeach the common enemy and oppressor of all!"

In spite of the oratory of Burke and other great speakers, Hastings was acquitted of all charges when the verdict finally came down in April 1795, but he was a broken man. He lived in retirement for many years, provided with a pension by the East India Company, but then he returned to the House of Commons once more in triumph in 1813 as a respected witness on Indian affairs at the debate on the renewal of the Company's charter. He had served his country, the Company, and India to the best of his considerable abilities; his impeachment reflected changing British attitudes towards government and Empire. His accusers wanted scrupulously honest government under firm parliamentary control—in Britain was well as in India. Hastings was tried as an arbitrary despot: the scapegoat for the old irresponsible Empire.

The growing involvement of the government in the Empire, which had previously been largely left to exploitation by individual adventurers and commercial companies, was dictated mostly by strategic considerations. Britain was involved in wars with Spain and Holland and, above all, with France. With her powerful navy, Britain attacked her enemies' colonies in order to distract them from their efforts on the continent of Europe and to gain bargaining counters for the eventual peace settlement. The British kept some colonies purely for their strategic value; they kept Acadia, for example, in the 1713 Treaty of Utrecht in order to defend New England against the French. Canada they regarded as a worthless tract of land, but they wanted to keep the French out of North America, and they also had a strong emotional reason for holding on to it—so that it should not seem that the popular hero General Wolfe had died in vain. Other colonies, such as Guadeloupe, were returned to France precisely because they were prosperous. British colonists elsewhere in the Caribbean feared the competition of Guadeloupe sugar within the protective imperial system.

In addition, Britain kept Dominica as a naval base and took Florida from Spain to complete the British occupation of the eastern seaboard. They took the Cape of Good Hope from the Dutch to guard the route to India and to provide security for the South Seas fisheries, now dominated by the British, as well as the

11

route to Australasia. The wine and sugar the Cape produced was also useful to have in reserve in case the Caribbean islands were lost. The colony provisioned ships stopping off on their way to India and the South Seas as well as the colonies in Mauritius and St. Helena. The same concern for the security of India dictated the occupation of Mauritius, the Seychelles, and the Maldives. The British kept Ceylon (now Sri Lanka) when they seized it from the Dutch because of the harbour at Trincomalee. Its cinnamon and pearls were an incidental bonus. Attempts to end the system of forced labour for cinnamon picking based on the caste system failed, and it was agreed that the Ceylonese were not sufficiently developed to be allowed free trade and freedom of contract. Britain bought Penang in 1786 as a strategic base guarding the route to China, and it acquired Singapore and Malacca from the Dutch for similar reasons. Indonesia, however, which was economically far more important, was handed back to them in 1815.

Few of the new colonies had any commercial significance, and many proved worthless as trade routes, so naval strategy changed. Penang, for example, was soon felt to be a white elephant, commercially worthless and strategically insignificant, undesirable as a settlement colony and a burden on the taxpayers. Singapore was a more suitable port for the China trade and had a population of twenty thousand by 1825. Lord Minto's secretary, Thomas Stamford Raffles, ransacked the royal palace in Java in 1811 and destroyed the authority of the Javanese aristocracy. He was appointed lieutenant-governor of Java, wrote the history of the island, established a settlement in Singapore on his own initiative, and on his final return to England in 1824 founded the London Zoo. Britain handed Java back to the Dutch in 1815, but it had already been penetrated by Chinese traders peddling opium from Bengal and the Dutch were unable to reassert their trade monopoly.

Two oddities among the new colonies were Sierra Leone in west Africa and New South Wales. Sierra Leone was first run by a group of high-minded philanthropists as a home for British slaves freed after Lord Mansfield's historic judgment in the Sommersett case in 1772. The colony was established in 1787, but within twenty years the company could no longer afford to maintain it. The British government took it over reluctantly, for it was unsuitable for settlement and seemed to have little strategic value.

Britain used New South Wales as a penal colony from 1788 onwards because convicts could no longer be sent to American colonies. Other immigration to Australia was encouraged simply to maintain the penal colony, and the expansion of the Empire in the Pacific from the harbour at Sydney was the result of private initiatives rather than of government design. By 1820, population was about eight thousand, of whom about 60 per cent were convicts. The Australian settlers were fiercely independent and interpreted the creed of the freeborn Englishman liberally. In 1805, Captain William Bligh (of *H.M.S. Bounty* fame) was sent to New South Wales to discipline these refractory spirits. They rejected his efforts, mutinied, and threw him into prison. In London the mutiny was taken as an indication of revolutionary discontent, and Lachlan Macquarie was sent out to put it down. He was as successful economically as he was repressive politically. Macquarie helped establish a prosperous yeoman class, built a large number of Anglican churches, controlled grain prices, and expanded trade relations throughout the Pacific. But his actions were not the result of a carefully considered blueprint for colonial development.

These new colonies, unlike the old, were not peopled by emigrants who had gone out of their own accord. Nor were British institutions generally transposed to them; more often, local laws and customs were adopted and modified. The inhabitants, whether native or European, automatically became British subjects, but they were not given the right to enjoy British representative institutions—not that this was a matter of much concern to most of them. The old colonial system survived in the Caribbean, Nova Scotia, and New Brunswick. In Québec, the British installed the old colonial system in the belief that British settlers would remain along the St. Lawrence and not move west where they were bound to come into conflict with Indian tribes. This hope proved to be an illusion, and Québec remained a colony of disaffected francophones. The Québec Act of 1774 gave Roman Catholics political and religious equality and restored French civil law. However, it also provided for an appointed governor with a nominated legislative council. The British colony of Québec was thus given autocratic French institutions, and similar methods of adapting foreign systems of government were applied in other conquered colonies.

After the American Revolution, English-speaking Loyalists moved north. They had no desire to live under French laws and demanded a restoration of the old colonial system. These demands were resisted both by the French, who felt that while the existing system might be autocratic, it was at least French, and by the British government, which felt that the American Revolution might never have happened had the colonists not been given too many rights in their local assemblies. Those who argued that the American Revolution resulted from too little freedom were in a minority, and henceforth the British were determined to keep a tight grip on what they held. As one official said: "It was better to have no colonies at all than not to have them subservient to the maritime strength and commercial interests of Great Britain."

Canada was the testing ground for this new approach. The Canada Act of 1791 divided Nova Scotia by detaching the western part where most of the "United Empire Loyalists" had settled, thus creating the province of New Brunswick.

Québec was also divided in two. Lower Canada, today's Québec, was predominantly French, whereas Upper Canada, now Ontario, was predominantly British. The interests of the strong British minority in Lower Canada clashed with those of the French majority. As merchants, the British wanted a tax on land, but it was resolutely opposed by the landowning French, who felt that import duties were a more suitable means of raising revenue.

Upper and Lower Canada had legislative assemblies elected by freeholders whose lands yielded at least forty shillings per year and legislative councils appointed by the governor. The object was to have conservative bodies that gave little scope for popular expression so that there would be no repeat of the upheaval in the Thirteen Colonies. Since the governors had the right to veto legislation and both provinces were controlled by reactionary cliques, the Family Compact in Upper Canada and the Château Clique in Lower Canada, the legislative assemblies had practically no power. In Lower Canada the French were virtually excluded from the upper house, and criticisms from the French-dominated lower house became increasingly strident. In 1807 the governor, Sir James Craig, suspended the assembly of Lower Canada. Much of the land was given to the Crown or to the Church of England, and favoured members of the ruling cliques also received large grants of land. G. A. Young, writing in 1839, referred to "the mimic sovereigns of Canada [who] enjoyed in a mediate state, some of the prerogatives of royalty." The British made a determined effort to create a strong hereditary class of landowning Anglican office-holders. High prices for timber were maintained by steep tariffs against foreign imports to Britain, and, as a result, land prices were greatly inflated. The settlers, who were coming in increasingly large numbers, found it difficult to buy land and resented the fact that they had to pay exorbitant prices to a privileged élite. As the population increased from one hundred and fifty thousand in 1773 to six hundred thousand in 1830, tensions mounted.

In November 1837 there was an uprising in Lower Canada in protest against the subjugation of the legislative assembly to the governor and his cronies in the legislative council. The rebellion was followed by a similar revolt in Upper Canada, its leader also demanding greater rights for the legislature. The uprisings were minor affairs and quickly crushed, but they caused great concern in Whitehall. The Thirteen Colonies had been lost, it seemed, because they had been given too much latitude. Now it looked as if Canada might be lost because it had been kept on too tight a rein. The rebellions triggered a major debate on the future of the Empire. Some argued that responsible government for the colonies was absurd since it would mean that the British Parliament no longer had any control. Others questioned the need for an Empire. It was expensive and brought few benefits; even the strategic argument was questionable. Overseas bases were needed to protect other colonies, not to defend the British Isles. As Lord Palmerston remarked, if one owned a house in London and another in York, one did not have to own every inn on the way. Thus, the upheavals in Canada in 1837 precipitated a debate over the future of the Empire that was to last for years to come.

Canada was, however, in many ways an oddity, its problems caused by cultural conflicts and the pressure of immigration. Elsewhere, autocratic adminis-trations, flavoured by foreign influences, were the rule. The experience of Québec was a warning that British institutions did not work particularly well in colonies with large foreign populations and a minority of English-speaking immigrants. Further-more, during the Revolutionary and Napoleonic wars it was uncertain whether the newly captured colonies would remain under British control after the end of hostilities. A decision about how the colonies should be governed could thus be postponed.

After 1815 it was generally decided that military governments had worked well in the past and that since local assemblies were fractious, they were best avoided. Even reformers supported this idea, for they did not want the colonies controlled by a handful of slave-owning whites. The result was the creation of "Crown Colonies" in which British institutions and laws were adapted and enforced without using local legislative assemblies. Ceylon and India were exceptions to this rule. In Ceylon, local laws and customs were preserved, and the lower levels of government were in the hands of the Ceylonese. A governor, supported by civil servants from Britain, ran the country autocratically but effectively and often with remarkable consideration for the well-being of the local population.

British colonies in Africa also underwent significant change. Originally, the British had thought of African colonies as sources of slaves and as a means of securing the route to India. The Royal African Company, chartered in 1672, was similar to the East India Company, and it was granted a monopoly of West African trade. But it ran into enormous difficulties. The expense of maintaining forts against attacks from Africans and rival Europeans ate into the modest profits of the slave trade. Rents had to be paid to African rulers, and African slave traders pushed up the price of their prized commodity. Company officials were often corrupt, and independent traders combined with African rulers to circumvent the company's monopoly to their mutual benefit. By 1730 the company was supported by government subsidies, and in 1750 it was relieved of its charter.

The British maintained a small force in West Africa, at Cape Coast Castle west of Accra, and appointed a governor and an administrative council. Slave trading was not the type of activity likely to lead to serious colonization or the development of further commercial activities. When Britain banned the trade in 1807, the West African colonies lost most of their importance. Trade was then being conducted by the Company of Merchants Trading to Africa, a corporation that any merchant could join on payment of a small fee, but it was unable to realize a satisfactory profit and was dissolved in 1821. Yet another company was formed in 1828 for trade with the Gold Coast.

Further up the coast, on the Gambia and the Senegal, the French had developed a lucrative trade in spirit gum, a substance needed for printing silks. In 1758 the British navy drove the French from West Africa, and almost all the French African colonies were retained by Britain at the Peace of Paris. The new colony of Senegambia was granted a constitution in 1765. It had a governor and executive and legislative councils that were appointed rather than representative. Courts enforced British law, religious toleration was guaranteed, and trade was open to all British subjects. This system, which foreshadowed the administration of Upper and Lower Canada, was far too ambitious and expensive for a backward colony, and it was soon abandoned. Senegal was returned to France in 1783, and Gambia was handed over to the Company of Merchants. To the distress of many politicians, it was impossible to get rid of Gambia because the inhabitants were British subjects under the terms of the constitution of 1765, and there was a powerful lobby of merchants who insisted that it should remain within the Empire.

Thus, in 1815 the British had two royal colonies (Gambia and Sierra Leone) and a chain of trading posts along the west coast of Africa. Now, bases for the slave trade were retained to suppress it. The determination to stamp out the slave trade and the defence of India were far more important than the development of commerce. There had been few European forays into the "dark continent" by 1815, apart from Mungo Park's adventurous trips up the Niger. The penetration of Africa still lay ahead, and most of the effort was to be the work of explorers and missionaries whose exploits were to capture the imagination of the Victorians.

From the French wars until the 1830s, British imperialism was fuelled by challenges from abroad and by unrest at home. Economic motives were used as excuses for imperialism; they were not decisive. The Empire had to be shown to be a profitable operation, whether for the state, British-based trading companies, or individuals in the colonies.

During the wars, the British navy had been greatly enlarged, and as a result, the Mediterranean became increasingly important strategically. Nelson declared that Malta was "the most important outwork to India," and the British temporarily occupied Sicily and the Ionian Islands to secure the route to Egypt and the Levant.

Britain went on the offensive against Egypt and the declining Ottoman Empire in response to French intervention in the area, but there were many who argued in favour of territorial conquest. After the war, the British retained Malta and the Ionian Islands as naval bases, and made Muhammad Ali of Egypt and the Ottoman Porte submit to their will, at least in matters of foreign policy. Colonel Hanmer Warrington made Tripoli into a British dependency, and a naval presence was also maintained in the Persian Gulf.

Trade followed the flag. The Mediterranean became a market for British manufactured goods and a supplier of raw materials. This "insular empire," as G. F. Leckie, its most fervent advocate, called it, was to guard the Mediterranean against French republicanism and the encroachments of the tsars. British principles of the rule of law and of ordered international commerce were to be respected throughout this British sea.

This process whereby the British exploited the economic possibilities of a region once they had gained control of it for strategic reasons can be seen in Asia, Africa, and the Caribbean. They seized large chunks of the Dutch Empire in order to deny them to the French. The destruction of Dutch monopoly in the East opened up the valuable market for Indian opium and also set the stage for attempts to sell British manufactured goods to the Chinese.

Much the same is true of the strengthening of the British position in India. Certainly, merchants were keen to exploit the cotton of Gujarat, which was prized in the China market, and the spices of the south were also in great demand, but politicians like Dundas and Wellesley wanted to strengthen the British position in India to offset the power of France in Europe. They also believed that formal rule was essential to overcome the tensions between the Company, British and Indian traders, and local rulers.

By the mid-nineteenth century, the driving force behind this type of imperialism was a curious mixture of nationalism, Christian missionary zeal, the search for profit, and the career objectives of Britain's civil and military officials. It met with resistance from native rulers, and it was also difficult to find an ideology that might make the Empire more palatable to those forced into it. Burke's "glories of the British constitution" were unlikely to be understood by Asians and Africans anyway and produced a form of government unsuitable for conquered peoples. The Anglican Church provided an example of piety to the infidels rather than a model of a religion that could hold the Empire together. The experience of sectarian violence and religious intolerance in Europe suggested that Christianity could hardly provide cohesion. The ideology of Empire became that of a white, Protestant master race, whose right to rule resided in its respect for the rule of law, its superior moral vision, its devotion to duty, and its gentlemanly virtues. It was agreed that some tributary peoples shared at least some of these qualities and could thus be encouraged to develop their own identities within the Empire. Sometimes this attitude worked, as at home in the United Kingdom. Elsewhere, in Ireland or among the Boers of South Africa and the French in Canada, it failed miserably.

The ritual associated with the Crown provided the outward symbolism of British superiority and the legitimacy of their rule. Impressive viceregal pageantry was introduced, with levées, investitures, infinite gradations of rank and status, and, above all, patronage. As governor general in India, Wellesley, although technically the representative of the EIC, not the British Crown, established an elaborate court based on that of the viceregal lodge in Dublin. It was therefore something of an embarrassment when he was awarded a mere "potato peerage," which underlined the Irish background of which he was ashamed. His brother, the Duke of Wellington, shared this feeling, arguing that "being born in a stable didn't make one a horse." Similar courts were established in Capetown, Nova Scotia, and Malta. In this last pleasant island, Sir Thomas Maitland established the elaborate rituals of the Knights of Malta, the Knights of St. John, and the Order of St. Michael and St. George, which were very much in the neo-gothic medievalist style of the times.

Expatriates who had previously been complaining that their rights were being trampled upon by the government in Westminster now outbid one another in displays of patriotism. Natives in the Caribbean, Loyalists in Canada, and independent merchants in India also hoped that the Crown would protect them against the arrogance of the planters, the pretensions of French settlers, and the privileges of the East India Company.

The Crown was represented as tolerant, understanding, and benevolent. It was the antithesis of the brutal and tyrannical Napoleon, the murderous Tipu Sultan, or the torturers who incarcerated innocents in the Black Hole of Calcutta. These personifications of evil served to strengthen British feelings of superiority, legitimized their civilizing mission, and provided an inspiring mythology to imperialists.

The wars against France and the fear of unrest at home necessitated a series of important reforms both in Britain and in the Empire. Pitt's India Bill of 1784 was designed to bring more order to the affairs of the East India Company. The governor general, Lord Cornwallis, was given greater powers, and a supervisory Board of Control was established in London. Cornwallis attempted to reduce the Company's debt, which had grown considerably during the wars against the Marathas and Tipu Sultan. He offered his solution in the Permanent Settlement of the Bengal Revenues in 1793. He appointed permanent, salaried, and accountable tax-collectors, a new type of civil servant, who was supposed to display the diligence and virtues of the ideal English gentleman. The Company's debt was not reduced, but the British received substantial revenues from this new source, and the Bengal model was soon applied in other colonies. In case these autonomous district officers did not live up to the high standards, local boards of revenue were established to supervise them. They, in turn, were subordinate to the governor general. At the same time, men like Henry Colebrooke, Lambert, and Francis Buchanan began the mammoth task of collecting statistical information about India along with materials on the peoples, customs, and political economy of the subcontinent. Typical of the practical application of the ideas of the Scottish Enlightenment, studies were also conducted in other parts of the Empire.

In India, Cornwallis and Wellesley set about increasing the size of the Company's armed forces by recruiting Indians from the warrior castes. The officers were mainly Anglo-Irish and Scots. In the Caribbean, blacks and mulattos were recruited for the militia, and in the Cape Colony, a Hottentot Corps was formed. Service in these colonial armies gave natives a chance to improve their social standing, and in India they saved the warrior castes from having to degrade themselves by entering inappropriate occupations.

Those who made a career in the Empire came in large part from the middle ranks of British society, although members of some of the leading aristocratic families of Britain as well as the gentry were to be found in the military, the diplomatic corps, and the colonial service, posted to the remotest parts of the globe. Some of them chose such service because they could afford to purchase a commission in the army or a place in the service of the Company. Others, however, like Lachlan Macquarie, who came from poor backgrounds, nevertheless were able to make great careers in the Empire. Middle-class imperial servants could aspire to a quasi-aristocratic life-style unavailable to them in Britain. The large number of Scots in the colonial service was largely the work of Henry Dundas. Scots, who in the late eighteenth and early nineteenth centuries were often better educated than their English and Irish counterparts, gave the service a particular flavour as they applied the ideals of the Scottish Enlightenment to political economy, education, and statistical research. The Anglo-Irish gentry, although less numerous, were also strongly represented.

These empire builders were agrarians with a distaste for "trade." They were also strongly attached to their churches, whether Church of England, Church of Ireland, or Presbyterian. Religion, they hoped, would act as a powerful antidote to radical ideas and strengthen the state. Although the Church Missionary Society was formed in 1799 to convert the heathen, the churches moved cautiously. They were more concerned to convert Catholics and other Christians to the truths of Protestantism than they were to convert Muslims or Hindus. Many felt that the heathens had to be educated first and that in the meantime they should be inspired by British examples.

These Protestant gentlemen were to form an élite, the lower ranks of which would be occupied by Anglo-Indians of stern orthodoxy and oriental Britons whose reconfirmed faith would save them from the lures of "brahminization." This élite was to be trained at public schools like Haileybury, which was founded by the East India Company, or Fort William College, created by Wellesley. At the Anglican cathedrals in India, pomp and ceremony would also provide inspiration.

This reluctance to convert non-Christians in India stemmed in part from fear of provoking rebellion and in part was the result of growing racism. Whereas membership of previous generations had gone native, keeping local mistresses and showing considerable interest in native culture, the new élite had a horror of miscegenation, which was more likely to occur if the natives were to adopt the same religion. Half-castes were now seen as a rootless and dangerous element, although some felt that a "touch of the tar-brush" would help Europeans survive in inimical climates. To the natives, the Protestant churches seemed to be instruments of British colonial domination, and those who converted were considered opportunists, eager to please their masters.

The old Empire had not championed racial equality. A man like Sir William Jones could admire Hindu philosophy, which had its Platos and its Aristotles, and the Hindu doctrine of rebirth seemed altogether more civilized to him than Christianity with its ghastly prospect of everlasting damnation. Yet he too could write that the Indians were of "low cunning" and "completely Jewish." Gradually, Indian life came to be seen as corrupting. Englishmen (Warren Hastings, for example) became prey to the depravity of the bazaar, and from the time of Cornwallis, the British practised a sort of commercial and political apartheid so that British gentlemen were not submitted to the harmful influence of the Indians. Even the Anglo-Indians were now excluded from European circles.

It was felt that self-improvement through virtue and industry was irreconcilable with the rigid caste system. Hinduism was seen as a cruel religion marked by superstitions and violence, widow-burning and infanticide. Similarly, the English believed Catholicism made the Irish and the Portuguese as idle and superstitious as the Indians. Within Islam, which was widely considered tyrannical, the English saw a wide spectrum. It extended from the utterly corrupt Turk to the noble, frugal, and independent bedouin in his modest tent in the desert. The Arabs, who had been seen as a race of cut-throats and thieves in the eighteenth century, were now romanticized as dashing heroes. In time, they too would settle down and devote their energies to commerce and industry, setting an almost British example of honesty and hard work for the Jew, the Turk, and the Hindu. Similarly, in the Caribbean there was an elaborate taxonomical hierarchy based on the amount of African blood. Octoroons, quadroons, and mulattos were placed on a minutely graded scale. In the newer colonies, such as Ceylon, even other Europeans were excluded: the Dutch because they were deemed to be of dubious loyalty; the Portuguese because they were Catholic and often of mixed blood.

This concept of interdependence underpinned Adam Smith's vision of free trade, which, far from being a rapacious free-for-all, was a market in which restrained autonomous beings dealt honourably with one another. There was no place for slavery, which was debasing to both master and slave and was economically inefficient since slaves had no money to spend and thus contributed nothing to the expansion of the market. Gradually, however, the individualist thrust of such arguments was lost, and a comfortable feeling of Protestant moral superiority was all that was left.

The educated gentleman, trained to serve the state and to look askance at the sordid world of business and the ostentatious displays of the nabobs, had to remain above the debased oriental world. He enjoyed financial independence so that he would not be corrupted by lesser beings. In return for this secure status, he was to do his duty, fulfil his obligations, lead a modest life, and set an example. It is an ideal that is still upheld in British public schools. It has produced first-rate civil servants and officers, but it has also created, all too often, men characterized by racial arrogance.

Racial stereotyping thus began well before the pseudo-scientific racism of the high Victorian era. It was rooted in ideas about "national characteristics," in Anglican triumphalism, and in romantic visions of the noble savagery. But in the eighteenth century, it was modified by a quite general assumption that human nature was much the same everywhere. Differences in culture and levels of development were attributed to the stage of civilization a society was believed to have reached. Adam Smith identified four main stages of social and economic organizations: first, hunting and gathering, second, pastoral and settled agriculture, third, the feudal, organizational stage, and fourth and finally, the stage of commercial interdependence of contemporary Western society.

Whereas it had once been feared that the lure of empire would depopulate Britain, by the end of the French wars emigration was beginning to be encouraged. Malthusian fears of chronic overpopulation were coupled with concern about the growth of rural violence, which reached its peak in the "Captain Swing" riots in the 1830s. Pressed at home, Scots and landless peasants from Ireland went abroad in large numbers. They were soon to be found everywhere from the St. Lawrence Valley to Australia, from the Cape to the South Pacific. In these colonies they found the Church and state already established, and they believed their diligence and loyalty would be amply rewarded. It was agreed that they should be independent freeholders, for any vestiges of feudalism would make it impossible for them to be morally independent. Throughout the Empire native rights to common lands were steadily eroded, company and crown lands were privatized, and the free sale of land was encouraged. There were some exceptions to the destruction of ancient customs, and freedom of contract did not sweep everything before it. In India, the caste system provided a welcome reservoir of labour. Primogeniture was often encouraged to stop land holdings from being parcelled into uneconomic units. In the Caribbean slavery continued for three decades after the slave trade was made illegal. The East India Company clung to its monopoly of the China trade until 1834, and opium remained a government monopoly.

The Empire was thus infused with the ideals of the reforming conservatives at home, the great landowners and squires whose example those in commerce and industry were eager to follow. They believed that their triumph in the wars against France was God's judgement on the justice of their cause, on the Protestant Church, and on the wisdom on the British political system. Their younger sons went off to the colonies as self-confident and well-paid officers of the colonial governors, proconsuls who ruled with little interference from Whitehall. They despised anyone who was not impeccably white, Anglo-Saxon, and Protestant.

All of these attitudes were evident on the Cape. The British regarded the Boers as barbarous slave-owners who should be discriminated against since, although Protestant, they were not Anglo-Saxon. Some Boers harboured suspiciously egalitarian ideas, and they were promptly brought into line. The slave trade was abolished, and the instruments of torture the Dutch used on their slaves were publicly displayed and smashed. Various modified forms of unfreedom continued long after slavery was formally abolished in 1832. The British showed some paternalistic concern for the Africans, Indians, and Malays whom the Dutch had enslaved, and a series of treaties were made with indigenous peoples. But those who objected to the terms of the treaties, like the Xhosa, were subdued.

The British imagined that the native people could be encouraged to become diligent and that they had been rendered idle by the appalling example of the Dutch. The "Hottentots," or Khoikoi, were formally Christian and therefore the target of

British missionaries. The Calvinist Dutch were left alone for linguistic rather than theological reasons.

Under Lord Charles Somerset, governor from 1814 to 1832, the intention was to colonize the Cape with British yeomen, and "Kaffrania," the Xhosa territory, was to be out-of-bounds to settlers. There were, however, powerful forces pushing for expansion into the rich lands to the north.

The basic ideas of British colonial policy in this period are clear. The aim was to use state intervention, if necessary, to create an improving landed élite and an industrious peasantry. Colonial authorities had to resolve problems created by the competing interests of the native people and the native-born whites (creoles), local systems of land tenure, and labour allocation. Often this project corresponded with the wishes of the local landed élite and trading classes and worked well. Where it did not, there was endless conflict or uneasy compromise.

2   The British Empire in the Nineteenth Century

By the 1830s it seemed that the paternalism of the Regency period was slowly being undermined by the reforming utilitarians, evangelists, and free traders. The enactment of the great Reform Act, the repeal of the Corn Laws, the ending of the East India Company's monopoly, and the gradual introduction of "responsible government" in Canada, the Cape, and Australia appeared to mark stages on this transition to a new régime that enshrined the ideas of the great political economists. But this view of a glorious age of liberal reform needs some modification. The Reform Bill, for example, hardly marked the triumph of the bourgeoisie; in fact, in many ways the power and influence of the aristocracy were strengthened by the deference shown to its members by the professional and industrial middle class. Land ownership was still the measure of status.

The imperialism of free trade was merely the privilege of a nation that had destroyed foreign competition and no longer needed protection. Slavery was abolished, but it was replaced by new and subtler forms of bondage. "Responsible government" gave more power to white élites in the settlement colonies in the interests of improving imperial defence, but it was only a minor step towards liberal democracy. In India, although there was much debate about educational and legal reform, little was achieved until later in the century, apart from Bentinck's efforts to economize by employing low-paid Indians in the junior ranks of the administration. Liberalism was most noticeable in its blanket condemnation of Indian culture and religion. A scientific racism was gradually replacing an unthinking chauvinism, just as faith in technology was replacing a belief in the capacity of mankind to improve his lot.

The reforms of this period were dictated more by the financial problems facing the rapidly expanding Empire than by the precepts of liberal political economists. As the frontiers were pushed forward, the British met the resistance of native peoples. The armed forces had to be strengthened, which required additional revenue. If the "rule of law" was to be upheld, it had to be administered and enforced. In many colonies, such as cinnamon-rich Ceylon, the costs of administration were not met. Attempts to increase taxes led to increased social tensions. Moreover, imperial trade did not prosper as hoped; there were slumps in world trade and more foreign competition; in some cases, there was also competition between different parts of the Empire. Uprisings, revolts, and outbreaks of violence called for increased vigilance and larger forces throughout the Empire. The British seemed to be trapped in a vicious circle: attempts to deal with problems only made them worse.

The armed uprising in Lower Canada in November 1837 and the smaller sympathetic revolt in Upper Canada exemplified these problems. At first, the British tried to placate Louis-Joseph Papineau and his supporters by making a number of concessions, but by 1837 they had decided to take a firm stand against any further demands from the French or from the English-speaking radicals. The rebellions were of little consequence militarily and were easily crushed. Indeed, the uprising in Upper Canada provided the governor with a welcome opportunity to suppress the radicals. In London, however, Lord Melbourne's administration was highly alarmed and feared that Canada might go the same way as the Thirteen Colonies. Melbourne, a reluctant imperialist, argued that "The final separation of those Colonies might possibly not be of material detriment to the interests of the mother-country, but it is clear that it would be a serious blow to the honour of Great Britain, and certainly would be fatal to the character and existence of the Administration under which it took place."

There was no obvious solution. The alternatives seemed to be either to assert rigid control from London or to set the colony free. The idea of responsible government within an Empire seemed absurd. It would mean that the governor would be controlled by the colonists and that the British Parliament would be powerless. The Empire would be a concept with no substance. Politicians like Lord John Russell, a leading Whig, felt that this was an exaggerated and excessively gloomy view. Colonies were expensive and could go their own way without hurting Britain's vital interests. None wanted to see the end of the Empire, certainly not the loss of India, but there was considerable sympathy for the idea that Britain could reduce her imperial commitments. The liberal imperialists argued that the ties between Britain and the colonies should be loosened. The colonies could be called upon to pay for their own administration and still maintain an affectionate respect for Britain. Might it not be possible to have liberty within the Empire?

The task of finding an answer to this difficult problem was entrusted to Lord Durham. "Radical Jack" Lambton, created Earl of Durham in 1828, had risen to prominence as a strong supporter of the Reform Bill. He was one of the outstanding politicians of the day and widely believed to be a future prime minister. Immensely wealthy, he was also vain and egotistical and an impossible colleague.

Melbourne had tried to get Durham to go to Canada before the revolts occurred, but Durham had refused on health grounds. Afterwards, Melbourne was desperate to get him to go, not only because Durham seemed to be the best man for the job but also because Melbourne needed the support of the Radicals to hang on to office. They were disaffected with his lack of reforming zeal and threatening to go into opposition. Melbourne disliked Durham personally and did not want to have him in his Cabinet. Sending him on an important mission to Canada would solve Melbourne's political problem. He waited anxiously for two weeks before Durham accepted his second and urgent request.

Durham arrived in Québec in May 1838. He entered the city dressed in a splendid uniform and mounted on a white charger, then established a magnificent court on which he spared no expense. His chief secretary was Charles Buller, a radical enthusiast for colonies and a popular character. Edward Gibbon Wakefield, a well-known political economist and advocate of increased colonization, was a close adviser. He had developed the "Wakefield principle" of colonization, whereby colonial lands were to be sold off, at a "sufficient price," to create a fund to encourage and subsidize further colonization. He had had ample time to ponder these matters while he was serving a three-year jail sentence for abducting a schoolgirl who was his ward. Durham was to make good use of Wakefield's principle to buy up one million acres at a very modest price. Thomas Turton, Durham's legal expert, also had a dubious past, having been involved in a spectacular divorce in which his wife had named her sister as co-respondent. To avoid scandal, Turton was not officially appointed to the mission, and, like Wakefield, he paid his own way.

Durham worked tirelessly to inform himself about Canadian affairs and to mend as many fences as possible. He pardoned all but 8 of the 161 rebels in Lower Canada, and those 8 he banished to Bermuda. This magnanimous gesture proved to be Durham's undoing. Lord Brougham, an old friend who had become his most bitter enemy, introduced a bill in the House of Lords revoking Durham's order on the grounds that Bermuda was not within his jurisdiction. Durham had many enemies in Parliament, who considered the appointment of such notorious characters as Wakefield and Turton to his mission scandalous. Fearing defeat, Melbourne refused to support Durham, and his Bermuda decision was reversed. Durham had no alternative but to resign, since the prime minister had promised him his full support. Thus, after a mere five months in Canada, Durham returned. He loyally did nothing to topple Melbourne's government, and he devoted most of his dwindling energies to the preparation of his famous report. It was completed at the end of January 1839, and Durham died in July of the following year. He was only forty-eight.

Durham's description of the problems facing Canada are of great interest, but his conclusions are of far greater importance for they had a profound effect on the development of the Empire. His principal recommendation was that Canada should be given responsible government and that the "present rude machinery of an executive council" should be scrapped. If the colonists had to choose their own law-makers, they would, he argued, have only themselves to blame if things went wrong and therefore would do everything possible to rectify the situation. This could not be said of a system that, at vast expense to Britain, left everything to the whim of a governor. Durham suggested that the constitution, foreign policy, and trade should remain under the control of the British government. Also, prompted by Wakefield's schemes for "systematic colonization," he proposed that the disposal of public lands be regulated by the Crown.

Durham recommended that Upper and Lower Canada should be united and that the Maritime provinces should be allowed to join at a later date. In a union, the French, whom Durham regarded as backward, ignorant, and easily led astray, would be outnumbered by progressive, forward-looking, and industrious English-speaking colonists. In his words: "I believe that tranquility can only be restored by subjecting the Province to the vigorous rule of an English majority." Durham hoped that the petty rivalries and hatred the French felt for the English would vanish as both peoples found a new and common identity as Canadians and that they would not then be tempted to allow themselves to be absorbed by their powerful neighbour to the South.

Durham was equally critical of the "Family Compact" in Upper Canada, which gave a small and irresponsible clique a monopoly of power. He therefore proposed that the executive council should be made responsible to the assembly. His conclusion was, thus, that the British government should put all the authority over the internal affairs of the colony in the hands of the men who enjoyed the confidence of a substantial and responsible section of the community. "Responsible government" was the key concept of the report. Durham insisted that if the governor's advisers did not enjoy the confidence of the people, the colony would eventually be lost.

Many considered Durham's proposals dangerously radical, for he was proposing that a colony should have rights, such as fully responsible cabinet government, that were not even enjoyed at home. Lord John Russell thought the ideas were absurd; it was theoretically possible that the advice of the executive council might be contrary to that of the Queen. Prompted by a further outbreak of rebellion in Lower Canada while Durham was on his way home, Upper and Lower Canada were joined together in 1840, but the Maritime provinces remained apart. Parliament, however, dragged its feet over the implementation of Durham's other proposals, and it was not until 1847 that the governor, Lord Elgin, was given instructions to act according to the advice of ministers who had the confidence of the legislative assembly. A responsible cabinet was first formed in Nova Scotia in 1848.

Still, the powers Durham was prepared to grant to a colony were limited. He insisted that responsible government could only be granted to a legislature in which

English-speakers, preferably of British stock, were in a majority, although he considered it possible for foreigners to absorb many of the virtues of the "English character." The "petty and visionary nationality" of the French settlers would, he believed, be swept aside by the vigorous British. Some of the limitations that Durham wished to impose were soon lifted. The Union Act of 1840 gave the Canadian legislature the authority to change the "form of constitution" and the right to sell crown lands. The protective tariff of 1859 was also contrary to Durham's free-trading convictions, which were enshrined in the report. The tariff was an important step along the road to full colonial autonomy because it established the principle that the colonial legislature had the absolute right to decide what taxes should be imposed, regardless of the opinions of the government in Westminster.

The Durham Report laid the foundations for the new British settlement Empire, and it did much to reconcile the anti-imperialist "Little Englanders" to the idea of Empire. It also strengthened the convictions of those who believed that the links between Britain and its English-speaking colonies had to be free from any coercion or that they should be broken by mutual consent. The Durham Report thus dimly foreshadowed the notion of dominion status and eventually of the Commonwealth. It was an outcome of which Durham would not have approved.

The immediate question was which colonies should be permitted to move towards responsible government? At first it was agreed that military bases, such as Gibraltar, or penal colonies, such as Australia, could not be allowed such freedom. Non-white colonies like India could not be considered, nor could colonies that were too poor or insignificant to stand on their own feet. But what of places like the Cape, New Zealand, and the planter colonies of the Caribbean, where a small white population dominated a non-white majority? Should such "mixed" colonies be ruled directly from Westminster in the interests of white settlers?

The Empire was now divided between "crown colony governments," where largely illiterate, propertyless, and non-European peoples were excluded from political power, and the "constitutional colonies" of Canada and Australia. The Cape and New Zealand had to be browbeaten into accepting responsible government, largely because it meant they would have to pay for costly native wars. "Responsible government" was thus to be granted to any colony that had a sizeable white population and that could be made to pay its own way.

India had a unique position within the Empire, and British attitudes towards India were complex, confused, and ever-changing. At first it had been a simple matter of profits. Then many saw India as a trusteeship, a country that had to be groomed for eventual self-reliance, with the British maintaining the peace in this divided and highly volatile subcontinent. A major problem was that however enlightened the intentions of British administrators might have been, they all too frequently came up against the Indian traditions and customs for which they professed so much respect. Colonial administrators wanted efficiency, prosperity, and the orderly collection of taxes. To achieve this, outmoded forms of land tenure and commercial practice had to give way to a European economy, laws, and institutions and thus to a European way of life.

A powerful bloc of radical liberals and evangelical Christians in England were convinced that political economy and Protestantism could bring salvation to the peoples of the world. William Wilberforce spoke for many when he said that the British should struggle for the "gradual introduction and establishment of our own principles and opinions; of our laws, institutions, and manners; above all, as the source of every other improvement, of our religion, and consequently of our morals." The great historian Thomas Babington Macaulay, law member on the Supreme Council of India, argued that Wilberforce's ideas could best be achieved by giving an English education to members of the Indian upper class, who would act as "interpreters between us and the millions whom we govern." A liberal, Macaulay told the House of Commons in a famous speech in 1833 that if such people were brought up as Europeans, they would eventually demand European institutions, which, when granted, would be "the proudest day in English history."

It was not the intent of the British to work towards this "proudest day"; it was merely seen as a possible consequence of giving the Indian élite an English education. For the time being British India was ruled despotically, much like the Mogul empire. The governor general, who was also viceroy for the Indian states that were British protectorates under "indirect rule," was answerable to Parliament in Westminster, to the East India Company until 1858, and then to the India Office. But it was a long way from Calcutta to London, and there was no telegraph link until 1860. Even when it came, it did not make much difference. The governor had absolute executive powers, and his legislative authority was extended to the Madras and Bombay presidencies in 1833. The council of senior officials was gradually enlarged although there were no elected members until 1909, and only after 1921 could it initiate legislation and act as a check on the government.

British rule in India in the early nineteenth century might have been despotic, but it was, by the standards of the day and probably by any subsequent standards, remarkably benevolent. The East India Company separated its commercial and political functions, and no administrator was permitted to own land or to engage in business in India. After 1833 the Company no longer engaged in commerce. Parliament insisted that the interests of Indians should take precedence over those of Europeans. Officials in British India defended what they believed to be the best interests of the Indian people against the encroachments of European merchants and speculators as well as against political demands from Westminster. The result was a curious Anglo-Indian identity, which was often at odds with the authorities at home and also with many of the British in India.

In 1833 Indians were made eligible for entry into the inner circle of the Indian Civil Service, the "Covenanted Service." No Indian took this important step until 1864, and by the outbreak of the First World War, only some 5 per cent of the Covenanted Service was Indian. Many Indians saw British rule as an indignity, the officials of the ICS as arrogant and aloof, and the pretensions to enlightened reform as a hypocritical cover for base self-interest. There were many local revolts and mutinies, but by far the bloodiest was the Mutiny of 1857–58.

It began among Indian troops stationed at Meerut near Delhi. Eighty-five sepoys of one of the finest native regiments, the 3rd Light Cavalry, were clamped in irons for refusing to accept a new issue of cartridges coated with a grease rumoured to contain a mixture of pork and beef fat. Pork is unclean to Muslims; the cow, sacred to Hindus. Several months earlier, cartridges greased in this way in Britain had been sent to India. Although they had been hastily withdrawn, the tension and mistrust that had been growing in Indian society generally, as well as within the sepoy army as a result of westernizing reforms, were escalated by this apparent disregard for the religious sensibilities of Indians. British officers were well aware of the heightened tension of the army, but most refused to believe that their own troops might be disloyal.

Muslim and Hindu, briefly, made common cause. They stormed the prison, released the mutineers, and went on a rampage, murdering British officers and civilians in an orgy of revenge. The British response was feeble and ineffectual in spite of the loyalty of many Indians, and the mutiny spread. The mutineers covered the forty miles to Delhi, where they proclaimed the aged Badahur Shah "Emperor of Hindustan," somewhat against his will. The mutiny spread to Lucknow and Cawnpore. The British soon lost control over approximately one-sixth of India in the north-central area. Elsewhere the uprisings were sporadic, isolated, and quickly suppressed.

The British recaptured Delhi in September and Lucknow in November, but it was not until late June of the following year that the uprising was finally over. The mutineers were hopelessly divided between aggrieved soldiers and civilians who were anxious to preserve traditional Indian society from the impact of the westernizing Company. There was no unity between Hindus and Muslims, and in some areas civil disorder was the result of violence between rival Indian groups rather than between British and Indians. It was not the progressive nationalist uprising that some have claimed. The mutiny did not spread to the Punjab, a recently conquered territory that supplied some of the toughest soldiers, and the Gurkhas of Nepal loyally supported the British in helping to restore their authority.

Racial hatred inflamed the fighting on both sides. Some mutineers slaughtered any European they came across and destroyed every vestige of European civilization. The British responded in kind with mass executions, sometimes burning mutineers at the stake or resorting to an Indian method: tying them to the mouths of cannons and blowing them apart. The result of all this bloodshed was that the gulf between Indians and Europeans grew wider and racial stereotypes became more grotesque. "Blacks" or "niggers" (a term that did not amuse Queen Victoria) were now seen, wrongly, as the brutish rapists of Victorian ladies, as idle and deceitful louts given to sudden outbursts of savage violence. The whites (Gora: pale-face) were said to sew their Muslim victims in pigskins before murdering them; they were hypocritical and brutal and detested Indian religions and traditions. English free trade had ruined the craftsmen, English education was an affront to the caste system, the free sale of land swept away the old system of land tenure and laws of inheritance.

The Indians who had benefited from the drastic changes wrought by the British remained loyal. They appreciated the advantages of a Western education, merchants in the towns profited from the increased prosperity of the few, and many landowners increased their holdings under the new system. Even the caste system helped Indians deal with the aloofness of the British, for the Hindu knew that their sense of superiority was not sanctioned by the divine order. Similarly, India continued to work its magic: the language, eating habits, and customs. Many Englishmen who were profoundly affected by Indian culture would confess that behind their brown skins a great many Indians were "pukka white-men."

The British government realized that the Mutiny had been the result of British misrule, a lack of respect, as Queen Victoria phrased it, for "the rights, dignity and honour" of the native princes and an intolerance shown towards native religions and customs. In her proclamation of 1 November 1858, the Queen insisted that her government would do everything possible to improve the moral and material welfare of Indians since their "prosperity will be our strength, in their contentment our security, and in their gratitude our best reward."

Much of this statement remained only a declaration of intent, and little was put into practice. There were, naturally enough, widely differing opinions on how best to deal with the Indians. Some argued that severe punishment was the only thing the natives understood, and they denounced the governor general, Charles Canning, for carrying out the Queen's instructions that only those who had been actively involved in atrocities during the Mutiny should be punished. Despite his ferocity in meting out punishment, he was soon given the contemptuous nickname of "Clemency Canning." Others, among them Gladstone, felt that the Mutiny was God's punishment on the British for failing to convert the Indians to Christianity and pointed out that Indian Christians had not joined the Mutiny. The majority agreed with Disraeli and argued the exact opposite. The frantic attempt to turn Indians into Christian Englishmen was bound to fail, as was the substitution of English laws and customs for those of an ancient and conservative civilization. They agreed that superstition, idolatry, corruption, incompetence, and vice were reprehensible, but they said also that the British had to turn a blind eye if they wanted to maintain their hold on this vast subcontinent with a mere handful of men.

The first of the major reforms after the Mutiny, in 1858, placed India under the Crown and made the governor general viceroy. The East India Company thus lost even its function as a government agency and was abolished, and Canning got a new, more exalted title. In the army the artillery was prudently made entirely European, and in the ranks the numbers of Indians were reduced and Hindus and Muslims were mixed in order to divide and rule. The activities of Christian missionaries were drastically restricted, their funds were severely cut, and the government insisted that the Hindus should be left to find their own way to salvation. Bible classes were forbidden in government schools, and a directive was issued insisting that "no pains should be spared in enforcing on all public officers the most stringent rules of toleration abstaining from any covert designs on their [the Indians'] religious feelings." The British were now less concerned with enlightening the Indians than with making certain that they were not provoked into another mutiny.

Attempts to strengthen Indian landlords in the interests of stability, however, were largely abandoned within twenty years of the Mutiny, and the main thrust of British reforming zeal was in the material sphere. Railway construction, irrigation projects, the postal and telegraph services, and road building all brought great benefits to the country and also strengthened the position of the British. Troops could be sent rapidly by train, information passed on instantly by telegraphic means, and any rebellion swiftly crushed. Nor was this development entirely the result of the Mutiny, for many of these projects had begun before 1857. Lastly, it should be remembered that large parts of India were unaffected by the Mutiny, and life continued much as before.

The other event that forced the British to examine their attitudes towards other races was the Jamaican crisis of 1865. Britain had colonized a number of islands in the Caribbean in the early seventeenth century, and Cromwell had taken Jamaica in 1656. Profits from the sugar trade were enormous. A small group of white planters, the "plantocracy," ruthlessly exploited their slaves, controlled a powerful lobby in the corrupt and unreformed House of Commons, and resisted any change in the social and political structure of the islands. But profits from sugar declined rapidly towards the end of the eighteenth century. Then the government first prohibited the slave trade and soon abolished slavery. Parliament agreed that the planters should be compensated for the loss of their slaves, and under the new system of apprenticeship, slavery actually continued for some years.

Apprenticeship involved long hours of back-breaking work and brutal discipline, and it clearly violated the spirit of emancipation. It was finally abandoned in 1838. As soon as workers were free to leave the plantations, they did so in droves, creating chronic labour shortages that were only partially overcome by the importation of indentured labourers from India and China. In 1854 Britain ceased to protect sugar, and the planters faced ruin. The plantocracy blamed the blacks, whom they denounced as idle, a view that found many supporters in Britain. The Colonial Office sympathized with the planters and refused to listen to black complaints about being forced off their lands. Instead, it suggested that the blacks work on the plantations as day labourers. White missionaries supported the blacks in their struggles with the planters, and some blacks who had prospered as free men were asking for a say in government.

In October 1865 a group of about four hundred black men protested in front of the court house at Morant Bay, demanding that they be granted land rent-free in the "back land" and forcibly securing the release of one of their number who was on trial. Local volunteers were called out to disperse the protesters, and seven men were killed on each side. In the sporadic fighting that followed the rebels killed eighteen men, half of whom were white. Another thirty-five were wounded.

The uprising was brutally repressed by the governor, Edward Eyre, a narrow-minded disciplinarian with no sympathy for the blacks. Eyre imposed martial law, ordering in soldiers from as far away as Canada. Four hundred and thirty-nine blacks were killed, 354 after having been court-martialled. Hundreds more were flogged mercilessly, and over a thousand houses were burnt to the ground. Among those executed was George William Gordon, a leading spokesman for the black cause. He was the son of a white planter and a black woman, a self-ordained Baptist minister, respected magistrate, and radical politician. Gordon was not personally involved in the mutiny, and the court-martial refused to condemn him to death. His execution was ordered by the governor.

A royal commission was immediately appointed to investigate these atrocities. Eyre, who had been suspended, was found to have been justified in acting swiftly to put down the rebellion but to have used excessive force. He was recalled in disgrace and brought to trial in England. His defenders on the "Eyre Defence Committee" included such illustrious names as Charles Dickens, Alfred, Lord Tennyson, Charles Kingsley, John Ruskin, and Thomas Carlyle. On the other side, the "Jamaica Committee" was equally distinguished and counted among its members John Bright, J. S. Mill, A. V. Dicey, T. H. Green, Herbert Spencer, Thomas Huxley, and Charles Darwin. Eyre was eventually acquitted and lived to receive a modest state pension.

The Jamaican rebellion provided a welcome opportunity to do away with the archaic constitutions in the West Indies. The Jamaican assembly was abolished, and the island became a crown colony. With the exception of Barbados, Bermuda, the Bahamas, and British Guiana, all the other colonies came directly under the Crown. The white settlers no longer ruled supreme, but the white man's concept of law and order remained, and the coloured majority were excluded from a say in the ordering of their lives.

Violent protests against British rule occurred not only in India and Jamaica but also in the Antipodes. At first, New Zealand was a dependency of New South Wales, and a resident was not appointed until 1832. He was to bring some order to a place infested with gunrunners, land speculators, and well-armed natives. The Islands were colonized by Edward Gibbon Wakefield's New Zealand Company, which was incorporated in 1839. Small isolated communities set about clearing the lush pastures that were to make New Zealand a prosperous farming community. Unlike Australia, which had a widely dispersed population of stone-age aborigines, New Zealand was inhabited by some one hundred thousand Maoris, a people with a sophisticated culture and a complex social order. They were agriculturalists, not nomads like the aborigines, and they had a strong sense of tribal land ownership. They were also fierce warriors. In order to have an ordered settlement of the colony, the British negotiated the Treaty of Waitangi in 1840. By its terms, about one hundred Maori chiefs acknowledged the sovereignty of Queen Victoria (Te Kuini Wikitoria) in return for guaranteed ownership of their lands. The British government was permitted to buy lands from the chiefs if they were prepared to sell.

The provisions sounded straightforward, but there were problems. The lands belonged to the tribe, and thus it was questionable whether an individual, even a chief, could sell them. The New Zealand Company had already bought and sold considerable tracts of land, and now it appeared that the settlers had no title to land they had bought in good faith. New settlers were hungry for land; the chiefs were

34

unwilling to sell. The stage was set for a series of conflicts between the Europeans and the Maoris. Both the New Zealand Company and the settlers tried to find ways to circumvent the Treaty, and the Maoris responded by fighting for their rights.

In 1845 Captain George Grey, a capable and valiant gentleman, was sent to New Zealand from South Australia to act as governor. He was remarkably effective, immediately taking the Maoris' main fortress and thereby earning their respect. He in turn showed respect for them, learnt the Maori language, and wrote a scholarly work on their mythology. Grey soon pacified the colony, and then he attempted to settle the land question and end corruption in the civil administration. He also built hospitals, schools, and model farms, and the constitution he drafted in 1852, the year before he left New Zealand, was remarkably progressive. It opened the way to responsible government, which was finally achieved in 1856.

Still, Grey had hardly left New Zealand before the Maoris began to lay plans to rid the islands of the white man (pakehas). A Maori king was elected in 1858, and war broke out between the king and the white settlers in 1860. Grey was sent back to New Zealand in 1861 to end the war, but he made a bad mistake by sending a punitive expedition from Australia. Doing so only served to push moderate Maoris into the king's camp. Although the Maoris were hopelessly outnumbered, they were immensely brave, and they were greatly admired by the British regiments that faced them. The war was effectively over by 1863, but sporadic fighting continued. The Colonial Office decided that the colonists should deal with the Maoris themselves and therefore withdrew the British troops. The last regiment left in 1870 while rearguard actions were still being fought. A peace was finally concluded in 1872, and although the Maoris had lost millions of acres and thousands of warriors, the settlement was not vindictive. They had been given representation in the general assembly in 1867, and in 1872 two chiefs were appointed to the upper house. Unlike the West Indies, the local white population was able to master the crisis and to accept responsibility for the colony's affairs. New Zealand was to develop as a prosperous and socially conscious colony, and it achieved dominion status in 1907.

In India, the West Indies, and New Zealand the struggles had been between whites and coloureds; in southern Africa it was a three-way clash between the British, the Cape Dutch (Afrikaners), and the African tribes. The British permanently annexed the Cape Colony in 1815 because of its strategic importance guarding the route to India. By that time there were twenty-seven thousand Afrikaners in the colony, and they had reduced the Hottentots and Kaffirs to virtual, and in some cases actual, slavery. The Bantus, a warrior people who had not been conquered, were kept at arm's length.

The Afrikaners were a mixed group of European settlers from the Netherlands. Most of them were of Dutch and German origin, and many of them were descendants of Huguenots. They were united in their staunch Calvinism, in their overbearing sense of racial superiority, and in their intense resentment of outside interference, whether from the Netherlands or from Britain. Although the British certainly did not regard the Africans as their equals, they felt that the harsh treatment meted out by the Afrikaners was excessive. The Afrikaners, in turn, became increasingly resentful of the high-minded liberalism of the evangelical missions and the humanitarian impulses of the British administrators. This explosive situation was made all the worse by the Afrikaners' determination to push into the Bantu lands of the interior to establish huge farms. The granting of certain legal rights to slaves in 1826 and the abolition of slavery in 1833 were further grievances. The Afrikaners complained that they had not been given sufficient compensation for freeing their slaves and that the British were similarly tight-fisted in redressing the damages caused during the Kaffir War of 1834-35, during which many homesteads had been destroyed and thousands of head of cattle slaughtered.

The Afrikaners decided to head north across the Orange River to what was to become the Orange Free State, Transvaal, and Natal. The Great Trek of 1837, the year of Queen Victoria's accession, saw some ten thousand Afrikaners escape from British rule to settle the northern pastures. It was an epic adventure. They had to surmount formidable physical obstacles, and the trekkers were constantly under attack from African tribes, the toughest and most disciplined of whom were the Zulu and the Matabele. The Afrikaners formed their ox carts into defensive laagers to fight off the attackers, and they finally achieved supremacy in a series of pitched battles, among them the Battle of Blood River.

The Great Trek presented the British authorities with a series of difficult problems. It had further exacerbated relations between whites and Africans and made a fresh round of wars seem highly probable. Because the Afrikaners were British subjects, they could not be allowed to establish autonomous republics. On the other hand, trying to subjugate the republics would be costly, and the resentful people would be difficult to administer. After much debate, the British decided to annex Natal in 1842, thus cutting the other two Afrikaner republics off from the sea. In 1848, the British annexed the remaining Afrikaner lands, but they proved unprofitable and tiresome to administer. In 1852 the Transvaal was granted independence, and two years later the Orange Free State was given full sovereignty. It seemed to be a workable solution. The British controlled the routes to the sea via the Cape and Natal; the Afrikaners had secured their independence. There seemed no reason why the two peoples could not co-exist peacefully, and the Afrikaners realized that they were likely to need the support of the British Army if the Bantus mounted a full-scale offensive.

In the Cape Colony this period witnessed the gradual development of responsible government. In 1825 an advisory council of officials was created to act as a check on the governor's absolute authority. In 1834 legislative and executive councils were added, and although the members of both were chosen by the governor, they did not act as mere rubber stamps. Representative government was first established in 1854 with two elected houses and with the franchise open to all races. The property qualifications were so low that a number of Cape coloureds and Bantus were able to vote. In the Orange Free State and the Transvaal, by contrast, rigid racial segregation was imposed. Full responsible government was not attained in the Cape until 1872.

In 1854, George Grey, now Sir George, was appointed governor of the Cape Colony in the next stage of his remarkable career. Grey was determined to create a federation of South African states that would include the Orange Free State and possibly the far less developed Transvaal. It was a bold scheme with a slight chance of succeeding, but it was sunk by the Colonial Office, which regarded Grey as a dangerous and overambitious man, and Lord Carnarvon, the undersecretary, who passionately believed in British supremacy and had no sympathy for federal solutions that might leave the Afrikaners with certain autonomous rights. Grey was dismissed in 1859 and later became prime minister of New Zealand.

A new chapter in the history of the region began in 1867 when diamonds were discovered on the Orange River; two years later there was a huge strike at Kimberley, in territory in dispute between Britain and the Orange Free State. In 1876 the British government purchased the Free State's claims for a paltry £90,000. Meanwhile, the Zulus were becoming increasingly threatening, and the Afrikaners of the Transvaal faced possible annihilation.

In this situation, Lord Carnarvon, who was back at the Colonial Office, saw the possibility of taking over the Free State and the Transvaal on Britain's terms. The Transvaal was virtually bankrupt, and President Burgers was unable to wring any tax money from the settlers. In 1877 the British once again annexed the Transvaal.

The long-expected Zulu War began in 1879. While British forces were initially routed, they rallied and crushed the Zulus, who never recovered from this catastrophic defeat. But now the Afrikaners no longer had any need of British support against the Zulus, and they were resentful that promises of local autonomy had not been fulfilled. In 1881, the Transvaalers rose up and defeated a British force at Majuba Hill. Once again the British granted the Transvaal its independence—in two ambiguously worded conventions signed in Pretoria in 1881 and in London in 1884. The British claimed that they retained a degree of suzerainty over the Transvaal; the Transvaalers under their forceful leader, Paul Kruger, denied that this was so. At the time the issue seemed academic, but it became of critical significance when gold was discovered on the Witwatersrand reef and turned Johannesburg in a city of fifty thousand Europeans, the vast majority of whom were British subjects. These foreigners (Uitlanders) almost equalled Afrikaners in number.

Kruger's government assumed that the Transvaal would soon have an English-speaking majority and therefore, adopted a discriminatory policy against the Uitlanders, imposing severe taxes and denying them civil rights. Casting a greedy eye on the riches of the Rand, the British exploited the plight of the Uitlanders to press for a South African Federation that would bring the Transvaal under their control. The chief advocate of this view was Cecil Rhodes, the premier of the Cape Colony, who by 1895 had come to the conclusion that force would be necessary to achieve this goal. Meanwhile, fearing that the British might be tempted to seize the Transvaal, Kruger had stockpiled a substantial amount of weaponry.

Rhodes had come to South Africa at the age of seventeen in 1870. After an unsuccessful attempt at farming, he had moved to the diamond fields of Kimberley, where he soon made enough money to return to England to study at Oxford. At university he developed his curious racist philosophy. Arguing that there was a fifty-fifty chance of God existing, he insisted that it was prudent to presume that He did. If it was God's will that peace, liberty, and justice should thrive throughout the world, then it was clear to Rhodes that the Anglo-Saxon race was His chosen instrument and that a global British Empire was part of His plan. Deeply fearful of women, Rhodes decided that marriage would divert his energies from the single-minded pursuit of his goals, which he believed he could only achieve if he became immensely wealthy. With this singleness of purpose, coupled with an acute business sense, he became the mastermind behind the creation of the De Beers Mining Company, which had a virtual monopoly over South African diamonds. He soon achieved a commanding presence in the Rand gold fields. The first part of his master plan, the accumulation of vast wealth, was rapidly accomplished.

For all his chauvinism and his passionate belief in the unique virtues of the Anglo-Saxon race, Rhodes believed strongly in co-operation between the British and the Afrikaners in South Africa. He was sharply critical of interference in colonial affairs by the Home Government, which he dismissed as the "imperial factor." As an indication of his beliefs, throughout his political life he represented the predominantly Boer constituency of Barkly West, where he was first elected in 1881.

Rhodes was the driving force behind the annexation of Bechuanaland (now Botswana) in 1884, a move designed to contain the Transvaal. In 1889 troops of his British South Africa Company crossed the Limpopo River and began the exploitation of the colony he named, with characteristic lack of modesty, Rhodesia. While its creation closed off the Transvaal to the north, the Boers built a railway from Johannesburg to Delagoa Bay in the Portuguese colony of Mozambique and thus secured a route to the coast that was not controlled by the British. With its increasing wealth and self-confidence, which was bolstered by the friendly attitude of the German government, the Transvaal began to feel that it might be possible to achieve a federation with the Orange Free State that would be dominated by Boers rather than Uitlanders

Nevertheless, supported by the Boers of the Cape Colony, who were led by Jan Hendrik Hofmeyr, Rhodes pushed ahead with his scheme for a South African Federation under the British flag. His plan was the ill-considered effort of a man failing in health and judgement, who was becoming more and more intolerant of advice. He planned that the Uitlanders of the Transvaal should rise up in defence of their rights and that armed forces from his British South Africa Company, stationed in either Rhodesia or Bechuanaland, would support the coup. Kruger's government would be overthrown and replaced by one chosen by Rhodes.

It was well known that the Uitlanders were poorly armed and that the rebels, in spite of blood-thirsty names, such as "the hellish twelve squad," were lukewarm in their enthusiasm for the enterprise, so Rhodes decided to postpone the coup. Dr. L. S. Jameson, a close friend of Rhodes, took no notice of those who urged caution, however, and mounted an attack on the Transvaal from Bechuanaland at the end of December 1895 with a force of six hundred men. The "Jameson Raid" was a hopelessly bungled affair. The Boers rounded the raiders up within a couple of days and handed them over to the British authorities for appropriate punishment.

This episode ruined Rhodes. He was forced to resign both as prime minister of the Cape Colony and as managing director of the British South Africa Company. He retired to Rhodesia, complaining of the "unctuous rectitude" of the British authorities and devoted most of his energies to the development of the colony that bore his name. By the time he died in 1902, at the age of forty-eight, he had been reinstated on the board of the company and been given an honorary degree by Oxford University. Part of his fortune endowed two hundred Rhodes Scholarships at Oxford for students from the self-governing colonies and the United States, which he sincerely hoped and believed would again become part of the British Empire.

The failure of the Jameson Raid greatly enhanced Kruger's prestige. He had beaten off an attack that the British government apparently supported, and he received a warm telegram of congratulations from Kaiser Wilhelm II. The high-handed antics by Rhodes and his cronies also outraged liberal opinion in Britain. "Ohm Paul" was thus more than ever determined to resist the Uitlanders' demands and the continued pressure from the British government.

The colonial secretary, Joseph Chamberlain, who almost certainly knew of the plans for the raid and who told the Commons committee that investigated the affair next to nothing, was determined to do everything possible to restore British prestige in South Africa. With Sir Alfred Milner, governor of the Cape, he set about isolating the Transvaal by negotiating a deal with the Germans over the future of the Portuguese colonies. In 1898 it was agreed that in the event of Portuguese bankruptcy, Mozambique would go to Britain; Angola, to Germany. The Germans untruthfully assured the British that they had no interest in the affairs of the Transvaal.

Chamberlain was unable to convince many of his cabinet colleagues that the Uitlanders had a reasonable case, and Kruger was unwilling to make any concessions until it was too late. Yet the issue of the Uitlanders was essentially irrelevant. The British wanted a united South Africa, and the grievances of the Uitlanders were mostly fabricated by the British press. Nor were the Boers a simple God-fearing folk fighting for their independence against the encroachments of the rapacious British. They wanted to drive the British out of South Africa. Kruger was as prone to brinkmanship as Milner was, but he was not as aggressive as some of the leading figures in the Transvaal. Chamberlain wanted to strengthen what he called "the weakest link in the imperial chain"; Kruger wanted to break it. Chamberlain was determined to guard the route to India, and he believed that Germany, which had just begun its massive naval building programme and which had invested the huge sum of three hundred million marks in the Transvaal, was determined to strengthen its position in South Africa at Britain's expense in spite of its protestations to the contrary. In his view, Kruger was the kaiser's stooge, and he had to be stopped. Milner reinforced this conspiratorial vision of the situation with his exaggerated concerns about the threat to British interests.

In May 1899 Milner confronted Kruger at Bloemfontein. The result was deadlock, and Kruger exclaimed, "It is our country that you want." Milner prepared for war, ignoring Kruger's belated announcement that he would agree to give the Uitlanders the franchise after five years' residence, provided that the British dropped all claims to suzerainty. Britain sent troops to South Africa and moved them to the frontiers of the Transvaal. On 9 October 1899, Kruger demanded that these troops be withdrawn within forty-eight hours. The British ignored the ultimatum they had provoked and went to war against the Transvaal and the Orange Free State.

Although the British eventually won the war, they were severely humiliated in the process. Almost half a million British and imperial troops took three years to defeat forty-five thousand Afrikaners, who used their brilliant and unorthodox tactics and showed superb marksmanship. At first the British Army was under the incompetent leadership of General Sir Redvers Buller, who had won the V.C. in the Zulu War. The Boers set siege to the strategically important towns of Kimberley, Mafeking, and Ladysmith. Then Buller was replaced by Field Marshal Lord Roberts, an illustrious figure who had won his V.C. in the Indian Mutiny, defeated the Afghans at Kandahar, and been commander-in-chief of the army in India. Ably assisted by the ruthless Kitchener, he relieved Mafeking, an event celebrated in jingoistic fashion in London, and Kruger hopped on the train to Delagoa Bay. It seemed that the war would soon be over, and Roberts returned to England to be fêted as a conquering hero. But the Boers still had some fifteen thousand commandos in the field led by men like Botha, Smuts, and Hertzog. The British countered this threat by a scorched earth policy, burning some six hundred farms and rounding up civilians in concentration camps in order to deny the commandos any support. Some twenty thousand people, mainly women and children, died in these camps, prompting the Liberal leader, Sir Henry Campbell-Bannerman, to speak of "methods of barbarism" and provoking widespread public protest in Britain.

The war dragged on until May 1902, when the Treaty of Vereeniging was finally signed. It forced the Transvaal and the Orange Free State into the Empire, but it also gave a number of major concessions to the Boers, the most important of which was to deny the vote to non-whites in the Afrikaner provinces. A fund was also established to rebuild the devastated farms.

The Boer War was a turning point in British imperialism. Many felt that it was a shameful episode, and criticism of British policy was widespread abroad. The country's prestige was severely damaged, but the government quickly took lessons of the War to heart. The army was reformed after a thorough examination of its shortcomings, and the Committee of Imperial Defence was established. Britain emerged from its splendid but precarious isolation and concluded an alliance with Japan and the Entente Cordiale with France.

In South Africa "Milnerism" failed. He negotiated a customs union that included Rhodesia, but he was unable to achieve a South African federation. The Afrikaners tenaciously preserved their language and their way of life and resolutely refused to assimilate. In 1906, Campbell-Bannerman's Liberal administration

41

granted autonomy to the Transvaal and the Orange Free State, and in the subsequent elections the Afrikaner nationalists Botha and Smuts and their Het Volk party triumphed. But what had seemed a severe setback for British interests was in fact the beginning of a era of co-operation between the Afrikaners and the British. The two ex-guerrilla leaders were moderates who believed that their nation's best interests were served by working with the British. Soon they brought their people into the First World War against the pro-German Boers, and Smuts became a statesman whose advice was prized by Winston Churchill, once a prisoner of the Boers. To everyone's surprise the old alliance between English-speaking South Africans and Afrikaner moderates had been restored.

3 The Heyday of Empire, 1876–1914

In 1876 Disraeli made Queen Victoria Empress of India. The governor general, Lord Lytton, was confirmed in his belief that the British were the true heirs to the Moguls, and he was further convinced that Britain's natural allies in India were the native princes, not the Western-educated commoners, the "babus," or intellectuals, whom he saw as potentially dangerous. Lytton's predecessor as viceroy, Lord Mayo, had argued that the British hold on India was precarious and that Indians should be encouraged to become involved in the government of their country. Lord Lytton held the more conventional view that Indians had no claim to representative government since they were not British settlers imbued with British values. Some felt that the Indians could be educated up to the point where they might be capable of running their own affairs, as Macaulay had suggested in 1833, but Lytton was not one of them. In any case, the question was hypothetical. It was agreed that the Indians had not yet reached that stage of development and that therefore they had to be ruled autocratically.

Gladstone and the Liberals had opposed the bill making the Queen Empress of India. They believed that India should be ruled for the good of Indians, not for the greater glory of the British. They saw the bill as a deliberate attempt to halt the process of recruiting Indians for the civil service, a policy that, in the long run, was likely to result in some form of responsible government for Indians.

Liberal opposition to Conservative policy in India and particularly to Lord Lytton grew when the viceroy ordered the invasion of Afghanistan to counter what he argued was a threat from the Russians. At first, the occupation of Afghanistan was peaceful, and a treaty was signed with the amir, but in September 1879 the British resident in Kabul was murdered, and the British forced the amir to abdicate. The situation was further complicated by a general election in Britain in 1880, which, much to the surprise of Queen Victoria and Disraeli, returned a Liberal government with a handsome majority. The new government faced an awkward situation. General Roberts fought a successful campaign to establish the rule of the British-backed amir, and Gladstone then ordered British troops out of Afghanistan. He preferred direct negotiations with St. Petersburg to hazardous military adventures, but his actions did little to assuage the fears of those who believed that the Russians were a real threat to the security of India.

The viceroy appointed by Gladstone's administration, Lord Ripon, gave more powers to local governments in India and eased the censorship of the press, much to the horror of the British in India and the Conservatives at home. This reforming policy was drastically slowed down when the Conservatives returned to office in 1886. Lord Salisbury's government ordered the conquest of Upper Burma in order to thwart French designs, and Burma was made a province of the Indian Empire. The Liberals supported a Conservative bill for the reform of the local councils in India in 1892, but the measure did little to enhance Indians' control over their own lives.

The British actually welcomed the founding of the Indian National Congress in 1885, not knowing it would become the great political force behind the independence movement. They saw it as a useful safety valve. Disaffected Indians could meet once a year, let off steam, and return to their submissive lives. At the same time, the Ilbert Bill, which had suggested that Europeans might be hauled up in front of Indian magistrates, was hastily squashed to placate an outraged British community.

India, with a population of some three hundred million by the end of the century and thus about one-fifth of mankind, was ruled by a mere handful of British officials. There were about fifteen hundred senior civil servants and about three thousand British officers in the Indian Army. There were hardly more than twenty thousand British residents in India, plus some forty to sixty thousand British troops. Yet, one-fifth of British overseas investments were in India, and almost one-fifth of British exports went there. The Indians paid for the administration of the Raj and for the army through their taxes, but they had no say whatsoever in how the country should be run. A determined nationalist movement would have had little difficulty in throwing the British out, but it did not happen. Most Indians lived in villages where life went on much as it had for centuries and political awareness was nonexistent. Even in the towns, the working class had not yet absorbed radical or socialist ideas. The Princely States in India, which contained about one-quarter of the population, were autocratic and conservative. The intellectual élite were mostly British educated and believed in gradual constitutional reform, their nationalism tempered by an admiration for British constitutional practice and the rule of law. British authorities felt any demands, however moderate, by educated Indians were impertinent. They believed they had manfully shouldered the white man's burden and ruled an inferior race fairly and selflessly. They lived apart from hot, dirty, superstitious, and disease-ridden India in their cantonments and hill stations and had little to do with Indians, however exalted or highly educated.

Lord Curzon, who served as viceroy from 1898 to 1905, regarded virtually all of humanity as inferior and put the Indians near the bottom of the scale. He told Balfour in 1901 that there was not one Indian in the entire subcontinent capable of serving on the executive council and reminded him that the British position in India, which he believed was the key to Britain's greatness as a nation, rested on the "extraordinary inferiority, in character, honesty and capacity of the [natives]." Curzon encouraged the improvement of an educational system, though it did little but produce clerks for the vast bureaucracy. Only one Indian boy in five and one girl in forty attended primary school, and little effort was made to train Indians in the sciences. However, elementary education had only been made compulsary in Britain in 1870, and there was little effort at home to train scientists or technologists either. Curzon did not set out to modernize India but to ensure that British administration was efficient and fair so that the superiority of the British way of life could be daily manifested. He did not intend to begin a new era but to reach the zenith of the old. He treated Indians with contempt, but he also demanded the highest standards of behaviour from the British so that their superiority should be clear. Thus, he would not tolerate the mild sentences passed by courts-martial on soldiers guilty of the rape and murder of Indians and intervened forcefully, much to the disgust of the military and the pleasure of the Indians.

With his conviction that Britain's greatness depended on the security of the Raj, Curzon was obsessed with the danger posed by Russia even though there was no longer any real threat. The Anglo-Japanese alliance of 1902 gave Britain a powerful ally against Russia, an ally that was to win a convincing victory in the Russo-Japanese war of 1904–5. Moreover, the Entente Cordiale of 1904 was made with Russia's ally, France. In the same year, the British government settled its differences with Russia in Tibet, Afghanistan, and Persia. Curzon regarded these developments with the deepest suspicion because he was convinced that they were motivated by a craven fear of Russia. He protested vigorously at the British guarantee of Afghan independence in 1905, regarding it as a "surrender" to Russia. He also demanded a more vigorous British policy in Tibet, a country under Chinese suzerainty. In 1902 he sent Colonel Sir Francis Younghusband, an extraordinary mixture of adventurer, swashbuckler, and mystic, to Lhasa to establish a military presence in the Chumbi Valley. Younghusband was instructed to offer a three-year indemnity to the Tibetans for this strategically important territory, but he disobeyed his orders and signed an agreement for seventy-five years. Balfour refused to accept the treaty, further infuriating Curzon.

In 1902 Kitchener, the hero of the Sudan and South Africa, arrived in India to take up his new post as commander-in-chief of the Indian Army. There ensued an impressive clash of wills between the haughty Curzon and the imperious Kitchener concerning the viceroy's authority over the expenditures of the Indian Army through the military member of the viceroy's council. After a three-year battle, the British government supported the commander-in-chief. Curzon fought a rearguard action against this decision, but when he saw that he had been defeated, he handed in his resignation in August 1905.

He left an India seething with discontent over the partition of Bengal. Curzon had decided to divide Bengal for reasons of administrative efficiency, but characteristically he did so without consulting Indian opinion. Educated Bengalis, the most politicized Indians, were outraged. They were convinced that partition was a sinister plot to crush Bengali nationalism by creating a predominantly Muslim East Bengal and a Hindu West Bengal in which the Bengalis were a minority among the Oriyas and Biharis. There were riots, a tax revolt, and political assassinations, with which the middle class sympathized. Bourgeois nationalists were now supported by popular opinion, and the nationalist movement that was to triumph within forty years was born.

Curzon's term of office marked the end of an era in British India. The Liberal victory in 1906 brought John Morley, Gladstone's biographer, to the India Office and Lord Minto to Calcutta from Ottawa. They were an odd pair, but between them they set about increasing Indian representation in the administration and the legislative councils in order to keep the radical nationalists quiet. In spite of Morley's denials, which were all the louder for fear of opposition from conservatives and traditionalists at home, it was a step in the direction of responsible government for Indians. This reforming work was continued by Lord Hardinge, who succeeded Minto in 1910. He reunited Bengal, created the new provinces of Bihar and Orissa, and moved the capital from Calcutta to Delhi. Thanks to the Morley-Minto reforms, by the outbreak of the First World War Indians formed the majority on the provincial councils and a minority on the all-Indian legislative council. Although they could debate and they could ask supplementary questions, authority remained firmly in British hands. But although few realized it at the time, India had begun the process of development from a dependency to a Dominion. This was finally acknowledged in 1917 by the secretary of state, Edward Montagu, who announced that his aim was "the gradual development of self-governing institutions with a view to the progressive realization of responsible government in India as an integral part of the British Empire."

The relative benevolence of British rule in India in the late nineteenth century was more the result of necessity than of virtue. The British Empire now extended over one-quarter of the earth's surface, and Britain could simply not afford to exert power all over the globe. From the 1890s the main area of concentration was Africa. There were two main reasons for this decision: the Suez Canal provided the essential link to India, and the riches—real and potential—of South Africa were a glittering prize. Africa was also more accessible; it was not bordered by a tiresome great power like Russia, and local tribes, armed with primitive weapons, could easily be subdued by small expeditionary forces.

Another problem, as Lord Salisbury complained in 1889, was that Britain seemed to be stuck with Egypt. Sir Evelyn Baring, later Lord Cromer, who had been sent to govern Egypt in 1883, pointed out that there was no popular strong local figure who could be relied upon not to flout Britain's wishes if he were given the responsibility of ruling Egypt. In 1887 Salisbury began a series of negotiations with the Turks, hoping that he might be able to get their agreement to a right of "re-entry" into Egypt if, after evacuation, the British decided that vital interests were at stake. France made sure that Turkey would not agree to this provision, and the negotiations broke down. Turkey, the so-called sick man of Europe, seemed about to expire, and the British feared that the Russians might be tempted to seize Constantinople and so threaten the Suez Canal in which they had bought a 44 per cent interest in 1875. Even when the French later indicated that they might accept the right of re-entry, Salisbury decided that it would be prudent to stay put.

Once the decision had been made to stay, the lands to the south had also to be secured. Baring pointed out that Egypt depended on the Nile and that therefore the Upper Nile had to be firmly in British hands.

At first it seemed that the question of the Upper Nile could be settled by diplomatic means. The Germans were prepared to recognize British claims to the Upper Nile, Zanzibar, and Uganda in return for Heligoland, an island in the North Sea. In the following year, 1891, Italy was bought off even more cheaply. It recognized British claims in return for recognition of Italy's claims to Abyssinia. Britain's position having been recognized by both Germany and Italy, Lord Roseberry proclaimed Uganda a British protectorate in June 1894. In order to keep the French at bay, the British government leased part of southern Sudan to King Leopold of the Belgians.

The French were not deterred by any of these diplomatic moves, and angered by their own self-imposed exclusion from Egypt, they decided to move into the Sudan. Hearing that the French were planning to send a military expedition, the British government issued a stern warning, but it was ignored. The French managed to persuade King Leopold not to stand in their way, and the Italians, who had been ignominiously defeated by the Abyssinians at Adowa in 1896, were in no position to offer any assistance to the British. A small French force under Captain Marchand left the Congo and reached the Nile at Fashoda on 10 July 1898. There it sat until 19 September waiting for the British to arrive.

47

Meanwhile, against the advice of Baring and many of his cabinet colleagues, Salisbury decided that the Sudan would have to be occupied. In 1896 Kitchener was sent out with a large force to crush the dervishes and destroy the powerful Khalifate. This he did in his characteristically thorough manner, defeating the khalif's forces at Omdurman on 2 September 1898, a battle that saw the British Army's last cavalry charge. Shortly afterwards he arrived at Fashoda.

The meeting at Fashoda was a curious incident. Marchand's small force, described by the British press as the "scum of the desert" was no match for Kitchener's army, and it was seriously short of ammunition. The encounter was polite, almost friendly. Marchand congratulated Kitchener on his great victory; Kitchener complimented Marchand on his skill and courage in successfully completing such a difficult journey. They both made ritual protests on behalf of their governments, and then they settled down to whisky and soda.

The French foreign minister, Delcassé, had hoped that Marchand would never get to the Sudan for fear that his expedition might lead to war. Great was his relief when he heard that the Fashoda incident had passed without a shot being fired. He bowed to superior force and gave Salisbury the French government's agreement to Britain's claim to the Nile. France received the Sudan from the Congo and Lake Chad as far as Dafur, but Britain controlled the Nile.

At the beginning of the twentieth century, the British Empire was thus the envy of the other great powers, the greatest empire the world had ever seen. Although little more than 10 per cent of its people were of British and European origin and although there were more Hindus and Muslims in the Empire than there were Christians, it was in a very real sense British. It was held together by the sometimes purely symbolic institutions of the monarchy, the English language, and the British legal system and administration, and it was watched over by the world's largest navy.

British rule took many and varied forms in different regions of the Empire, but there were two basic approaches. The white settler colonies of Canada and Newfoundland, the Cape and Natal, Australia and New Zealand were self-governing with constitutions based closely on the Westminster model. Although they were subordinate to the British Parliament, these colonies ran their own domestic affairs, and although they had no say in foreign affairs, they were defended by Britain, largely at Britain's expense. Some settler colonies in the West Indies and in Africa were not given such freedom, and the future of the Orange Free State and the Transvaal, which had been seized from the Boers, had yet to be decided. Elsewhere, the colonies were administered directly without consultation with the colonized.

The colonial Empire stretched across the globe from the impoverished sugar plantations of the West Indies to the strategically important Mediterranean possessions of Gibraltar, Malta, and Cyprus, which in turn protected British interests in Egypt, the Sudan, Uganda, Kenya, and Somaliland. Across the Persian Gulf were Aden and Gulf States, which were felt to be equally important in guarding to route to India via the Suez Canal. The final point in this strategic chain was Ceylon with its naval base at Trincomalee.

Other colonies had more mundane commercial reasons for their existence, among them the old slave-trading colonies of West Africa and Rhodesia and Nyasaland ruled by Cecil Rhodes's British South Africa Company.

India, the jewel in the crown, was a case apart. Queen Victoria had been made Empress of India, and her viceroy—helped by a handful of British administrators backed by the Indian Army—ruled the Raj as a absolute monarch, even though he was answerable to Parliament thousands of miles away. This tiny band of white men subjected an entire subcontinent to their rule.

The foundations of this great empire were far from healthy. The Boer War had shown that Britain could no longer afford to go it alone and reluctantly had to set about looking for outside support. The workshop of the world had lost its preeminent position and been overtaken by Germany as Europe's greatest industrial power. This uncomfortable fact was underlined by Germany's determination to challenge Britain's naval supremacy, an arms race that proved to be cripplingly expensive to both countries.

Some, most notably Joseph Chamberlain, felt that the Empire provided an answer to Britain's increasing difficulties. A system of imperial preference, diplomatically called tariff reform, would throw up a tariff wall around the Empire and protect it from foreign competition. The resulting prosperity would be used to pay for social reform at home. It was an attractive vision, but critics quickly pointed out that only one-third of Britain's trade was with the Empire and that the risks of abandoning the traditional free-trade policy that was accepted by all political parties were far too great.

In 1902 the budget contained a provision to impose import duties on corn, meal, and flour. Chamberlain hoped to secure remission for Canadian grain as a major step towards tariff reform and as a gesture of thanks to the Canadian government for giving Britain a 33.5 per cent advantage over foreigners on import duties. The chancellor of the exchequer, C. T. Ritchie, an orthodox free-trader, threatened to resign if the remission were granted. Chamberlain felt betrayed and stormed up and down the country preaching tariff reform. Balfour managed to secure Chamberlain's resignation and also those of Ritchie and two other of the leading free-traders in his cabinet. The prime minister wanted to keep the lines open to Chamberlain for fear that his campaign might win widespread popular support, in which case he would be a useful ally in the forthcoming election. Balfour therefore appointed Joseph's son Austen to the chancellorship.

It soon became obvious that Balfour's stratagems had failed. Chamberlain's Tariff Reform League became enormously powerful—to the point that it seemed that it might take over the conservative Unionist party. Others in the party fought for free-trade. Winston Churchill left in protest and joined the Liberals. Balfour, his party split in two, saw no alternative but to call an election in 1906; in it the Unionists were soundly defeated. The Liberals had a huge majority; only 157 Unionists were returned to Westminster, two-thirds of them supporters of Chamberlain. Poor Balfour lost his seat and had to agree to tariff reform in principle in order to remain as leader of the party. Later in the year, however, Joseph Chamberlain suffered a stroke, which ended his political career. The Liberal government remained faithful to their free-trade ideals, often to the point of madness, for example, when Lloyd George insisted that tariff reform amounted to tyranny. Chamberlain's great scheme was never put into effect, and some of the Dominions, tired of waiting, tried to make their own arrangements. Canada, for example, agreed to a reciprocity agreement with the United States in 1911, but Laurier's government was defeated on the issue.

It was also questionable how far the great proconsuls of the British Empire would co-operate with such a centralizing scheme dictated by Westminster, for they were prone to ignore any orders that ran contrary to their strongly held personal views. Sir Alfred Milner in South Africa, who referred to the House of Commons as "rabble," was forced to abandon his scheme for the federation of the four South African provinces after lengthy protest. In India, Lord Curzon, whose belief in his superior judgement was unshakeable, did all he could to deceive and outwit the Cabinet when his views ran contrary to theirs. Another such figure was Sir Frederick Lugard, the great proponent of "indirect rule," an approach developed by his predecessor in Nigeria, Sir George Goldie. By it, Britain was to exercise its rule indirectly by ruling according to local principles through local rulers. Lugard was sparing in the information he sent back to London, and in the course of extending British rule in Nigeria, he involved Balfour's government in a colonial war against its will.

Attempts were made at the Colonial Conferences of 1902, 1907, and 1911 to ensure a greater degree of centralization and co-operation between the various parts of this sprawling Empire, but they came to nothing. A Committee of Imperial Defence was formed in 1902 in the aftermath of the South African War. It was a purely advisory body without executive functions. It was a British rather than an imperial body, and it was left up to the Dominions to decide what use they wished to make of it. In fact, they asked no questions and sent no delegates to it, although a Canadian minister once attended a meeting while in London on other business. The committee met regularly, but it achieved little since it had no real power. Few agreements could be reached or decisions taken since the army and navy were deeply suspicious of one another.

In 1907 there was general agreement that it was desirable to establish an Imperial General Staff, but the Dominions would not make any definite military commitments. This lack of support did not greatly worry the British, who had a low opinion of the contribution they were likely to make. New Zealand's 1911 proposal to create an imperial defence council was rejected out of hand by the Canadians and the South Africans and did not even win the support of British Prime Minister Asquith. The colonies wanted more power, some even dreamt of statehood, and they resisted any move towards centralization.

The British government felt that since the Royal Navy defended the Empire, the colonies should help defray the cost. In 1887, Australia and New Zealand agreed to contribute, and in return a naval squadron was stationed in Australasian waters. The Cape and Natal also made a contribution to ensure naval protection on the eve of the Boer War. The Canadians saw no reason why they should pay a penny to the British admiralty since they did not feel threatened and were convinced that the United States would defend them should the need arise.

In spite of this penny-pinching attitude towards defence, the Canadian government decided to build a Canadian Navy. The two naval bills of 1909 and 1912 triggered off fierce parliamentary battles, but by the outbreak of World War I, Canada had an embryo navy, which it placed at Britain's disposal. Canada was following the example of Australia and New Zealand, who had begun to build their navies in 1909.

Although the Dominions had rallied to Britain's support during the Boer War and had sent some seventy thousand volunteers to South Africa, they were reluctant to make unconditional commitments. The colonial conferences were informal and powerless meetings, and the adoption of the impressive new title of Imperial Conference did nothing to alter this fact. The 1907 Imperial Conference bestowed the title of "Dominion" on Canada, Newfoundland, Australia, and New Zealand. The Cape, Natal, Transvaal, and the Orange Free State were described as "self-governing colonies" until 1910, when they were united in the Union of South Africa. Dominion status underlined the fact that nationalism was growing within the

Empire, that ties were weakening, and that Britain needed the Empire more than the Empire needed Britain.

Critics of the Empire abounded, but no serious politician, whatever reservations he might have about certain aspects of imperial policy, seriously thought of abandoning it. Some prominent Liberals had been strongly opposed to the Boer War and had been falsely denounced by the government as unpatriotic Little Englanders. Almost all Liberals were proud of the imperialist traditions of their party, and they were determined not to allow the Conservatives to outdo them in their professed enthusiasm for the Empire. This "Liberal imperialism," professed by the likes of Herbert Asquith, Sir Edward Grey, and, J. B. S. Haldane was fervent enough to satisfy the most enthusiastic Conservative imperialist. With regard to the Empire, Conservatives had no cause for alarm about the 1906 Liberal Cabinet, which counted such stalwarts of Empire among its members, although there was some concern about what John Morley would do at the India Office.

There were, however, certain distinctions between Liberal and Conservative imperialism. The Liberals had no time for Milner's racism and contempt for democracy, and one of the first things the new Liberal government did was to remove him, after having censured him for using Chinese indentured labour. They did not wish the Empire to become any larger and promptly put an end to territorial expansion in Somaliland. They also had little sympathy for Conservative obsessions about the strategic defence of the Empire and believed that there was an alternative to force that could serve to keep it together. If the peoples of the Empire were reasonably content, prosperous, and free, they would be prepared to continue the existing arrangements and not be tempted to resist. The Empire should, above all, be collaborative, not coercive.

The Liberals had no great vision for the Empire; most simply wanted to muddle through. Their attitude is summed up in the words of John Morley, who said: "I can answer for today; I can do pretty well tomorrow; the day after tomorrow I leave to providence." This Liberal view of Empire was diametrically opposed to that of Curzon, who was obsessed with the Russian threat and wanted to turn the Persian Gulf into a "British Lake" and to secure Tibet, Afghanistan, and southern Persia. The Liberals had few quarrels with his administration of India—after all, he stood for equality before the law for Indians and Europeans, had reformed the educational system, done his best to remove the threat of famine, and improved irrigation and the transportation network. He resigned before the Liberal government took office, and Morley was thus saved from any unpleasant confrontation with the viceroy, but he took over responsibilities for an India seriously disrupted by the partition of Bengal in 1905, a situation that was ably fanned by the Indian Congress, some of whom argued for complete independence, the majority for self-government within the Empire.

The leader of the moderate wing of Congress, Gopal Krishna Gokhale, welcomed Morley's appointment to the India Office and described him as "the reverent student of Burke, the disciple of Mill, the friend and biographer of Gladstone" who would apply their lofty principles to the government of India. Morley, whose idealism had worn somewhat thin with age, disliked Congress, but he thought it was desirable to co-operate with Gokhale in order to keep the radical camp down. He was convinced that without reform the Raj could not be saved; with reform, there was still some chance of preserving the British connection.

Minto, who was on the spot, felt that the situation was much more serious. The Indian Civil Service was highly alarmed and felt seriously threatened by the possibility of another Indian Mutiny. Minto advised that any protest movements should be crushed and that law and order should be maintained so that Indian hotheads would learn a lesson. Morley was appalled, arguing that a repressive policy would be likely to provoke the very mutiny that Minto wished to avoid.

Morley, the man of reason and moderation, sat in London, but in India intransigents in the Indian Civil Service faced intransigents in Congress. The two sides hardened in their positions. Indian nationalists threw bombs and assassinated their opponents. The British authorities responded with more repression, which, in turn, led to more bombs and further assassinations. The Morley-Minto reforms, which brought more Indians into the government, were thus designed as a sop to Indian opinion, not as a step towards democracy. For all his idealistic credentials, Morley specifically denied that he wished to transplant British parliamentary democracy to India.

At best, British policy in India was one of the lesser evil; at worst, it was one of divide and rule. It was tempting to play the moderates in Congress off against the radicals, the princes against the middle-class intellectuals, and Hindus against Moslems. Such a policy caused further tensions in the long run, but for the time being the combination of carrots, like the Morley-Minto reforms of 1909, and sticks, such as the Press Act of the following year, secured the peace.

Elsewhere in the tropics the Caribbean colonies declined into destitution and backwardness. The protective tariff on sugar, which had given them some relief, was removed in 1908, the government arguing that the colonies' dying agonies should not be unnaturally prolonged.

Some of the African colonies were more profitable. British West Africa was a rich source of palm oil, hardwoods, and cocoa. The trade in gold and ivory still thrived, and the copper deposits of Northern Rhodesia brought considerable profits. There was hope that the British farmers of the "White Highlands" of Kenya would soon be prospering. The fact that they had grabbed the most fertile lands and caused endless misery to the African population could be forgotten. The white settlers of Southern Rhodesia at least paid for the administration, and in spite of Liberal misgivings about this small and largely racist minority, they were seen as racial support for their blood-brothers against the Boers in South Africa.

None of these colonies experienced indirect rule in the form it was intended. Even in Northern Nigeria, which was administered by Lugard, the inventor of the idea, its principles were abandoned whenever it was deemed necessary. Other colonies, like Egypt or the Malay States, were ruled through a khedive or accepted advice, not for any ideological reasons but simply because that seemed to be the easiest way to do things. Some colonies, like the British High Commission Territories in South Africa, were largely ignored and thus experienced virtually no rule at all.

In much of the Empire the quality of government depended on individual governors. They had few resources at their disposal, little support from Whitehall, and vast areas to control with a skeleton staff of white men and a few trusted natives. Indirect rule here was a matter of expedience, of indolence, and sometimes of desperation, not a deliberate policy. Britain lacked the resources to establish firm centralized government throughout the Empire, even if it had wanted to. Whitehall could do little but make suggestions, admonish, and hope for the best. This hands-off policy was cheap, the natives were appeased, and the Empire was relatively peaceful. The Liberals had no colonial philosophy or policy and bent such principles as they had according to local circumstances. The Conservatives were more prone to expound their ideology and cook up plans, but they were rarely put into effect. The British prided themselves on their pragmatism and common sense, but they were often an excuse for failures to implement policies or merely for lack of imagination, energy, and foresight.

Liberals never shared Joseph Chamberlain's enthusiasm for tropical colonies, which were central to his ideas about 'constructive imperialism,' the aim of which was to lead to imperial self-sufficiency. Most of them found these notions bizarre, for they believed in the international division of labour rather than imperial autarky, but that did not mean that they were blind to certain advantages to be gained from tropical colonies. They felt that they were desirable as secure sources of raw materials and foodstuffs. They recognized the need for Malayan rubber, encouraged the growth of cotton in Uganda, looked for sources of oil, and were gratified as the price of cocoa climbed.

Even socialists knew which side their bread was buttered on and salved their consciences by complaining bitterly about ruthless exploiters like King Leopold of the Belgians, whose brutality in the Congo had caused widespread disapprobation and resulted in the surrender of his African kingdom to the Belgian parliament in 1909. Cecil Rhodes was also seen as an example of the worst type of monopolizing imperialist, the likes of whom the socialists were determined to put out of business; but they still thought of colonialism as a means of bringing progress, prosperity, and enlightenment to backward and impoverished regions.

This was a central dilemma for all political parties. All believed in the desirability of progress and prosperity, but they had to face the fact that these were scarcely possible without the intervention of capitalists. Given the tight-fistedness of successive governments, development was liable to have the effect of making a number of undesirable characters exceedingly rich. It was a dilemma to which there was no easy answer. Capitalists argued that without a monopoly, their risks were too high, and they would be forced to take their money elsewhere. The Colonial Office had little sympathy for monopolists, but it desperately wanted capital for the undeveloped colonies. Offers of substantial investment in return for the grant of a monopoly were often hard to resist, and the liberal conscience could be once again assuaged by insisting that some regard should be paid to the interests of the colonized.

A solution favoured by a number of Liberals was to encourage peasant proprietors who would trade with the Europeans through native middlemen. Development was likely to be less rapid and less spectacular but also far less open to abuse. Some colonies managed to do quite well without the injection of large sums of capital and thus could resist the approaches of the monopolists. In much of West Africa, local peasants sold their crops to African merchants, who in turn sold them to European factors. The system did not lead to industrialization and modernization, but it encouraged the development and strengthening of a vigorous peasantry and thus avoided the terrible abuses of the Congo or Ireland. It was well adapted to local needs and customs, and it provided powerful arguments for the proponents of indirect rule.

Peasant proprietors enjoying the benefits of indirect rule and happily trading with British agents were an attractive vision, so attractive that Sir Charles Lever was sent packing when he asked to set up a large-scale palm-oil operation in West Africa in 1907. Sir Charles moved to the Congo where the Belgians had no such scruples. West Africa was one of the most prosperous parts of the Empire, and peasant proprietorship seemed to work very well. Trade with the region grew at a spectacular rate in the years immediately before the Great War. Whether modernizing capitalists like Lever would have done any better, and at what cost, was hotly debated at the time and long afterwards.

Within the Empire, Egypt was something of an oddity. It was never called a colony, and it was supposed to be handed back to the "natives" once its finances were put in order. Egyptian nationalism was inspired in part by the example of the revolutionary Turks, and it was fanned by British insensitivity over issues of race and religion, by the savage repression of dissent, and by British determination to hang on to the Suez Canal for as long as possible. The British were slow to realize the strength of Egyptian nationalism, a cause that was taken up by the landed élite, who resented the heavy taxes placed upon them by the British, but they eventually saw the need to win the moderate nationalists over to their side. Cromer's heavy-handed approach had even pushed the khedive into the nationalist camp. Up until then he had been despised as a British lackey. Cromer's successor, Eldon Gorst, won the khedive back and gave Egyptians a greater say in local government; but his actions were too little and too late. Nationalism grew in intensity, and Gorst felt obliged to resort to such measures as rigorous press censorship and imprisonment without trial. By 1911, when Gorst had to resign because of his poor health, he had earned a reputation for illiberal repression. He was followed by Kitchener, who continued his predecessor's policy of giving the Egyptians a greater say in the legislative assembly, an opportunity they used to agitate against the British. This agitation strengthened the conviction of old-style imperialists that any concessions were bound to lead to trouble. They took some comfort in the certainty that Kitchener was the man to take care of any difficulties.

Egypt was not the only area were there was violence. The Zulu rebellion in Natal, which lasted from 1906 to 1908, resulted in thirty-five hundred African deaths. There were also uprisings in Kenya, Nigeria, and British Guiana in which many were killed. The Indians continued to assassinate officials, and some die-hard Boers persisted in the struggle for freedom; but, on the whole, the Empire was remarkably peaceful in the years before World War I, and when it is compared to the savage brutality of the Germans in the Herero and Maji-Maji rebellions, British rule seemed extremely mild. Radical critics of the violence attributed it largely to Milner and hoped that his foreign ideas would die with him. They spoke too soon, for the war was to end the period of Liberal drift and begin a new chapter in the history of the Empire.

The Boer War had poisoned relations between the Afrikaners and the British, and it needed considerable magnanimity to win any of them back. In December 1906 the Liberal government granted full self-government to the Boer republics of the Transvaal and the Orange Free State. It was a remarkably successful move, and in May these two republics agreed to form the Union of South Africa with the Cape and Natal.

The new Union was deplorably racist. Only "British subjects of European descent" could become members of the Union Parliament. Many Liberals thought it regrettable that three-quarters of the population were excluded from the political process and feared that sooner or later there would be conflict between Africans and Europeans in South Africa. But the British could not rule South Africa without the consent of the Boers, and the Boers would not be placated if the Africans were to have a share of political power. Without a colour bar, there could be no union. The most that Liberal critics could do was to hope that at some time in the future it would be possible to give the Africans a voice in running the country.

The province with the most embarrassing problems was Natal, which Winston Churchill described as the "hooligan of the British Empire." Indian immigrants suffered endless humiliations and discrimination, but they had an eloquent and forceful spokesman in Gandhi, whose campaign on their behalf won him a great reputation in India. He was absolutely loyal to the Empire and had served with great distinction in the ambulance corps during the Boer War. He helped the British crush an African revolt in 1906, and he enthusiastically supported Britain's war effort in 1914. The British were thus exceedingly embarrassed when he asked for protection against the outrageous behaviour of the Natal whites. They were doubly embarrassed because there was precious little they could do to help the Indians.

South Africa was thus a constant reminder that the British Empire was held together by expediency and compromise, not by principles. It was, however, widely assumed that if an attempt were made to impose liberal principles on the Empire, it would simply fall apart. Since no one wished to get rid of the Empire, it was reluctantly agreed that one had to turn a blind eye to some of the more unsavoury examples of bigotry and racism and hope that enlightenment would eventually prevail.

Many imperialists were appalled at the state of the Empire. With his South African experiences, Milner thought it was at best a mess and at worst a tyranny. John Buchan complained of the vulgarity, materialism, and lack of dedication in an Empire in decay. There were varying prescriptions for reform, most of them singularly illiberal. Milner and the members of his "Kindergarten" passionately believed in the virtues of tariff reform and felt that parliamentary democracy had to stand aside when the needs of the Empire were at stake. They were supported by Leopold Amery and the "Compatriots," who had similar ideas and agreed that the House of Commons should have its wings clipped. Buchan believed in racial superiority tempered with a conscientious attitude towards the lesser breeds. The "Round Table" group hoped to revitalize and consolidate the Empire, on the whole by slightly less drastic means, although as élitists they were far from being convinced democrats. Critics of these approaches harped on Milner's German origins and denounced him as a Bismarckian, a Prussian, and a militarist.

The distinction between Milner's group and the Round Table members was made quite clear over the issue of Irish Home Rule, the suggestion that Ireland should enjoy a degree of autonomy. F. S. Oliver, who was an enthusiastic federalist and author of the influential *Life of Alexander Hamilton*, proposed a federal devolution of powers to the four component parts of the United Kingdom, an idea that was endorsed by his Round Table colleagues. It was a hopelessly unrealistic proposal because it was utterly unacceptable to the Irish, who rightly saw it as a means to retain a union dominated by England under a slightly different system of government.

Ireland became a major issue in domestic and imperial politics just prior to the outbreak of World War I because of the third Home Rule Bill, which was introduced in April 1912. The bill was bitterly opposed by the Conservative, or Unionist, Party who, along with their Ulster Unionist allies, denounced "Rome Rule." Home Rule was placed on the statute book in October 1914, but its implementation was delayed until after the war, thus postponing a major political crisis.

For the Conservatives, Home Rule was a betrayal of Empire. For Milner it was a "horrible nightmare," and he promptly organized the Ulster Defence League, which had nearly two million members by 1914, and collected considerable sums of money to finance an armed struggle against Home Rule. For Milner and his followers more was at stake than the fate of Ireland. The unity of the British Isles was the essential precondition for the unity and greatness of the British Empire, and for Milner dedication to the greatness of the Empire was a greater concern than British politics, which he loathed, or the House of Commons, which he despised, or even his party colleagues, whom he considered pusillanimous.

The experience of the imperial conferences showed that hopes of binding the Empire closer together were illusory, but they still persisted. Indeed, had the Liberals attempted any drastic reform of the Empire, they would almost certainly have provoked strong nationalist reactions. The Liberal policy of compromise was anything but heroic, but it succeeded in keeping the peace. The support given to Britain by the Empire during the war was ample testimony to its success. In economic terms the policy of collaboration paid handsome dividends, and imperial trade was far more vigorous under the Liberals than under the Conservatives.

Britain's need for the Empire was both economic and emotional. Economically, the Empire was enormously important. Thirty-five per cent of Britain's exports went to the Empire in the years before World War I. Forty-two per cent of foreign investment was in the Empire. Britain depended on Malaya for rubber, Egypt for cotton, and India for the traditional cup of tea. Maybe these vital economic links would have continued even if Britain had divested itself of the Empire, but it was a risk no one was prepared to take.

Emotional ties with the Empire were equally strong. The Empire stood for so many things. It was proof of Britain's standing as a great, many would even say the greatest, power. It was exciting, exotic, romantic, the inspiration to poets like Rudyard Kipling, who was born in Bombay, and novelists like G. A. Henty, who had been a war correspondent in the Crimea, India, and Africa, to say nothing of the countless purveyors of popular culture who inspired generations of young Britons. It provided not only jobs but also a vocation for those twenty thousand colonial administrators and the experts, educators, and policemen who were prepared to shoulder the white man's burden. These young men on the whole did a good job. The majority were trained in the minor public schools to serve their country, to do their duty, and to lead the lesser breeds onwards and upwards. Most were honest, hardworking, and dedicated, but there was no place else for them. They needed the Empire not simply because they were trained from earliest childhood to administer distant lands, but also because the Empire confirmed their sense of superiority, their authority, their mission, their purpose in life, their dearest and deepest values. Lower down the social scale, the Empire was also a home for millions who emigrated from Britain to seek their fortune or simply to earn a living.

None of this activity was essential. Marxists who claimed that imperialism was necessary for the survival of capitalism were proved wrong, as were those who argued that without the Empire, the monarchy, the churches, the middle class, and the public schools would lose the justification for their existence. Not that the Empire was in any sense threatened. The Boers were defeated, admittedly at a cost. The ententes with France and Russia settled most of the more pressing problems. The major threat, from Germany, was to Europe rather than to the Empire. The fringes of the Empire were secure, and within it a handful of administrators held things together with tact, diplomacy, and compromise. It was a brilliant achievement at minimal cost. Had it been held together by force, it would have fallen apart—this was the lesson of the Boer War. The Empire was reasonably tolerant and thus reasonably tolerable. The small minority who found it intolerable could be controlled by a handful of soldiers and policemen. To keep the Empire together Britain had to continue being tolerant and reasonable, and that was the limit of its powers. It was a limit that was readily accepted, but it was also one that made the whole concept of power increasingly questionable.

Although the seeds of the independence movements had been sown, the Empire was remarkably free from the radical anti-European and anti-imperialist nationalist movements that were so prevalent in other parts of the world in the immediate prewar years. Japan had become a world power and was increasingly contemptuous of the West. Chinese nationalism was on the move, the Young Turks revolted in 1908, and Marcus Garvey's black nationalist movement in the United States gathered momentum. There were echoes of such movements throughout the Empire from the Hindu revival in India to Calvinist nationalism among the Afrikaners in South Africa, from the fanatical disciples of the late Mahdi in the Sudan to the Gaelic League in Ireland. It remained to be seen whether the British would be able to contain these movements, but when the war came, many of these issues were shelved.

4 The Empire in War and Peace, 1914–1939

Lenin proclaimed that World War I was an imperialist war, and a number of imperialists would have agreed with him, though for quite different reasons. Many had warned for a long time that German ambitions from Morocco to the Pacific were a constant threat that would eventually have to be met. When war broke out in 1914, it came as no great surprise, and there was general agreement that a principal aim of the war was the defence of the Empire. Australians and New Zealanders, supported by their Japanese allies, seized the German colonies in the Pacific and China. In southern Africa an imperial force, largely South African, did the same with somewhat greater difficulty. In Mesopotamia, a larger campaign was mounted against the Turks, which brought rich pickings after the war. But none of these colonial campaigns were anything other than side-shows, and it was never doubted that Germany could only be decisively defeated and the Empire preserved on the Western Front.

The Dominions of Canada, Australia, and New Zealand did not question Britain's declaration of war, their navies were placed under the command of the Admiralty, and armies were recruited to send to France. In South Africa the situation was somewhat different. A large number of Afrikaners, seeing no reason why they should be called upon to die for the detested British, remembered the support given to their cause by the kaiser and rose in revolt. The uprising was quickly crushed by two leading Boer generals, Prime Minister Louis Botha and Minister of Defence Jan Smuts, who continued the "great and urgent imperial service" requested of them— the conquest of German South-West Africa. Afrikaner opinion was divided between those who felt more could be gained by actively accepting the king's declaration of war and those who felt that Botha and Smuts were traitors to their national cause.

Other national groups that might have been expected to object were surprisingly enthusiastic in their support. The Irish Nationalist MPs supported Asquith's government, and thousands of Irishmen from the southern counties volunteered to fight in France. In Canada the French Canadians voted for the government to ensure a unanimous vote. Even extreme nationalist Indians did not oppose the war, and many Indians were active and enthusiastic in their support.

This support was more than purely verbal. The Canadians recruited 628,964 men, of whom 56,639 were killed. Of 412,953 Australians, 59,330 lost their lives. New Zealand called 128,525 men to arms, of whom 16,711 never returned. South Africa recruited 136,070 whites, of whom 7,121 died. Such sacrifices were not only made by whites. India sent 1,440,437 volunteers and lost 62,056. Of the 59,000 men from British East and West Africa, almost 3,000 were killed. Eighty-two thousand Egyptians, 8,000 West Indians, 1,000 Mauritians, and 100 Fijians served in non-combatant units. A total of some 2.5 million colonials fought for Britain. By comparison 6,704,416 Britons served in the war, and 704,803 lost their lives.

This seeming unanimity was superficial, and it was unlikely to last unless Britain made substantial promises and concessions. The situation was summed up by the brilliant New Zealand cartoonist, David Low, then at the beginning of his career. His drawing showed politicians solemnly burying the hatchet. The caption read:

Here lies

party

government

buried but not buried

very deep

because there will be a

glorious resurrection.

The apparent unanimity of the Empire in supporting Britain's war against Germany and the vital support, both in men and materials, given to the war effort, confirmed the old-style imperialists in the belief that the Empire was indeed a cause with a future. In 1917, Milner, now a member of Lloyd George's war cabinet confidently announced that if the Empire was bound closely together and avoided getting too involved with Europe, it could in future stand up to anyone. Many agreed.

The imperialists were in a strong position. They had been on the outside since 1906 and then were brought into the wartime cabinet by two Liberal prime ministers, Asquith and Lloyd George. Curzon and Balfour were appointed in May 1915. In December the following year, Milner joined them, and Smuts was added to their number in June 1917. Furthermore, Curzon and Milner were members of Lloyd George's inner cabinet. A host of other imperialists were close to the prime minister as well, among them Lionel Curtis, Philip Kerr, Leopold Amery, and John Buchan. Curzon chaired a special cabinet committee on "Territorial Desiderata," which came up with extensive plans for expansion in the Middle East and East Africa for the defence of India.

Of course, Curzon's aims could not be achieved, none of the plans for the future of the Empire realized, unless the war was won. To win Britain needed the Empire and had to make concessions to ensure its continued support. The need for troops on the Western Front was so great that colonial garrisons had to be stripped to the minimum. There were only fifteen thousand British troops left in India, considerably less than half the number at the time of the Mutiny. Moreover, Britain depended increasingly on the goodwill and support of the United States, a country whose high-minded denunciation of British imperialism was tiresome but could not be ignored. The Bolshevik revolution placed a great power in the hands of professed revolutionaries and anti-imperialists, and their example inspired many nationalists throughout the Empire. While statesmen dreamt of a glorious future with Britain firmly in control of a closely knit Empire, they expediently made concessions and promises that were likely to have a quite different effect.

It took a long time for the heady spirit of August 1914 to wear off, and there was a widespread sense of false security. India was peaceful until 1916, thanks in part to the skilful policies of the viceroy, Lord Hardinge, whose reform measures were endorsed by his successor, Lord Chelmsford, and by Edwin Montague, who became secretary of state for India in 1917. Quiet was also maintained by serious divisions within the ranks of the Congress Party and the imprisonment of a number of nationalist leaders.

In 1916 Bal Gangadhar Tilak, who had been freed from jail in 1914, was readmitted into the Congress Party, and he soon took control. Under his leadership, aided and abetted by an extraordinary Englishwoman, Annie Besant, Congress adopted a far more aggressive policy. Under the terms of the Lucknow Pact of December 1916, Congress patched up its differences with the Muslim League. The nationalist movement was now united and on the offensive. The seriously concerned Indian government ordered the arrest of Annie Besant, a move that only served to provoke further protests.

Montagu, who faced this highly explosive situation on his appointment as secretary of state, decided that concessions were necessary. He therefore told the House of Commons that he favoured responsible government for India, which would remain an integral part of the British Empire. These brave words caused an uproar in some circles and a number of resignations in India. How, they argued, could the secretary of state make such far-reaching concessions when Indian nationalists were stabbing Britain in the back? How, replied the others, could he refuse to do so when Indians were fighting and dying in large numbers for the common cause? In November 1917, Montagu travelled to India, met both Tilak and the Muslim leader, Jinnah, and worked out the details of a reform programme with Lord Chelmsford.

The Montagu-Chelmsford Report, which was published in August 1918, proposed a number of major steps towards self-government. Indians were to take care of education, public health, and agriculture. The British would still maintain control of the finances and the forces of law and order. The resulting division of power was given the title of "dyarchy."

The reforms were not implemented during the war; Montagu hoped that the promise would keep the peace until the fighting was over in France. They were finally put into effect in 1919 in the Government of India Act. More elected members were allowed in provincial legislatures, and Indians were given government portfolios on the basis of the division of powers in the dyarchy. India was granted partial democracy at the provincial level, although the central government remained authoritarian; but the calming effects of these reforms were largely nullified by the Rowlatt Acts, which called for harsh punishment for sedition, and by the Amritsar massacre in which nearly four hundred Hindus were killed by British soldiers.

India was not the only place in the Empire where there was trouble during the war. Although many French Canadians were sympathetic to the fate of Belgium, they were never particularly enthusiastic for the Entente. In 1917 there was rioting in Québec in response to the introduction of conscription. In Britain itself, the Easter Rebellion in Dublin in 1916 was suppressed with such savagery that "Home Rule" was no longer acceptable to Irish nationalists. They now demanded complete independence. Lloyd George's "Black and Tans," sent to Ireland in 1920 to pacify the Irish, completed the process of alienation.

Although the Dominions were co-operative, they used the Imperial War Conference of 1917 to demand a conference after the war to change constitutional relations with Britain. In future, co-operation was to be between sovereign nations sharing common interests and assumptions. The Dominions were recognized at the peace conference and signed the treaties. So did India, but its signature was somewhat hypocritical since the government of India in no sense represented the people. The French were in this case justified in its accusation that Britain was trying to pack the conference with its subject nations. The Dominions were accepted as full members of the League of Nations, and Australia, New Zealand, and South Africa were given their own mandated territories.

The situation in Egypt was more complicated. Egypt was nominally under Turkish suzerainty, and Turkey went to war on the side of the Central Powers. The British responded by declaring a protectorate over Egypt, promising to consider Egyptian self-government once the fighting was over. Egyptian nationalists were not impressed. They wanted something more concrete than a mere promise to consider.

The British also had to deal with the Turks, who threatened the Suez Canal and the oil fields of the Gulf. Fronts were established in Palestine and in Iraq, but they made little progress. Churchill's Gallipoli campaign, designed to knock Turkey out of the war, was a disaster. The Australians and New Zealanders lost terrible numbers, which caused much bitterness in the Antipodes. Anzac Day on 25 April, the anniversary of the landings, is a day of remembrance in both countries and often an occasion for the expression of anti-British sentiment. Canadian memories of Vimy Ridge and South African feelings about the campaign against General von Lettow Vörbeck in East Africa are not tinged with such rancour, but they were victories.

Britain lacked the manpower to do the job in the Middle East, and therefore it was tempted to ally with the Arabs, who wished to shake themselves free from the Turks. The Arab revolt, supported by the British, began in June 1916, and the results were spectacular. By the end of the year, Allenby had taken Jerusalem. In the following year, he occupied the rest of Palestine and pressed on into Syria. Iraq was taken by General Maude and his Indian troops.

Suez and the oil supply had been secured, but Britain was faced with the problem of what to do with the Middle East. In April 1916 Britain and France signed the Sykes-Picot Treaty. Under the terms of this agreement, Britain was to take Palestine and most of Iraq and the Persian Gulf; the French, Syria. It is hardly surprising that the terms were kept strictly secret until they were revealed, to the great embarrassment of the signatories, by the Bolsheviks, who for a brief moment preached the virtues of open diplomacy.

The Arabs had not struggled to free themselves from the Turks only to be subjected to French and British rule, and the Americans, who had convinced themselves that they were fighting for democracy and self-determination, took an equally dim view of the treaty. The British therefore felt constrained to make a number of promises to the Arabs in a series of declarations that sounded impressive but contained little of substance.

By far the best known of these declarations was made not to the Arabs but to the Jews. The Balfour Declaration of November 1917 was typically vague; it promised British support for "the establishment in Palestine of a national home for the Jewish people." The motives behind this declaration, like those in the other cases, were mixed. It was supported by Zionists as a firm commitment, by imperialists who wished to establish a client state in Palestine, and by others to win the support of Jews for the cause of the Entente. Balfour and the prime minister, Lloyd George, were honest enough to describe the declaration as "propaganda." There were also considerable differences of opinion within the British government over these declarations. Montagu strongly disapproved of the Balfour Declaration, and Balfour returned the compliment by disapproving of Montagu's declaration that India was to be granted responsible government in the foreseeable future.

Britain thus made a series of vague and often contradictory promises that were obviously designed to deceive the Arabs and probably the Jews as well. Moreover, the policy it pursued was clearly contrary to the principles expounded in President Wilson's fourteen points. In his best-selling account of the Arab revolt, the *Seven Pillars of Wisdom*, T. E. Lawrence (Lawrence of Arabia) openly admitted that he deliberately misled the Arabs with promises he knew he could not fulfil. To what extent his superiors were equally cynical is hard to determine. Most probably acted unthinkingly, on the spur of the moment, hoping that it would be possible to muddle through once the time came to make good on the promises.

With the defeat of the German and Turkish empires, there were rich pickings for the powers at the peace conference. With the Americans piously anti-imperialist, the Italians deemed undeserving of reward for their modest contribution to the war effort, and the Japanese interested only in their corner of the Pacific, the British and French could divide up South-West Africa, Tanganyika, Togoland, the Cameroons, Arabia, Syria, Iraq, Persia, Lebanon, and Palestine, along with more distant and exotic spots, such as Samoa, the Bismarck Archipelago, and Kaiser Wilhelmsland (the latter two became part of New Guinea). With Milner in the Cabinet as colonial secretary, Balfour as foreign secretary, and Curzon as lord president, it was obvious that the British intended to get as much as they could. In order to placate the Americans and others, these colonies were called "mandated territories," held as a "sacred trust" on behalf of the League of Nations until they were able to "stand by themselves under the strenuous conditions of the modern world." British imperialists thought this verbiage was silly, but they accepted the concept of mandated territories on the grounds that the League simply demanded standards of conduct that the British already respected in all their colonies.

In the Middle East the Sykes-Picot treaty formed the basis of the division of the spoils, leaving Britain with a sizeable addition to the Empire that almost satisfied Curzon's ambition for a land bridge from the Mediterranean to India, but it was to cause the British government endless headaches. In addition to Egypt, Aden, and Cyprus, Britain now controlled Palestine, Transjordan, Iraq, and the Persian Gulf states.

Cecil Rhodes did not live to see the fulfilment of his dream of a route from the Cape to Cairo controlled by Britain, but it was achieved by the annexation of Tanganyika. In West Africa much of Togoland and the Cameroons became part of the Empire, and South Africa took over South-West Africa (Namibia). The German Pacific colonies were divided up between Australia and New Zealand.

While Britain was thus adding to its Empire, relations with the self-governing Dominions were becoming strained. Sir Robert Borden, the prime minister of Canada, remarked in October 1918 that he had entered the war a devout imperialist and had ended it an insistent nationalist. He had become increasingly irritated by the failures of the consultative process during the war, and he was determined that Canada should have a voice at the peace conference. The Dominions were in fact granted dual status at the peace conference. As part of the British Empire delegation, they were given all the papers of the greater powers and served on the important committees and commissions. They were also given the status of smaller allied powers, which were not always privy to the deliberations of the Big Four. Meanwhile, in India the British found themselves obliged to negotiate with the nationalists. For the first time the Indian Civil Service was unable to acquire sufficient recruits from Oxford and Cambridge and had to make do with people from a lower social status. The élite from Oxbridge via the Public Schools preferred the Colonial Service, which, under the determined direction first of Milner and then of Churchill, greatly enhanced its prestige. Many now felt that since British influence in India was declining, the future lay in tropical Africa.

The experience of the war convinced the Dominions that some form of association of sovereign states under the British Crown was desirable. In 1917 Borden argued that "the dominions fully realize the ideal of an imperial Commonwealth of United Nations." General Smuts warmed to this theme and added: "People talk about a league of nations and international government, but the only successful experiment in international government that has ever been made is the British Empire, founded on principles which appeal to the highest political ideals of mankind." Smuts argued that this fact was not reflected in the constitution, which made the Dominions, in theory at least, "subject provinces of Great Britain." It was agreed at the Imperial War Conference in 1917 that the first postwar conference would address this issue; but by 1921, when the conference met, the British government had more pressing problems to deal with than a new constitution for a Commonwealth.

In April 1919 there was a riot in Amritsar in the Punjab triggered by the passions of Sikh, Hindu, and Muslim fundamentalists. The small local police force was unable to handle the situation, two banks were attacked, and the managers were beaten to death. An assistant manager of one bank, a railway guard, and an electrician were also murdered, and a woman missionary came within an inch of losing her life. The British authorities, fearing that this might be the beginning of another mutiny, ordered the nearest army brigade, commanded by General Dyer, to restore order. Dyer marched through the streets sounding the drum and ordering the mob to disperse, warning that if they did not they would be fired upon. The troops then fired at the crowd in a public square, the Jalianwala Bagh, killing 379 people. Dyer further ordered the flogging of six men and made all those who passed the spot where the missionary woman had been attacked crawl.

Reaction to the Amritsar massacre was varied. The crowd was Hindu, and thus the Sikhs thought Dyer a hero and made him an honorary member of their sect. After pressure was applied by Indian nationalists, an enquiry was held in Lahore under Lord Hunter. It censored Dyer, who was forced by the viceroy's council to leave the army. This decision was upheld by the British Cabinet, although it was unpopular with the army council. The British community in India was outraged and treated Dyer like a hero. Back in London, he was strongly supported by the House of Lords and by the majority of Conservative MPs. The *Morning Post* established a fund for him and collected £26,000 within a month. Although Edwin Montagu, the secretary of state for India, condemned the massacre as an act of "terrorism, racial humiliation and frightfulness," the majority of the British people sympathized with Dyer. Churchill also spoke of the "frightfulness" of the massacre and insisted that this was "not a remedy known to the British pharmacopoeia." In India it confirmed the fears of those who felt that the British promise of self-government was insincere and that "dyarchy" was a fraud that concealed absolute British control over the subcontinent. Gandhi, who had recruited Indians to fight for Britain in the trenches of France, now took over the political leadership of Congress and began his campaign of passive resistance and non-co-operation campaign of "satyagraha." The British continued to make concessions to the nationalists along the lines of the Montagu-Chelmsford Report, while still keeping the Indian government subordinate to Whitehall. Indians were now permitted to join the civil service, as had been proposed by the Lee Commission in 1917, and they could also become officers in the Indian Army. Indian representatives had been admitted to the Imperial War Cabinet and the War Conferences of 1917, and India was a member of the League of Nations, in spite of not being self-governing, a requirement of the League Covenant. All these reforms undermined the morale of the British in India. They realized that the writing was on the wall; but the concessions were not enough to appease the nationalists, who could point out the incongruity between the notion of India as a full member of the British Empire and the discrimination against Indians living in other parts of the Empire. There were many outbreaks of violence, usually spurred by religious hatreds, but the British, remembering Amritsar, were reluctant to intervene. For example, a violent clash between Muslims and Hindus near Madras in 1921 resulted in five hundred deaths. In February the following year a police station at Chauri-Chaura in the United Provinces was attacked; the police did not use their firearms, and twenty-two of them were brutally murdered. The main aim of British policy in India now was to uphold law and order, but it was difficult to know how to do so without provoking further resistance.

Britain was able to hold the line in India for the time being. The success of Gandhi's tactics at least meant that self-rule would not be attained by revolutionary violence. Furthermore, the country was seriously divided on religious lines, the Muslims fearing that a British Raj might well be replaced by a Hindu Raj, which was likely to be an even less attractive prospect.

Things were quite different with Britain's oldest and most intractable colonial problem. The Irish nationalists refused to compromise and could not be suppressed. Lord Birkenhead, the lord chancellor, regretted that he lacked the means to crush them; the British Army, the Royal Irish Constabulary, the Black and Tans, and the Auxiliary Division or "Auxis" had all failed to stop the Irish Republican Army, ably commanded by Michael Collins and generously financed by American sympathizers. The army and police had no idea how to combat the I.R.A's guerrilla tactics, and the Black and Tans and Auxis answered terror with terror. In Britain, many, including King George V, were disgusted at the behaviour of the British forces. The chief of the Imperial General Staff, Sir Henry Wilson, argued that peace could only be restored by full-scale war. Few relished this prospect, preferring to make a last attempt at conciliation, a course of action strongly supported by the king. Complex negotiations between Eamon De Valera, president of the provisional republican government, and Lloyd George finally resulted in the foundation of the Irish Free State. Since it did not include the six counties of Ulster, the Free State was not acceptable to a sizeable section of the I.R.A., and the fighting continued until April 1923.

Some wanted to give Ireland dominion status. Lloyd George wanted to do so as a symbolic effort to save the Empire. Smuts, who was in England for the imperial conference, felt that the Irish would accept dominion status just as the Boers had done. The political party of the nationalists, Sinn Fein, insisted that dominion status was irreconcilable with independence and that republicans could not owe allegiance to the king. De Valera wanted external association with Britain. Much of this argument had no point, for it was unclear what it actually meant. Lloyd George, for instance, was unable to define it. Still, there was no doubt that however vague the concept might be, dominion status did have great symbolic significance. Britain's "Other Island" had broken away, a colony had fought for its independence, and it had won. It reminded imperialists that the Empire was declining; renaming it a "British Commonwealth of Nations" was an admission that Britain's power was waning. The Irish Free State was fully self-governing but not fully sovereign. However, the Irish refused to acknowledge the existence of the imperial tie, and it became meaningless. When De Valera became prime minister in 1932, he set about severing the constitutional ties with the Commonwealth at once. It was not until 1949, when India became an independent republic and yet was admitted as a full member of the Commonwealth, that a solution was found to similar difficulties.

Events in Ireland also showed that the British lacked the forces needed to keep peace throughout the Empire. The massacre at Amritsar in April 1919 occurred at the same time as serious clashes between Jews and Arabs in Palestine. In May, the British were at war in Afghanistan and on the brink of war with Turkey. In July, there was a full-scale revolt in Iraq, and it seemed that Persia might also rebel. It was clear that the British government had to loosen its hold over much of the Middle East.

When the revolt in Iraq was crushed, the country was given a degree of self-rule, subject to British "advice." King Faisal was surrounded by British advisers, the RAF maintained a huge airfield at Habbaniya, and a financial agreement tied the country closely to Britain. Britain unilaterally declared Egyptian independence in 1922, acting on the recommendation of Lord Milner, but it continued to control Egypt's foreign affairs and maintained a large garrison to protect the Suez Canal. It was not until 1936 that an Anglo-Egyptian treaty gave the Egyptians some degree of real independence. Persia was abandoned, but the oil-rich Gulf states were retained. Arabia was handed back to the Arabs, except for the south coast, which was felt to be strategically vital for the defence of the canal. British control of the region was thus eased, and Balfour spoke of "unostentatious co-operation with the Arabs," but it was nonetheless a form of control that the British were determined to enforce.

Whereas the British were in retreat in Ireland and the Middle East, in Africa they continued their advance. Many influential figures dreamt of a great white Dominion in east-central Africa, the key to which was the wealthy colony of Southern Rhodesia. Here the whites held all the trump cards. They had the economic power, and they had not been administered by Whitehall but by an immensely wealthy company. When the company gave up the administration of the colony immediately after the war, it was assumed that the white settlers and their legislative council would take control. The British government tried to incorporate Southern Rhodesia into South Africa in order to minimize the cost of administration and also to counterbalance the Boers by an influx of prosperous British settlers. The proposal was rejected by a referendum of Rhodesian whites in November 1922. The government, anxious not to be locked in battle with the settlers and equally eager to save money, handed Southern Rhodesia over to the legislative assembly in October 1923. The Colonial Office reserved certain rights to object to legislation, but in fact the colony was now governed by the white settlers.

The East African Protectorate, soon to be known as Kenya, had a quite different structure. The population comprised some ten thousand whites, more than twice that number of Indians, and close to one million Africans. It was an explosive situation. The whites had a dramatic leader in Lord Delamere and enjoyed considerable support from the Conservatives, who approved of his ambition to create a white Dominion in Kenya. The Indians were determined that they should not become a subject people. They were politically organized and had the support of the government of India, which was sensitive to the problems of Indians elsewhere in the Empire whose cause was also loudly championed by the Indian nationalists. For them the fate of their fellow Indians in Africa was seen as clear indication of the sincerity of British policy in India itself.

The Indians strongly resisted the whites. They demanded equal voting rights for the legislative council, the abolition of all forms of segregation, and equal access to the rich farmlands of the White Highlands. Meanwhile, Harry Thuku organized the Kikuyu, who protested against the requirement that adult male Africans carry identity cards and also against the increase in taxes. Thuku's arrest in 1922 was followed by a riot in Nairobi in which twenty-five Africans were killed.

In addition, church leaders and humanitarians, supported by the powerful voice of Lord Lugard, demanded that the rights of the Africans should be respected. The British government tried to find a way out of this dilemma by publishing a white paper in 1923 that insisted that the interests of the Africans were more important than the conflicting claims of immigrant communities. But the statement amounted to a limited victory for the whites since the "Devonshire Declaration" argued that only the agents of the imperial government could act on behalf of the Africans. The Indians, who were not such agents, were thus not granted equal voting rights. Nevertheless, this concept of trusteeship also excluded the possibility of responsible self-government by the whites.

The whites were encouraged when Amery was appointed colonial secretary in Baldwin's Conservative government of 1925. Amery dreamt of an East African Dominion made up of Kenya, Uganda, Tanganyika, the Rhodesias, and Nyasaland, all dominated by the whites, who would nevertheless be mindful of their function as trustees. He was strongly supported by the governor of Kenya, Sir Edward Grigg, whom he had appointed and who worked hard for federation. Amery's white paper of 1927 proposed that the trust, hitherto held only in theory by the agents of the imperial government, should now be shared with the white settlers.

Amery's colleagues were less than enthusiastic about the vision of a Great White Dominion and proposed a royal commission under Sir Edward Hilton Young to examine the issue. The commission's report, published in 1929, argued that African interests had to be paramount and that the white settlers were not the best trustees of those interests. This was a severe blow to Amery and the settlers, but a worse one was to follow. In May 1929 the government resigned, and the new Labour government appointed the Fabian Sidney Webb (Lord Passfield) colonial secretary. He reasserted the Devonshire Declaration and insisted that responsible government could only be granted when all had adequate representation.

The settlers were furious at this rejection of white supremacy, and their supporters at home were determined not to give up the struggle. A joint committee of both Houses, dominated by the Conservatives under Amery and his former undersecretary, William Ormsby-Gore, managed to modify the definition of paramountcy to mean that the interests of one group should not be subordinated to those of another. This was an important step back towards the "dual policy" of trusteeship by both settlers and Whitehall and gave considerable encouragement to the settlers.

Although some colonial administrators supported the aspirations of the whites, many still believed in "indirect rule." They saw co-operation with tribal authorities as the best insurance against political unrest, and they felt the Africans were to be led gently but firmly onto the road to self-government. These principles did not please the educated urban élites, the "educated natives," "black Europeans," and "Afro-Saxons," who wanted the vote, jobs in the upper echelons of the civil service, and full and equal rights for Africans. They became the basis of the nationalist movements, which rejected the principles of indirect rule and which the colonial administrators found difficult to contain. These young Africans pointed out that "trusteeship" did not involve concern for the welfare of the natives, who scarcely benefited even from the copper boom in the barren bushlands of Northern Rhodesia and British Somaliland. The British made no effort to offer social services to Africans until the late 1930s, and then they were largely in response to violent protests against intolerable conditions. The enactment of the Colonial Development and Welfare Act in 1940 marked the beginning of a serious attempt at economic and social planning for the colonies.

Amery's enthusiasm for white settlers extended to the Jewish settlers in Palestine, whom he would have welcomed into the Commonwealth. Many imperialists felt that Zionists, especially secular ones, could provide the British with a useful ally in the Middle East. They also viewed Zionism as a civilizing force, and many anti-imperialists on the left shared their opinion. The problem was that the Palestine Arabs resisted the Jews, and Britain was obliged under the terms of the mandate to guarantee the civil and religious rights of the non-Jewish peoples in Palestine.

At first there was very little trouble in Palestine, and it was not until 1929 that the Arabs revolted in protest against Jewish immigration. The Jewish settlers retaliated violently. The Labour government produced a white paper in 1930 in which Lord Passfield threatened to cur back on Jewish immigration and to restrict the sale of Arab land to Jews. This possibility triggered off a massive protest from Jewish groups at home and abroad that the British government was rejecting the Balfour Declaration. It was supported by Conservative imperialists and by left-wing sympathizers with the Zionist cause. The government was forced to repudiate the suggestions made in the white paper, and there was a sharp increase in Jewish immigration, especially after Hitler was appointed chancellor of Germany in January 1933.

The Arab Rebellion from 1936 to 1939 resulted in some five thousand deaths, mostly Arab. In 1926 there had been about one hundred and fifty thousand Jews in Palestine; by 1936 there were about four hundred thousand, or one-third of the population. The more Jews there were in Palestine, the weaker the position of the Arabs and the greater their frustration. Increasing violence on both sides was the inevitable result. Since Palestine was a mandated territory and since the Arabs would resist fiercely, the British could not hand over even a part of Palestine to the Jews, as many wanted to do and as Lord Peel's Royal Commission suggested. They thus were faced with the increasingly difficult problem of keeping the peace and trying to find an equitable solution to an insoluble problem, a task made all the more difficult by the fear that the Arabs might join forces with Hitler during the coming war if Jewish immigration were not drastically reduced. The Jews, it was argued, would always fight Hitler, and their protests would thus have no strategic impor-tance. For the Zionists Britain's new policy was a dastardly betrayal, which few were ever able to forgive.

Compared with Palestine, the Caribbean was a haven of peace. The situation in the West Indies was unique in that it was a multi-racial society but that all the peoples—Africans, whites, Indians, and Chinese—were immigrants, and most were of varying degrees of mixed blood. Some non-whites were able, thanks to their exceptional abilities and determination, to get an education, become successful in the professions or business, and even win a seat on the legislative council. Others, like the great cricketer Learie Constantine, were greatly loved and respected and reminded countless Englishmen of the iniquity of the treatment of blacks in the Empire. This élite of African origin was insistent that blacks in the West Indies should be given the right to govern themselves and that they should not be treated as primitive tribesmen.

The oligarchical society of the West Indies would not give way to these demands, and only a small minority of the population were given the right to vote. The terrible economic conditions in the Caribbean worsened during the Depression, and there were widespread strikes, effectively organized by trades unions, and a number of violent riots. In 1938 the Moyne Royal Commission proposed far-reaching reforms that were to pave the way to creating a black commonwealth in the Caribbean.

This process advanced much further in Ceylon, where it seemed that the non-white population might soon achieve self-government. The Donoughmore Report of 1928 recommended that the vote should be given to all men over twenty-one and all women over thirty. They were to elect the members of the legislature, to which Ceylonese ministers would be responsible. This process permitted the development of democratic institutions before independence was granted, an example that unfortunately was rarely followed elsewhere in the non-white Commonwealth.

Most colonial administrators agreed with Lugard, who insisted that the aim of colonial policy should be to improve the moral and educational standards of the inhabitants of the colonies and to exploit the wealth of the colonies for their good and for the good of Britain. In the interwar years precious little was done about economic development in the colonies. Colonial medical and agricultural research councils were established, a few stretches of railway built, some harbours improved, but the total amount of money spent was minuscule. The Labour government introduced a colonial development bill in 1929, but contemporary economic theory argued that the best way to get out of a recession was to save money, so the funds available for colonial development were strictly limited. At the same time, the colonies were cruelly affected by the world depression, and most increases in output were offset by falling prices.

Little was done for the moral and educational needs of the colonies. In most of black Africa only 5 to 15 per cent of the children went to school, and most of these schools were substandard. Throughout vast parts of the Empire health care was primitive, sanitation deplorable, and housing totally inadequate. Successive British governments, which felt that they had little to spend on social welfare at home, spent even less on social welfare in the colonies. Schemes for colonial development, even when put forth by such forceful characters as Leopold Amery, got nowhere because the money for their realization was never made available.

That the purse-strings were not loosened was partly the result of disagreements about the direction colonial policy should take and partly the result of an increasing lack of interest in and enthusiasm for the Empire. Should India be seen as the centre of the Empire, or should the emphasis be on the development of Africa as a key part of a multi-racial commonwealth? Many efforts were made to stir up popular enthusiasm for the Empire, but most of the population, particularly the working class, remained apathetic. The efforts of people like Amery or Beaverbrook, who hoped that the working class could be weaned away from socialism by a thrilling vision of Empire, were fruitless. Those who wanted better housing, higher wages, and increases in unemployment benefits found it difficult to accept the argument that their standard of living would be improved by capital investments in distant parts of the Empire.

There was also a growing uneasiness that much of the talk about the moral mission in the Empire was hypocritical. The old imperialism of free trade had proudly contrasted the openness of the British Empire with the selfishness of other empires, which, it was argued, simply served selfish national interests. Britain could afford to keep the door open because as the wealthiest industrial nation it feared no competition and free trade suited her best. This sense of moral superiority was thus reinforced by self-interest; but now the basic justification of Empire was that it was in the national interest, not that it was moral. Indeed, it was increasingly questioned whether it might even be immoral. Were the rights of native peoples being respected? Was the Empire simply a means whereby greedy whites exploited local populations who were forced into submission by the civil and military authorities? Was not internationalism, isolationism, socialism, or some other -ism a more worthy ideology than imperialism?

An increasing number of people believed that the Empire could regain some of its moral probity by offering a framework within which colonies could be encouraged to develop to the point that they could become self-governing members of a multi-racial commonwealth. The white settler colonies had become self-governing Dominions. India had been promised that it would be allowed to follow suit. Imperialists in the Round Table group, many Liberals, and most of the Labour Party agreed that self-government should not be granted only to whites and that the Empire would fall apart if the principle were not applied to all its members. For the time being, however, much of this was theoretical, confined to the pages of *The Round Table* or to high-minded Fabian pamphlets for the simple reason that there was little serious pressure for change. In Africa, nationalist movements were only just beginning to organize, and elsewhere the local police and army garrisons could keep the peace. Even in India and the Middle East a few timely concessions were felt to be sufficient to postpone fundamental decisions about the future of the Empire.

There was also general agreement that most of the colonial peoples were not yet mature enough to run their own affairs. Many questioned whether India, in spite of the promises that had been made, would be ready for self-government in the foreseeable future. Most felt that self-government in Africa could only be considered when fundamental changes in the social fabric of the colonies had taken place, when African leaders had been educated to accept political responsibility, and when the masses would not be misled by self-seeking leaders. Racial prejudice was still deeply engrained, but at least the idea of self-government for the non-white Empire was now widely discussed.

Enthusiasts for indirect rule argued that British parliamentary institutions could not simply be transplanted to the colonies. This was not because the local population was necessarily too stupid or too backward but principally because they believed that different societies had different needs, different values, and different political cultures. Political institutions should be allowed to develop within each society to meet its own needs. The problem with this approach was that local institutions showed little sign of developing, and anthropologists warned of the evils of meddling with traditional societies. These warnings provided some comfort to colonial administrators who preferred to leave well enough alone as they had no blueprint for the future. The pros and cons of indirect rule were endlessly debated, but in practice the status quo was preserved and strengthened. Self-government seemed a distant prospect indeed.

The status quo suited most of the white Dominions. As Australian Prime Minister Billy Hughes argued in 1921, they had already achieved virtually all the rights of independent nations, and there was therefore nothing serious to discuss. Only Smuts, who was under pressure from South African secessionists, had any quarrel with this view. But Hughes was also adamant that there should be close consultation between Britain and the Empire over the formulation of common foreign policy goals. In many areas this was easy to achieve; in others, it was not. In 1921, for example, Australia argued strongly in favour of the renewal of the Anglo-Japanese alliance. The Canadians, who wished to appease their American protectors, opposed the suggestion. These differences were smoothed over during the Washington Conference of 1921–22, but the problem still remained that there was no machinery available for the implementation of a common imperial policy. Britain wished to keep a free hand; the Dominions were reluctant to pay their full shares of the cost of a common defence policy.

These problems were dramatized during the Chanak Crisis of 1922 when Britain seemed about to go with war with Turkey and Lloyd George and Churchill made an appeal for support from the Dominions. Whereas Australia and New Zealand responded immediately, the Canadians replied that the matter would first have to be debated in Parliament. The Canadian prime minister, Mackenzie King, won this round, and at the conference in 1923 the British government made no attempt to limit the Dominions' freedom of action in foreign policy. Indeed, the Dominions were given the right to have their own diplomatic representation abroad and to make treaties independently. The British reserved the right to deal with European affairs without consulting the Dominions. Thus, at Locarno in 1925, which guaranteed the borders between France and Germany, the Dominions were not consulted, did not expect to be consulted, and were not bound by the treaty.

The Empire no longer existed as a united diplomatic entity. Most of the Dominions felt that automatic support should be given to Britain in times of acute crisis, although General Hertzog of South Africa argued that the Dominions at least had the right to remain neutral. Hertzog got some support from Mackenzie King, who had been locked in battle with the governor general of Canada, Lord Byng, over the royal prerogative to dissolve Parliament and was in an isolationist mood. The Irish Free State could also be counted on to demand complete independence for the Dominions.

To the surprise of some, the British government conceded most of these points at the Imperial Conference in 1926. The "Balfour Definition" of inter-imperial relations clearly stated that the Dominions, although they owed a common allegiance to the Crown, formed a free association of autonomous states. This definition was given further expression by the appointment of British high commissioners to the Dominions, who acted, to all intents and purposes, as ambassadors. The governors general were now simply representatives of the Crown, substitute heads of state.

The problem remained that as long as the Dominions were subject to British statutes, legislation passed by the 'imperial' Parliament in Westminster, they were not fully sovereign. A conference of constitutional experts was convened in 1929 to examine this problem. Its recommendations were discussed at the Imperial Conference of 1930 and finally embodied in the Statute of Westminster of 1931. Henceforth, the Dominions were not bound by any past or future British act, unless they "requested, and consented to, the enactment thereof." By the same token, dominion acts could not be invalidated by the British Parliament. There was now no requirement for membership in the Commonwealth, as the Dominions had been formally called since 1926, other than that they owed allegiance to the Crown. The Statute of Westminster put an end to the "imperial parliament" and for this reason was greatly regretted by some conservatives and imperialists. Churchill denounced the statute as "pedantic, painful, and, to some at any rate, almost repellent." The Australian statesman R. G. Casey complained that "we have torn down a castle to build a row of villas." Most people felt that Churchill's objections were silly expressions of a long past imperial romanticism, sour grapes from a man who had recently resigned from the shadow cabinet over the appeasement of Indian nationalism and who was now in the political wilderness. The Statute of Westminster gave legal status to Balfour's formula and was widely accepted. The Commonwealth was now a very exclusive club within the Empire. Membership offered many advantages and demanded no obligations. It is for this reason that newly independent nations readily joined. In fact, Burma was the only ex-colony that declined the offer, and the Irish Republic decided to leave in 1948.

The Statute of Westminster was made at the height of the Depression, and much of the Commonwealth's efforts were now devoted to dealing with economic problems. In 1930 Mackenzie King was defeated in the Canadian general election by R. B. Bennett, who advocated a scheme of imperial free trade—a curious contradiction in terms that had been made popular by the British press barons Northcliffe and Rothermere. The British Labour government, which was impeccably orthodox in its belief in free trade, rejected the proposal out of hand. By 1932, when an economic conference was convened in Ottawa, the new Conservative chancellor of the exchequer in the coalition National government, Neville Chamberlain, was sympathetic to the proposal. He was, after all, the son of "Radical Joe," and Empire free trade was a revised version of tariff reform. The major result of the conference was the signing of the "Ottawa Agreements," a series of bilateral agreements on tariffs between members of the Commonwealth. It was a step in the direction of Empire free trade, but it was not quite the all-encompassing economic system its advocates had envisioned. Another important step towards making the Commonwealth into an economic rather than a political unit was the creation of the sterling area. It was formed in 1931 when Britain was forced off the gold standard, and it made sterling the monetary standard throughout the Empire, with the exception of Canada.

Defence soon became as much a matter of Commonwealth concern as economics with the increasingly serious challenges from both Germany and Japan. But once again it was difficult to forge a common policy. Canada and Ireland were reluctant to make any commitments that might result in their getting involved in a European war. South Africa wished to show its independence by emphasizing its role as an independent member of the League of Nations. The result was some confusion over such issues as the abandonment of sanctions against Italy in 1936 and the appeasement of Hitler. British governments quoted "dominion opinion," even though it was virtually never unanimous, as an excuse for a particular action or, more often, for inaction.

None of this was at all surprising since the Dominions were vastly different in the degrees of independence from Britain. Canada under R. B. Bennett looked to

Britain as a counterweight to the economic power of the United States and was an equal rather than a dependent. Similarly, South Africa was immensely rich, and her trading links with Britain were more the result of choice than of necessity. Both countries faced the problem of containing significant groups who were determined to preserve their identities. Boers and French Canadians harboured grudges against the British that could not be overcome within the framework of the Commonwealth. In the case of South Africa, these problems were further compounded by the determination of many statesmen to create a rigid segregation between whites and Africans.

Australia, New Zealand, and the Irish Free State, by contrast, needed British capital and British markets. During the Depression the volume of their exports to Britain fell, and their debts grew considerably. This situation was particularly resented in Australia where the Australian Labor Party insisted that it was the result of a deliberate policy by British capitalists to subjugate the country. Most people, however, believed that the link with Britain was essential for economic survival, particularly during a world depression. Coupled with this feeling of dependence were more positive ties of family and political culture.

Many statesmen felt that too much had been given away to India, the result, Lord Birkenhead suggested at the beginning of his four-year term as secretary of state for India in 1924, of "malaise" rather than weakness. They hoped to put off self-government for as long as possible and disingenuously argued that dyarchy amounted to responsible government and should satisfy Indian demands.

It is no wonder that Gandhi did not trust the British. His illusions about the British Empire, which he had trusted, admired, and even loved had been shattered by the Amritsar massacre. Now he denounced the British government in India as "satanic" and insisted that paying taxes to it was to subsidize atrocities. He called for non-violent protests and civil disobedience and collected a mass following. But the campaign soon got out of hand, and after the murderous attack by his followers on the Chauri-Chaura police station in the United Provinces, Gandhi was arrested and jailed by a young judge, C. N. Broomfield, who, in passing sentence, referred to Gandhi as a "great patriot and a great leader" and spoke of his "noble and even saintly life." Gandhi was soon released, much to Broomfield's delight.

Many felt that Gandhi had been tamed and that Indians could be appeased by liberal reforms. The major problem now seemed to be not Congress but the British Labour Party, which gave the impression of being determined to give India away. In order to meet this threat, Birkenhead set up a Statutory Commission, headed by Sir John Simon, in 1927. Under the terms of the 1919 act, it was to report in ten-years' time on how the act was working and on the prospects for the future. Fearing that Labour would win the next election, the government appointed this commission, which did not include a single Indian, two years ahead of time. Gandhi and the Congress boycotted the commission, which they saw as a deliberate insult, and wherever the commission travelled in the six months it was in India, it was greeted with mass demonstrations and riots. A committee of Congress, chaired by Motilal Nehru, father of Jawaharlal, drew up a constitution for a fully independent India and presented it to the British government in spite of the objections of the Muslim League, which felt that the provisions for communal elections were unfair.

Even before the Simon Commission published its report, the viceroy, Lord Irwin (later Lord Halifax), a man in whom Gandhi had absolute confidence, announced that the government intended to give India full dominion status. For Gandhi this status probably would have been enough, but the radical young Congress leaders Jawaharlal Nehru and Subhas Chandra Bose rejected the suggestion out of hand and demanded complete independence. Determined not to be overtaken by the radicals, Gandhi responded by his dramatic salt marches. This hugely successful publicity stunt was ostensibly directed against the salt tax and the prohibition against the unlicensed manufacture of salt. Once again, his non-violent protest led to the violence that Gandhi abhorred. Gandhi was jailed along with sixty thousand others, but he was soon released by Irwin, who invited him to discuss the situation at the vice-regal residence in Delhi, a palace then under construction that was to be even larger than Versailles. Winston Churchill expressed his disgust at "the nauseating and humiliating spectacle of this one-time Inner Temple lawyer, now turned seditious fakir, striding half-naked up the steps of the Viceroy's palace to parley on equal terms with the representative of the King Emperor." On the other side, many Indian nationalists also protested that Gandhi had consented to talk to Irwin.

Both the Conservative prime minister, Baldwin, and his Labour successor, MacDonald, agreed with Irwin that a compromise solution had to be found and that major concessions would have to be made to Congress. Baldwin stood up to Churchill and his imperialist cronies, who wanted no such concessions, and MacDonald resisted the Labour left's demands for immediate independence for India. Three Round Table Conferences were held with Indian representatives, and for the second of these Gandhi travelled to London. King George V invited him to tea and warned him that he would not have any attacks on his Empire. Gandhi made a considerable impact on British public opinion, but he did not greatly impress those in power. While he was in London, the truce in India broke down. In 1931 the National Coalition government appointed Lord Willingdon viceroy. He disliked Gandhi and took a firm line against civil disobedience when the Mahatma mounted a fresh campaign in 1932. Much to Churchill's delight, Gandhi was sent to prison and the civil disobedience campaign was called off; but it was clear that there could be no turning back and that the argument was now about the speed at which the changes should be made. In Britain there was general agreement that progress towards dominion status should be slowed down.

Baldwin and MacDonald's proposals for limited reform in India were grudgingly accepted by Gandhi, who was able to convince Congress to accept them in spite of vigorous protests from Nehru and the radicals. These proposals formed the basis of the Government of India Act of 1935, the longest act in the statute book, passed after 15.5 million words had been expended upon it in parliamentary debate.

The Indian provinces were now given responsible government, the governors being reduced to mere representatives of the Crown, although they were given substantial reserve powers in an emergency under section 93. Nehru proposed a boycott of provincial elections, but the majority of the Congress thought otherwise, and as a result the party won eight of the eleven provinces.

In the provinces the act was a success; with the central government it was not. The problem was that the princes had proposed a federal solution whereby they would preserve their autonomous powers; it was a solution warmly welcomed by the British, since most of the princes had banned Congress, and they would be valuable conservative allies against the Congress radicals. Congress, naturally enough, protested vigorously. The princely states were overrepresented in the bicameral federal legislature, and the delegates were not elected but appointed by the princes. Furthermore, certain important matters, such as defence, foreign affairs, the protection of minorities, and tariffs on British imports, were still reserved to the viceroy. The British, aided by their princely allies, thus maintained their rule under changed conditions.

The British die-hards felt that these reforms went too far and would lead eventually to independence for India. Churchill, for example, was determined to scupper the new constitution and managed to persuade the princes to have nothing to do with it, arguing that it was a sinister plot to hand over power to the firebrands in the Congress. The new viceroy, Lord Linlithgow, sent three officials around India to explain the new constitution and to convince the princes that it was in their best interests to accept it, but to no avail. They refused to accept the new constitution so that at the centre the viceroy and his council were in charge, a situation that many British officials found admirable.

In the provinces the governments found, much to their surprise, that the governors hardly ever interfered and that the British civil servants obeyed their instructions. The major problem in the provinces was that the Muslims, with the exception of Muslim members of Congress, were largely excluded. This was the inevitable result of the British electoral system of election by constituencies rather than proportional representation, but it led to widespread anger among Muslims. The leader of the Muslim League, Mohammed Ali Jinnah, was the reverse of a religious fanatic. He enjoyed drinking whiskey, and his wife was a Parsee. He had left Congress when he failed to convince Gandhi to make the concessions needed to reassure the Muslim community. Jinnah felt that as a mass party Congress was prey to Hindu fanaticism, and he left India in 1931 and became a successful barrister in London. He was persuaded to return to India in 1934 to become leader of the Muslim League.

In the 1937 provincial elections the Muslim League did very poorly, getting a mere 5 per cent of the Muslim vote. It is hardly surprising, therefore, that the League did not get any share in government. The antics of some Hindu extremists in the new provincial parliaments convinced Jinnah that the British Raj was about to be replaced by a Hindu Raj, not a pleasing prospect for India's Muslims. Nehru hoped that Jinnah and the Muslim League, having been trounced at the elections, would return to the fold of Congress. Congress could then shake off the image of being essentially a Hindu party and reassert its nonsectarian character. Congress could also then claim to be the party of all Indians. Jinnah, an immensely proud man, felt insulted by these suggestions, and Gandhi and Nehru made no attempt to appease him. He therefore set about the Herculean task of making the Muslim League into a mass political movement. It was a tragic turn of events, for it meant that an independent India, which virtually everyone agreed was soon to come into existence, would be partitioned and would be the scene of some of the most terrible mass killings in human history.

Looking back at the Empire on the eve of the World War II, it seems clearly to have been on the brink of collapse. The white Dominions were independent nations, India was soon to be a sovereign state, other colonies in Africa, Asia, and the Caribbean were to follow suit. But at the time it seemed quite different. Even anti-imperialists in the Labour Party imagined that the end of Empire, for which they professed to yearn, would come in the distant future and seemed as remote and nebulous as the classless society. Few imperialist die-hards could bring themselves to even contemplate the prospect. The British still regarded themselves as a world power with worldwide obligations and commitments. As such, they could not devote all their attention to European affairs. The case for appeasing Hitler was strengthened by the argument that it was not possible to resist both Germany and Japan. The case for resisting Japan was much more compelling. The Dominions had nothing to fear from Germany; Australia and New Zealand had a great deal to fear from Japan. The staggering sum of £60 million was spent on improving the defences of Singapore in an attempt to secure this vital base against the Japanese threat. But even if Singapore was mistakenly thought to be impregnable, the Japanese menace was still very real.

The consequences of this illusion of imperial power were ironic. The British found themselves fighting for their lives in Europe and were to lose their Empire. The Dutch-American popular historian Hendrik van Loon was almost alone in suggesting that "What until a few years ago constituted the heart of a mighty empire, will rapidly transform itself into an over-populated island lying somewhere off the Danish coast." The vast majority believed that the Empire would be around for at least as long as they were likely to be and that Britain, for all its problems, was still a truly great power. This illusion of power might now seem ridiculous, but it was the source of tremendous pride and strength in the dark days of the coming war.

5 The Empire and Commonwealth at War, 1939–1945

When World War II began, it seemed to many that the Commonwealth and Empire were more a liability than a source of strength. It was even larger than it had been in 1914, but its enormous size was out of all proportion to Britain's strength. Britannia no longer ruled the waves, and it could not maintain a convincing military presence in both Europe and the Pacific. The Empire did provide five million men to fight Britain's war, but most of these were used to defend the Empire, a task that could never have been effective without the massive, and often reluctant, help of the Americans. Furthermore, the British used more of their own men to defend the Empire than the Empire sent to Europe.

In 1939 the Empire was seething with unrest. India and Egypt were full of nationalist turmoil. In Palestine Arabs and Jews were at each others' throats as were Turks and Greeks in Cyprus. In the West Indies and in some of the African colonies there were the first signs of nationalist revolt. In the white Dominions there were problems too. Ireland had virtually left the Commonwealth, and South Africa was an unwilling ally. Canada had not always been compliant during the interwar years, and French-Canadian attitudes were unpredictable. Australia and New Zealand depended on British military support, for they only had modest reserves of manpower.

The war was at first exclusively European. Hitler's rapacious intentions were not directed against the Empire, and there seemed little that the Commonwealth could do to save Poland, to which the British government had given a guarantee. Nevertheless, Australia and New Zealand, conscious of their need for British protection should the Japanese continue their aggressive policies but also mindful of their ties to Britain, promptly joined the Allied cause. Canada insisted on the right to debate the issue in the House of Commons; then, a week after Britain's declaration, voted almost unanimously for war. In South Africa, Smuts, who was strongly anti-German and quite strongly pro-British, succeeded Hertzog as prime minister and won a majority of thirteen for war. Most Afrikaners were opposed, and some were even vociferously pro-Nazi. Three future prime ministers of South Africa were among those interned for advocating the cause of Adolf Hitler. The Irish Free State proclaimed itself neutral and thus denied the British bases that would have been very useful against the Atlantic U-boats; but it offered no help or encouragement to the Germans. Many Irishmen volunteered for the British armed forces, and only a handful helped the Nazis, the most infamous of whom was "Lord Haw-Haw" (William Joyce), who made Nazi propaganda broadcasts from Berlin and was hanged for treason in 1946.

In India the viceroy simply announced that war had broken out. Most of the Congress party heartily detested Nazi Germany, and Gandhi and Nehru sympathized with the British cause, but they argued that if they were going to be called upon to fight in defence of democracy, they ought to have a democracy to defend. When the British government refused to make any statement on its plans for the future of India, the provincial governments resigned in protest. The British governors then invoked section 93 of the India Act and ruled the provinces by decree.

Obviously, some major concessions would have to be made to Congress if Britain was to win Indian confidence and support. Linlithgow proposed an expansion of the viceroy's council to include Indians and a guarantee that India would be granted dominion status after the war. Churchill, who had announced that he had "not become First Minister of the Crown in order to preside over the liquidation of the British Empire," rejected these proposals out of hand. In October 1940 Gandhi began another campaign of civil disobedience.

In the Middle East the majority of the population was anti-British. In Egypt, officials prepared to welcome Rommel's Afrika Korps. There was a rebellion in Iraq in 1941 that was temporarily successful, and Britain and the U.S.S.R. invaded Iran to chase away its German advisers and to secure its oil. Palestine remained in permanent and bloody turmoil.

The situation became even worse after the Japanese attack on Pearl Harbor. Hong Kong fell within days. The Japanese swept through Malaya, and the great fortress of Singapore, on which the defence of the Pacific hinged, fell almost without a fight. It was one of Britain's most ignominious defeats. Churchill called it "The greatest disaster and worst capitulation in the history of the British Empire." Rangoon was occupied in March, the Burma road to China was cut off, and the Japanese soon held most of Burma. With the collapse of General Wavell's command, the East Indies lay open to the invaders. Britain's power and prestige were shattered by these defeats. The white man's vaunted superiority was seen to be a hollow boast. It was only the racist horrors of Japan's "Great East Asia Co-prosperity Sphere" that convinced many Asians that they preferred the somewhat humbled British to the brutal Japanese.

The British knew that the Empire in Asia would never be the same again. The Labour Party mounted a spirited attack on the Conservatives for failing to keep their promises, particularly to India, and demanded that self-government be granted as soon as possible. Most Conservatives agreed, some with considerable reluctance, that it would not be possible to return to Asia after the defeat of Japan as if nothing had happened.

The consequences of Pearl Harbor were not all catastrophic for Britain, for now Britain and the Empire no longer fought alone; they had the United States— a mixed blessing. The British thought Roosevelt's dislike of colonial empires foolish and hypocritical, but they had to take it into account. The United States championed the cause of national liberation and so gave enormous encouragement to the nationalist movements within the Empire.

The British collapse in Asia further called into question the nature of "trusteeship," which was the basic doctrine of the British colonial administration: a legacy of nineteenth-century imperial thought that was increasingly hard to justify. The old paternalism had to be replaced by the idea of partnership, and the war forced the British to take colonial aspirations seriously. Britain could no longer wait until the colonies reached the age of consent; it had to promote their welfare and development actively. These views were eloquently expressed by an exalted mandarin, Lord Hailey, a retired Indian civil servant, former governor of the Punjab and later of the United Provinces, and an influential writer on imperial and commonwealth affairs. They found an increasing resonance in the Conservative party and complemented the rekindled concern for progressive welfare legislation at home.

What self-government meant was now also called into question. Previously, internal autonomy was considered self-government, and the fact that Britain kept control of foreign affairs and defence was not seen as a limitation. Hailey, however, insisted that self-government implied dominion status, and he suggested that Asian and African colonies could become Dominions.

Hailey was fully aware of considerable difficulties attached to such a programme. It was generally agreed that some colonies were not ready for self-government and that their peoples could not be abandoned to ruthless chieftains or their minorities left to the whims of majorities. Native administrators had to be taught how to govern honestly and impartially, and this training was even more important than the introduction of parliamentary institutions. The viability of such changes was an issue that had played an important part in the deliberations of the Paris peace conference after the World War I.

Could a small African colony or remote Caribbean island survive on its own as an independent state? Here federation seemed to be the best solution. India's federal constitution of 1935 seemed to point the way. A West Indian federation and an association of African states suggested a possible solution. During the war a number of regional centres were established to co-ordinate military and economic efforts in Central America, the Middle East, West Africa, and the Pacific. General

Smuts proposed an East African federation under South Africa in an explosive article in *Life* that attacked the United States' strong criticism of colonialism. Further encouragement for federations came from the Australian W. K. Hancock in his influential book, *Survey of British Commonwealth Affairs,* which attacked the British for investing little in the Empire and for failing to encourage self-government. From the West Indies W. M. Macmillan declared that trusteeship was an "anaemic" doctrine and recommended the establishment of development commissions along the lines of Roosevelt's Tennessee Valley Authority. Macmillan argued that they should be backed up by an intensive education programme; indirect rule, he said, had propped up the old élites and blocked extension of the franchise and the creation of an administrative class.

Round Table agreed that trusteeship was inadequate; the speedy collapse of the British Empire in Asia had shown how shallow its roots were. The paper suggested that it was unreasonable to expect all the colonies to adopt parliamentary governments and follow the path of the Dominions. This being so, they could never be integrated into the Commonwealth, and some other form of affiliation would have to be worked out. There was a hint here that certain residual powers would remain in British hands. Many, however, did not see inherent dangers in a multiracial Commonwealth. The former colonial minister and staunch imperialist, L. S. Amery saw no reason why the African colonies should not eventually be included in the Commonwealth. Young Conservative reformers went much further. In his introduction to the pamphlet "Forward from Victory," R. A. Butler charged the government with having starved the colonies of capital and with neglecting education. He called for federations in the West Indies and East Africa and for full dominion status for India and other colonies.

All these critics wanted an active colonial policy that would abandon indirect rule and speed up the process of self-government. Parliament, which showed little interest in the Empire, and a tight-fisted Treasury would have to change their ways. The British people would have to accept that the Empire gave the nation only an illusion of power. The object of colonial policy should thus be decolonization, a word coined by Hailey. Decolonization was never confused with independence; it implied a change of status within the Empire, not a separation from it.

The government was slow to react to these promptings, and colonial issues were not debated in the House of Commons until June 1942. Harold Macmillan, then undersecretary of state, insisted that the lesson of the war was that independence without adequate defence was meaningless. It was pointless to break up the Empire into a series of small countries. Only larger groupings, in close partnership with Britain, could provide the necessary security. The British Empire was not an exploitative institution as the Americans seemed to imagine; it provided defence, encouraged trade, and provided a stable monetary system and a modern transportation network. It was a partnership for mutual benefit. The colonies would have a far brighter future within the Commonwealth than as helpless little independent nations.

But Macmillan's speech was still vague on details. He had avoided any mention of dominion status, and talk of "the greatest divergence of local responsibility" could mean almost anything.

Later in 1942, Viscount Cranborne made a more specific statement of government policy towards the colonies. The aim, he stated unequivocally, was that the colonies should become self-governing nations like Canada, Australia, New Zealand, and South Africa. This was not the end of the Empire but a new phase in its history. "We, the citizens of the British Empire, whatever our race, religion or colour, have a mission to perform, and it is a mission that is essential to the welfare of the world. It is to ensure the survival of the way of life for which the United Nations are fighting, a way of life based on freedom, tolerance, justice and mutual understanding, in harmony with the principles of the Atlantic Charter." Cranborne did not make any promises or set a timetable, and he stressed that in certain colonies progress was "inevitably slow." He made the retreat from Empire appear to be a glorious civilizing mission rather than a surrender.

The government did not just make statements of intent; it also undertook a number of reforming measures. The crisis in the West Indies had resulted in the appointment of a royal commission in 1938, and its proposals for economic and social improvements were adopted. The formation of labour unions was actively encouraged, and they became the basis of new political parties. In 1944 universal suffrage was introduced in Jamaica, and a semi-responsible government under Alexander Bustamente was formed. Similar changes took place in Trinidad, Barbados, and British Guiana, but efforts to form a West Indian federation with dominion status were not successful. A federation was finally patched together in 1958, but it fell apart four years later.

In Africa reforms concentrated on local government and the inclusion of a larger number of Africans in the administration. Two Ghanaians were admitted to the executive council of the Gold Coast; British trade unionists advised Africans on how to establish unions, which had proved such a successful method of political education in the West Indies. The Gold Coast and Nigeria were given new constitutions, and regional councils were established in Northern Rhodesia. But there were also reminders that Africa was not ready for full self-government. When Nana Sir Ofori Atta, the Ashanti paramount chief, member of the Gold Coast Legislative Council since 1915 and one of the first Africans to receive a knighthood, died in 1943, a human sacrifice was offered at his funeral. Where such practices occurred, the British felt that democracy was a distant prospect. Serious efforts were made to improve education, and a number of African universities were founded, with degrees to be granted by London University. Such training would develop an African élite who could take on the responsibilities of self-government. In early 1945, the government established a Colonial Development and Welfare Fund, and efforts were made to improve the African economies. During the war the achievements were necessarily limited.

In spite of these changes, there was considerable unrest in Africa. The 1941 Atlantic Charter, which promised all peoples the right to choose their own form of government, encouraged nationalists, and they were tempted to act while Britain was fighting for its life. The Kenyan Kikuyu Central Association was banned because it was thought to be conspiring with the Italians, and nationalist political parties were formed in Nigeria, Nyasaland, and the Cameroons in 1944. There was a violent strike in the copper mines of Northern Rhodesia. Two divisions of West Africans had fought the Japanese in Burma, and the sixty-five thousand troops returning after the war ended in Europe had expectations of major improvements at home. Britain's postwar prime minister, Clement Attlee, promised that the Atlantic Charter applied to all peoples.

In Asia during the war years, with the Japanese on the Burmese border and the Royal Navy no longer able to protect the east coast, the situation in India was critical. Roosevelt and Chiang Kai-shek pressured Churchill to make a generous offer to ensure the loyalty of the subcontinent. A committee on India, chaired by Attlee, proposed that India should be guaranteed dominion status after the war in return for its support. Churchill sent Sir Stafford Cripps out to put these proposals to the Congress leaders. Cripps was more than willing to go. He was on friendly terms with Nehru, sympathized with his cause, and was determined that his mission would succeed. Churchill, on the other hand, resented being pushed into giving up India, he did not want the Indians to have any say in the running of the war, and his very position as prime minister was being challenged by Cripps. Churchill had made Cripps leader of the House of Commons on his triumphant return from Moscow, where, as ambassador, he was seen as the architect of the Anglo-Soviet alliance.

The British proposals were that the Indians should decide their constitutional future after the war and that a number of Indian politicians should immediately join the viceroy's executive council to help run the war. These recommendations were not enough for Congress. Gandhi said the proposals amounted to drawing a "post-dated cheque on a crashing bank." Congress insisted that the government of India should be handed over immediately and that it should have full dominion powers.

Cripps, a brilliant negotiator, tried to persuade Congress that if they had a majority on the viceroy's council, their powers would equal those of a dominion government. At this point Linlithgow objected that Cripps was "baiting the trap with my cheese" and secretly began to correspond with Churchill in order to undermine Cripps's position. Churchill, furious that Cripps was now supported by Roosevelt's envoy to Delhi, Colonel Louis A. Johnson, claimed that Cripps had exceeded his instructions. Taking the chair of the cabinet India committee, the prime minister insisted that Cripps could only present the government's proposals, which he knew were utterly unacceptable. He then telegraphed Linlithgow assuring him that the viceroy's constitutional powers would not be limited. This marked the end of Cripps's mission.

The failure of the Cripps mission gave further ammunition to those Indian nationalists who, under the leadership of the Bengali extremist Subhas Chandra Bose, believed that their cause could best be served by allying with Germany and Japan. Bose had travelled to Berlin, via Moscow, in early 1941, where he told Ribbentrop that he was eager to support Germany. Hitler, however, admired the British Raj, which he saw as the perfect example of how racially superior people could lord it over hundreds of millions of subhumans—an example he intended to emulate in eastern Europe. On the other hand, he felt that Bose had a certain nuisance value. The Germans gave him propaganda facilities, including the "Free India" radio, helped him organize an Indian Legion out of Indian prisoners of war, and permitted him to co-operate with the anti-British Faquir of Ipi in Afghanistan.

The Germans soon tired of Bose and sent him off to Singapore, where he proclaimed a new government of India, called Azad Hind, organized an Indian National Army under the Japanese, and continued his propaganda efforts. The Japanese found Bose as tiresome as the Germans had. His army disgraced itself in battle, his propaganda had little tangible effect, and his fortunes waned with those of his Japanese patrons. He was killed in a plane crash while he was attempting to escape to Moscow. What fate would have awaited him there can be imagined.

Bose was a man of exceptional intelligence: he had scored highly in the ICS examinations, and he had been Congress's president despite Gandhi's opposition. In his native Bengal he had a considerable following, but his alliance with the Germans and Japanese was misguided. Gandhi, Nehru, and the majority of Indians could not bring themselves to side with Britain's enemies. They profoundly respected many aspects of British civilization, detested Nazism and everything it stood for, and realized that India would be considerably worse off under Japanese rule.

Congress was at a political stalemate. Then Gandhi came up with one of the gnomic slogans that secured his continued leadership of the popular mass movement. "Quit India" was a vague response, and there is no evidence that Gandhi had any idea of what he intended to achieve. Proclaiming that India should be left in God's hands, that non-violence would "sterilize" the Japanese, and that his followers should "do or die" did nothing to clarify the situation. Linlithgow did not wait to see what would happen. He had Gandhi and other Congress leaders arrested and banned the party. Widespread violence followed. The railway from Delhi to Calcutta was blown up. Supplies could no longer get to the Burmese front. Telegraph lines were cut, policemen were killed, and it seemed that India was on the brink of a full-scale revolt. But the British authorities stood firm, and the violence soon subsided.

The main beneficiary of the Quit India movement was the Muslim League. With Congress unable to function, they were invited to form governments in four provinces—Bengal, Sind, North-West Frontier Province, and Assam. In 1940 Jinnah had issued the Lahore resolution, which called for the creation of a separate Muslim state to be called Pakistan. In Urdu "Pak" means pure and "stan" land, and this "Land of the Pure" was also a mnemonic of Punjab, Afghania (North-West Frontier Province), Kashmir, Sind, and Baluchistan. To these were to be added Bengal, Assam, and the Muslim areas of the north-east.

Jinnah's scheme, which seemed hopelessly impractical in 1940, was given a boost by Cripps, who had promised that any province could secede from an independent India should it so wish. Churchill supported the opt-out clause because it would make life more difficult for Congress and would, he hoped, secure the loyalty of Muslim soldiers, of whom there were disproportionately large numbers. Linlithgow and Wavell, the commander-in-chief in India, had serious reservations. Jinnah was determined to seize the opportunity, and he now proclaimed that he was not merely leader of the Muslim League but also of all Indian Muslims. Many Muslim leaders protested at his dictatorial aspirations and at the probable disastrous consequences of a religiously divided India, but they feared that Jinnah would appeal for popular support and that he would succeed. Unable to beat him, they joined his cause. The British also accepted this suave lawyer as the spokesman of the Indian Muslims, which greatly enhanced his stature.

In 1943 Churchill appointed a new viceroy—Lord Wavell, a one-eyed warrior rumoured to be something of an intellectual who was taciturn to the point of being virtually mute and thus not very adept at communicating with politicians. Churchill counted on him to do nothing, but he had miscalculated. Far from continuing with Linlithgow's policies, Wavell was determined to give Indians a far greater share in the government and to prepare the way for independence as soon as the war was over.

One of Wavell's first acts was to release Gandhi, but London ordered Wavell not to talk to the Mahatma. Gandhi's situation was radically altered, since Congress had fallen apart, and most of its leaders were still in jail. Jinnah dominated the political stage, and discussions centred on the campaign to create a Muslim state. Gandhi resolved to meet Jinnah and in effect agreed to the Lahore declaration. Jinnah responded by raising the ante. He demanded that Gandhi accept an independent Pakistan.

Jinnah's intransigence prompted Wavell to action, but the India Committee refused to agree that a major political initiative was needed and even refused Wavell permission to travel to London to state his case. When he did go, he was kept waiting for days and hardly got a hearing. Eventually, in May 1945, the government did agree to allow Congress and the Muslim League to appoint representatives to the viceroy's council.

Wavell's argument was that if Britain did not secure a friendly partnership with India, it would also lose its influence in China, Burma, Malaya, and the rest of the Far East. He pointed out that the promise of self-government had been made by Montagu in 1917 and by Cripps in 1942 and that it would be unthinkable to go back on that solemn undertaking. He was supported in his view by the commander-in-chief, Sir Claude Auchinleck, and by the vast majority of the British in the ICS. Churchill finally gave way when a general election had been called and he feared that India might become a damaging issue.

Once again, Jinnah disrupted the negotiations. He insisted that only the Muslim League be allowed to appoint the Muslim members. Congress had many Muslim members, and its president, Maulana Abul Kalam Azad, a Muslim, was appalled at the suggestion that Congress was a purely Hindu party. Furthermore, since the Muslims were allotted half the Indian seats on the council, although they accounted for only one-quarter of the population, Jinnah would receive disproportionate power. Wavell turned Jinnah down flat since he could not afford to alienate the Punjab Unionists. The Punjab, with its large Muslim population, provided half the Indian Army, and it was India's bread basket. Jinnah promptly announced that he would refuse to co-operate if Wavell did not meet his demands. Wavell's situation was impossible. If he gave way to Jinnah, the council would not be representative. If Jinnah would have nothing to do with it, the results would also be unrepresentative.

The overwhelming victory of the Labour Party at the elections of 1945 and the victory over Japan completely altered the situation. Prime Minister Attlee wanted Indian independence as soon as possible and called for nationwide elections for a constituent assembly. These elections, held at the end of 1945, resulted in a triumph for Congress. The Muslim parties, other than the League, and notably the Punjab Unionists, went down to a crushing defeat. Jinnah was in a good position to claim to speak for all Indian Muslims, an opportunity he was quick to exploit. The struggle was now no longer between the Indians and the British, but between Hindus and Muslims.

The constitutional developments in Burma in the interwar years were similar to those of India. A dyarchy was established in 1923, and in the 1930s semi-responsible government was granted. The governor held significant reserve powers and controlled the administration, but the cabinet was largely Burmese, and it was responsible to an elected parliament.

At the beginning of the war, Burmese nationalists, prompted by the Indian example, demanded immediate independence as a precondition for their support for Britain. The British government spoke vaguely about dominion status after the war. The Burmese, supported by the governor, Sir Reginald Dorman-Smith, demanded a definite promise to this effect. Churchill, however, insisted that no promises be made.

The young Burmese nationalists, led by Aung San, who had organized an anti-British student strike in Rangoon in 1936, welcomed the Japanese invasion. The Japanese made him head of the Burmese National Army (BNA) and encouraged the independence movement. The Burmese soon lost any illusions that they might have entertained about the Japanese. Clearly, were the Japanese to win the war, Burma would become a colony. Japanese rule in Burma, for all the talk about co-prosperity and Asian brotherhood, was brutal. The nationalists therefore began talks with the British secret service at the end of 1943, offering to help drive the Japanese out if they were guaranteed independence.

The British were now in an awkward quandary. Should they accept the offer, or should they put the nationalists on trial as collaborators and traitors? The Burmese Chamber of Commerce, representative of British economic interests, had no doubts. They demanded that the nationalists be put on trial and that the property of Indians who had fled Burma be restored to them. Some progressives in the Conservative Party pointed out that the Burmese economy was almost entirely controlled by foreigners and that the Burmese had been ruthlessly exploited. It was time that the wealth of their country be given back to them. *The Times* agreed, arguing that Burma should be granted independence immediately after the war and that it would be wrong to treat the country differently from India. The British authorities, however, felt that Burmese independence would have to be postponed for several years after the war in order to build up the economy so that, as Dorman-Smith put it, the British could "hand over a country for which we have done a good job of work."

93

In spite of the objections of the British government, of the British administration of Burma in their exile in Simla, and of his political advisers, Lord Louis Mountbatten, the commander-in-chief of South East Asia Command, insisted that Aung San and the Burmese National Army be welcomed as allies. He argued that he needed their help to drive out the Japanese and that postwar reconstruction would be impossible without their active co-operation.

In May 1945 the government at last published its white paper on Burma, which stated that Burma should be given the right to decide on a new constitution three years after the end of the war. Eventually, Burma would get dominion status, provided that certain British interests were guaranteed. This offer was too little, too late. Mountbatten had recognized the army that marched under the Burmese national flag, but London did not recognize that a return to the situation prior to December 1941 was impossible. Even the Labour spokesmen, Sir Stafford Cripps and Arthur Creech-Jones, found the white paper admirable. Once again *The Times* took a remarkably progressive line, criticizing the white paper and pointing out that Burma was the first British colony to be liberated and that British actions there would be closely watched throughout Asia.

The Burmese nationalists predictably denounced the white paper, and Aung San's political party, AFPFL, which was infiltrated by communists, demanded to be recognized as the provisional government of Burma. Dorman-Smith turned down this proposal. Mountbatten tried to mediate, but he failed. Burmese affairs were returned to the colonial administration, which had no sympathy for the young nationalists around Aung San. Aung San then organized a party army, the People's Volunteer Organization, which threatened to launch a civil war. Britain had no choice but to leave Burma, which became fully independent in January 1948.

In Ceylon the situation was quite different, and the Ceylonese were prepared to accept dominion status. There had been no Japanese occupation; the British had not been ignominiously driven out, leaving the field to the occupiers and the nationalists. The leaders were older men, members of a British-trained élite, not young firebrands with mass popular support.

Ceylon had been granted a degree of self-government in 1931 with an elected council of state forming a government analogous to that of a British county council. Many found this arrangement unsatisfactory. The minorities, particularly the Tamils, felt that it discriminated against them. Others demanded full dominion status and asked why they could not have a parliamentary system on the Westminster model.

Demands for constitutional reforms became louder when the war began. When Cripps went on his thankless mission to India, the Ceylon council of state asked that he also visit the island and called for a promise of dominion status as soon as the war ended. These proposals were turned down. It was not until May 1943 that the British government, mindful of the strategic importance of Ceylon, finally made some concessions. Ceylon was offered "full responsible government under the Crown in all matters of internal administration," but the British were to remain firmly in control of foreign policy, defence, and the economy.

The British tried to avoid taking responsibility for the contentious issue of the minorities by handing it over to the Ceylonese, who were invited to submit their own proposals. The vice-chancellor of Ceylon University, Sir Ivor Jennings, helped draft proposals; but even this expert constitutional lawyer was unable to offer a solution that could get the required two-thirds majority on the council.

In an attempt to break the deadlock, the government appointed a commission to examine the proposals. The Ceylonese felt, with some justification, that this was simply a delaying tactic and boycotted the commission. Its report, published in September 1945, called for a constitution on the Westminster model, even though the commission felt that the Ceylonese had not yet reached a sufficient level of political maturity. A white paper published in the following month supported the commission's findings. The new constitution was approved, virtually unanimously, by the council of state in November 1946.

The prime minister, Don Stephen Senanayake, demanded dominion status, and since the Labour government wanted to make sure that he would win the forthcoming elections, they eventually gave in. Dominion status was granted on 11 November 1947, and an independence bill passed three months later. Independent Ceylon opted to remain within the Commonwealth. There had been a minimum of violence or even protest. It was hoped that this admirable example would be followed elsewhere within the Empire.

In Malaya, the full horror of Japanese occupation was revealed. Malaya had a large and prosperous Chinese population, and they were subjected to appalling brutality that even exceeded the disgusting treatment meted out to British and Indian prisoners. For the Japanese all Chinese were real or potential enemies, a reasonable assumption given that the Japanese had indulged in mass murder on a spectacular scale in China. Many Malays showed indifference to the fate of the Chinese. They were jealous of their economic success, and, as Muslims, they intensely disliked Buddhist infidels. At first they believed the Japanese promises of "co-prosperity," but soon, like everyone else in Asia, they became disillusioned.

When the Japanese were driven out, the British were greeted by all, Malay, Chinese, and Indian, as liberators. The British were genuinely popular in Malaya, and the small nationalist party could make no headway. The Malays looked to the British to save them from economic and political domination by the Chinese. The Chinese, in turn, were grateful to be delivered from the unspeakable horrors of the Japanese occupation and knew that under British rule they could get on with their business affairs without undue interference. The Indians felt that British rule would save them from domination by either the Malays or the Chinese.

Another country of vital strategic importance during the war was Egypt. Under the terms of the Anglo-Egyptian treaty of 1936 Britain took over formal control of Egypt in time of war. For the first three years Egypt was the centre of British military operations. When he could spare the time from slaughtering vast quantities of wildfowl, the colourful Sir Miles Lampson, who had been given the title of ambassador in 1936, ensured that King Farouk and his ministers danced to the British tune. He was assisted by Oliver Lyttelton, a close cabinet colleague of Churchill's, who remained permanently in Cairo. The headquarters of British Middle East Command was close to the embassy, and the Royal Navy's headquarters were in Alexandria.

At first all went well for the British in the Middle East as Wavell's forces inflicted a series of defeats upon the Italians. Their successes did not sit well with Farouk, who liked Italians and who had a number of Italians in his court. Sir Miles Lampson asked the king to dismiss these enemy aliens, but he promptly made them Egyptian citizens—an elaborate process rumoured to involve ritual circumcision. As Rommel's Afrika Korps marched towards the Egyptian border, Farouk appointed Ali Maher, a man known to be sympathetic to the German cause, prime minister.

Lampson was determined that Nahas Pasha, a pro-British politician who had played a critical role in securing the Anglo-Egyptian treaty, be appointed prime minister in his place. When Farouk flatly rejected Lampson's request for the change, Lampson delivered an ultimatum. Unless Nahas Pasha were appointed prime minister within hours, the king would have to accept the consequences. Farouk replied that the request was a breach of the Anglo-Egyptian treaty. Lampson then ordered tanks and armoured cars to surround the royal palace, marched in, and told Farouk that he was no longer fit to occupy the throne. Farouk was about to sign a declaration of abdication when a court official whispered into his ear that he should give way and appoint Nahas Pasha rather than lose his throne.

The British had won this round, but at a price. Egyptian nationalists were appalled by Lampson's actions—though they despised Farouk. They were determined to end colonial rule, but for the moment, the nationalists, particularly in the army, were forced onto the defensive. Nahas Pasha interned most of those suspected of pro-German leanings, including Ali Maher, and the country remained docile for the remainder of the war.

Churchill had complained that it was intolerable that Cairo should contain "a nest of Hun spies, that the canal zone should be infested by enemy agents." He could have said much the same thing of Iran. Reza Shah, a ruthless and no longer efficient despot, had lost the support of his people, and while claiming to be neutral, he was on increasingly good terms with the Axis powers. Iran teemed with German businessmen, technicians, and spies. The Germans had encouraged the shah's determined but ill-advised efforts to modernize his country, and they had supplied him with aircraft, all manner of weaponry, and other such trappings of modern civilization. In the summer of 1941 Iran became centrally important to Allied strategy. The Soviet Union, which had been allied to Germany until June 22, was fearful that the Germans might eventually use Iran as a launching pad for an attack on the Caucasus, and they also wanted to use the Iranian railway to carry supplies. The British had long wanted to get the Germans out of Iran, but they had not had the troops available to do the job, and they had not wanted to alienate the Soviet Union.

Repeated requests to the Iranians to remove the Germans achieved nothing, so after lengthy deliberations, the British and Soviets invaded in August 1941. The shah, realizing that resistance was pointless, ordered the army not to resist. With British and Soviet troops in Teheran, the shah's position became intolerable. He was forced to abdicate in favour of his son and died in his South African exile three years later.

Wartime Iran was a curious place. The British and Soviets were deeply suspicious of one another. The British found themselves allied with a corrupt and unpopular ruling class; the Soviets, with the politically inexperienced poor, whom they encouraged to join the communist (Tudeh) party. Neither power showed particular interest in the country, and as long as the oil was secured and the railway to the Caspian Sea ran efficiently, they were content to leave well enough alone. This gave the young shah and the Iranian parliament, the Majlis, an opportunity to exploit the situation by appealing to Britain for support against the Soviets and to the Soviets for support against the British. The chief player in this intricate game was an upper-crust radical nationalist, Dr. Mohammed Mossadeq. He was astute and incorruptible. His histrionics, his spiritual qualities, and, above all, his impeccable breeding infuriated the British, and he was later to become one of the prime villains in the British chamber of foreign horrors. In 1944 Mossadeq managed to get a bill through the Majlis that made it illegal for any official to discuss oil concessions with a foreigner.

The Russians were reluctant to leave Iran after the war as had been agreed in 1942, but when they were faced with a united and determined Anglo-American front, they backed down and left, some months after the deadline. Much to the horror of Mossadeq and his following of nationalists from the professions, the shah co-operated closely with the British and Americans. The Anglo-Iranian Oil Company had its concessions confirmed, and the Americans sent arms. Mossadeq and the nationalists complained that Iran was more dependent on the West than it had been under the shah's father. But for the moment the British had few worries. The shah, who could be easily manipulated, was in their pocket, and most of the Majlis, with the exception of Mossadeq and his friends, queued up outside the British legation to be bribed. The Anglo-Iranian Oil Company, Britain's largest overseas corporation, was the principal source of the Iranian government's revenue, and the future seemed secure.

The Jews in Palestine had welcomed the appointment of Winston Churchill as prime minister, for he had made frequent assertions that the British should hold good the pledge they had made that Palestine should become a national home for "that vast, unhappy mass of scattered, persecuted Jews." They were soon disappointed. Once in office, Churchill began to fear that the unlimited entry of Jews could push the Arabs onto the side of the Axis.

This dilemma was dramatized by the fate of a passenger ship, the *Struma*, which had set sail in December 1941 from the Romanian port of Constanza with 769 Jews fleeing German-inspired pogroms. The ship was in an appalling condition, and when it reached Turkish waters, the Turks wished to send it back as unseaworthy, but first they consulted the British ambassador. Sir Hugh Knatchbull-Hugessen showed considerable compassion, despite his own anti-Semitism, which was common to his class and profession. He suggested that the *Struma's* passengers, although they were clearly illegal immigrants, might be admitted to Palestine for humane reasons. The Foreign Office was furious when they heard of this advice and ordered him to get the ship sent back to Constanza.

By now the ship's engines had quit, and the vessel was stuck in Turkish waters. Weeks passed with passengers living in horrific conditions before the British consented to allow children under the age of sixteen to go to Palestine. However, they would not provide any shipping, and the Turks would not let them travel overland. The Turks then towed the ship out into the Black Sea where it mysteriously exploded and sank. Only two passengers survived, and the British let them enter Palestine as "an act of clemency."

The case of the *Struma* was the most dramatic of many incidents in which shiploads of refugees were turned back. The Zionists now saw the British as their enemies, and the Hagannah, their armed force, decided to use the weapons they already had to protect themselves from the Arabs to fight for their liberation. The British authorities had a vexing problem. On the one hand, they wanted to forbid both Jews and Arabs to carry arms, but, on the other, Hagannah activists were often useful as informants on conditions in Germany and occupied Europe, and their absolute determination to rid the world of Nazism could not be called into question. Arabic-speaking Jews, such as Moshe Dayan, who had narrowly missed being hanged for carrying arms (he claimed they were for use again the Germans), were invaluable as intelligence agents in Syria, Lebanon, and Iraq.

David Ben Gurion, the Jewish leader, was convinced that the British would never honour their promise for a national home for the Jews, but he was not prepared to attack the representatives of a country that had been at war with Nazi Germany from the outset of hostilities. Two terrorist groups had no such scruples. The Stern Gang, one of whose leaders was Itzhak Shamir, set about murdering Britishers in the vain hope that this would win concessions for the Zionist cause. Another group, the Irgun, made up largely of Polish Jews, was led by Menachem Begin. In the 1930s the Irgun was financed by right-wing anti-Semites in Poland who wanted them to murder Arabs in order to make room for the immigration of Polish Jews. Begin arrived in Palestine from Brest-Litovsk in 1942. He argued that since the British and Americans had done nothing to save the European Jews, they were accomplices in their murder. In 1944 Begin ordered the Irgun to concentrate their attacks on British government offices and police stations rather than on individual Arabs. The subsequent wave of violence by the Irgun and the Stern Gang horrified the moderates in the Jewish Agency, who feared that the British would lose any remaining sympathy for the Jewish cause.

Chaim Weizmann, president of both the Zionist Organization and the Jewish Agency, had long pleaded for the creation of a Jewish armed force that would fight the Nazis like the Free French, the Poles, or the Czechs and that would help the national cause as the Indian troops had done. Churchill was sympathetic, but the Foreign Office and the Colonial Office had serious misgivings. They harped on the effects on the Arab world and on the danger of giving Zionists military training. It was not until September 1944, when the danger from Nazi Germany had gone, that a Jewish Brigade was formed; its members proudly wore the Star of David on their shoulder flashes.

Two months later, the Stern Gang murdered Churchill's close friend Lord Moyne, the minister of state for the Middle East. The Jewish Agency and the Hagannah, in a frantic attempt at crisis control, hunted down members of the Stern Gang and the Irgun, tortured them, and handed them over to the British. These efforts did little to melt Churchill's heart; nor did the grim details of Nazi extermination camps, which created a wave of sympathy for the Jewish people throughout the civilized world. But the fact that the leader of the Palestinian Arabs, the Mufti of Jerusalem, had been an active supporter of Adolf Hitler diminished the persuasiveness of the Arab cause. Still, when Labour came to power, the new foreign secretary, Ernest Bevin, who had initially been sympathetic to the Zionists, changed his views. He saw no compelling reason for a major change in policy.

In Black Africa the war had far less dramatic effects than in the Middle East or Asia. If anything, the war slowed down the process of constitutional change. Malcolm MacDonald, son of the first Labour prime minister, was appointed colonial secretary in 1938, and he was determined to carry out most of Hailey's suggestions. He told the British officials in Africa that major changes would have to be made and that the Africans would have to have a far greater share in running their lives. When the war began, these ambitious schemes were put on hold, not to be revived until after the election of the Labour government in 1945.

In Kenya, the government banned the Kikuyu Central Association, a nationalist movement under the leadership of Jomo Kenyatta that had widespread and growing support. Kenyatta was in London and thus escaped internment. But the British needed Kenya to supply their armies in the Middle East as well as the seventy-five thousand soldiers stationed in Kenya, and so they could not afford to alienate the Africans. Africans were appointed to the production boards established to make sure that targets were met. In 1944 the son of a Kikuyu medicine man, Eliud Mathu, was appointed to the legislative council where his Oxford education stood him in good stead.

The white settlers were appalled. They had hoped that Kenya would be recognized as a white colony. The governor appointed in 1944, Sir Philip Mitchell, was openly contemptuous of the white settlers, whom he thought self-seeking, politically short-sighted, and vulgar. In the new Labour government, the settlers had to face a colonial secretary, Arthur Creech Jones, who was known to be on good terms with Kenyatta, who had been sharply critical of Kenya's labour laws in the past, and who promptly proposed equal representation on the legislative council for Europeans, Indians, and Africans. The whites were outraged and determined to fight back, but they were few in numbers. Only nine thousand settlers faced the ninety-seven thousand Kenyan Africans who had fought in the British Army during the war. These men were skilled and self-confident, and they were determined to share in the rewards of victory. It was a highly explosive situation.

Rhodesian politics were dominated by white demands that Northern Rhodesia (now Zambia) and Southern Rhodesia (now Zimbabwe) be amalgamated. The

Colonial Office held the view that uniting them would not be in the best interests of the African tribes, to whom certain promises had been made. Perhaps more important was that Northern Rhodesia's copper was an important strategic raw material, which the Colonial Office did not want to be in the hands of some rather dubious whites. Direct control from Whitehall was preferable. Southern Rhodesia, which lacked this valuable commodity, could be left to the settlers to run.

The result was that Southern Rhodesia applied a colour bar on the South African model, whereas in Northern Rhodesia, as elsewhere, the Colonial Office would not tolerate such racist policies. Nevertheless, Southern Rhodesia was efficiently run. It prospered and contributed significantly to the war effort. Had it asked for dominion status after the war, it would have almost certainly have been granted, but white Rhodesians still insisted on "amalgamation" with the north.

In spite of the fact that Britain's two great allies, the United States and the Soviet Union, looked askance at the Empire, it was undiminished when the war was over. But there had been great changes. The war had driven home the fact that things could not go on as before. Britain was no longer a great power; that it was not simply a little island off the coast of Europe was due in no small part to the remarkable performance of Winston Churchill. The Americans were also slowly beginning to realize that they were a great power with interests and commitments all over the globe. They felt that these interests were threatened by communism and realized that in their struggle against this peril, they would do well to use the expertise and resources of the British Empire. Churchill outlined his idea of the "special relationship" in his famous speech at Fulton, Missouri, in March 1946: "If the population of the English-speaking Commonwealth be added to that of the United States, with all that such co-operation implies in the air, on the sea and in science and industry, there will be no quivering, precarious balance of power to offer its temptations to ambition and adventure." Anti-imperialism, Churchill shrewdly calculated, would have less influence on American policy than anti-communism.

Had Churchill won the election in 1945, he would probably have tried to hang on to the Empire, reneging on promises made during the war, just as Lloyd George had done earlier, using the spectre of world communism to justify his actions. But the Labour Party cautiously set about dismantling the Empire amid the ruins of the domestic economy. Most Labour politicians regarded the process of decolonization with equanimity. Few were strictly speaking anti-imperialists, but most were eager to loosen the ties with the colonies. They had little choice. Britain was virtually bankrupt and heavily indebted to the Americans. Attlee believed that in the age of air power and the atomic bomb the Empire could no longer defend itself on its own. Even if Britannia had still ruled the waves, its power would not have been sufficient.

Any thought of imperial expansion, such as the proposal to establish a trusteeship over the Italian colonies, had thus to be dismissed. Those countries, such as India, Ceylon, and Burma, that were ready for independence should be granted it as soon as possible. For the rest, the government would exercise a responsible trusteeship in order to enable the colonies rapidly to learn how to stand on their own feet. It was a realistic approach to which few could object.

6 Labour and the Empire, 1945–1951

At the Potsdam Conference Churchill had shown considerable interest in the Italian colonies. Stalin had tried to head him off by suggesting that they should be placed under a three-power trusteeship. The thought of the Russians established in North Africa was enough to convince even the Americans that it would be best to leave Tripoli and Somalia in Italian hands. After all, the Italians had ended up fighting on the Allied side. Bevin, the new Labour foreign secretary, was determined that the British should not leave the Middle East. He insisted that the Italian colonies were strategically important and should not fall into the hands of a power inimical to British interests in the area. He therefore argued that a British trusteeship should be established over Somalia and Cyrenaica in spite of Prime Minister Clement Attlee's objections to any further commitments, to say nothing of American complaints about "the painting of any further red on the map." The Colonial Office supported Bevin's position and argued that it was in the best interests of the Somalis that their country should be united.

Attlee, an unrepentant Little Englander, had no sympathy for Bevin's imperial ambitions. He believed that Britain could not afford to maintain a military presence in the Middle East and that the area should be policed by the United Nations. Somaliland he described as "a dead loss and nuisance to us." In the end, after lengthy debates and a defence review, the result was a compromise. Bevin's schemes for painting a few more areas red had to be abandoned, but Britain maintained an impressive presence in the Middle East, securing the oil and guarding the gateway to a soon to be independent India.

In Asia, problems with the Americans were considerable. They had long accepted Chiang Kai-shek's imaginative assessment of his military prowess and assumed that he was a freedom-loving democrat. British diplomats despaired, feeling that the "dawn of intelligence" in the American view of China was long overdue. Towards Indochina Roosevelt had entertained a scheme of trusteeship that would have involved Americans, Russians, Filipinos, and the Chinese, but it was disavowed by the Truman administration at the meeting to found the United Nations in San Francisco in June 1945. At least the British did not have to fight off the suggestion that such schemes would be suitable for Malaya or Burma.

American hostility to British imperialism may have been a factor hastening postwar decolonization, but it was hardly critical. The British had lost interest in the Imperial Mission. Many leading figures in the Labour Party were on friendly terms with such nationalist leaders as Jawaharlal Nehru, Krishna Menon, Hastings Banda,

Kwame Nkrumah, and Jomo Kenyatta. The colonial secretary, Arthur Creech Jones, was on particularly close terms with the African nationalists. He was on the left of the party and had been imprisoned for his pacifist stand in World War I. He was an innovative and imaginative politician who came up with some excellent long-term plans for development. Unfortunately, Creech Jones lacked any sparkle so that most, including Attlee, were blind to his considerable talents. He lost his seat in the election of 1950 and virtually disappeared from the pages of history.

Creech Jones was not appointed colonial secretary until October 1946. His predecessor, George Hall, was a trade union hack, responsible for the affairs of an undiminished Empire. Britain dominated the Middle East from Iran to Libya and from Abyssinia and Eritrea to the Persian Gulf. It controlled Africa from the Cape to Suez. In Asia there were countless Pacific islands along with the major territorial possessions. There were patches of red on the globe from the Caribbean to the Falkland Islands and from Saint Helena to the Seychelles. Throughout these vast possessions nationalist movements were seething, complicated by struggles between Hindus and Muslims, Arabs and Jews, and African tribes.

The British knew that they could not possibly deal with their own problems, let alone those of the Empire, without the support and co-operation of the Dominions. Consultation with the Dominions was frequent, detailed, and thorough. Lord Addison, an experienced older statesman, was a excellent choice as secretary of state for the dominions (an office that was renamed the Commonwealth Relations Office in July 1947).

Like the other Labour leaders, Addison pursued an active imperial policy and had no sympathy with those who wished to scuttle the entire enterprise. Some were shocked at the frequent outbursts of imperial enthusiasm from British socialists. Attlee lectured Truman and his secretary of state, Dean Acheson, on the superior understanding that the British had of the Oriental and Asiatic minds as a result of centuries of imperial experience. Bevin was second to none in his enthusiasm for Britain's role east of Suez, and Herbert Morrison, who became foreign secretary in 1951, even spoke of "the jolly old Empire." The Dominions were also eager to preserve the Empire to ensure a viable imperial defence. Smuts, for example, who was seriously worried that the British would withdraw from Egypt, insisted that the Suez Canal was the lifeline of the Commonwealth and warned that if the British moved out, the Russians would move in.

The Commonwealth was equally important economically. The British fed on Canadian wheat and meat; their dairy products were from Australia and New Zealand. More than 40 per cent of British exports in 1950 went to the Commonwealth. The sterling area, although it excluded Canada and included such countries as Iceland and Iraq, was essentially a Commonwealth concern, and it was central to Britain's financial policy. Problems over the sterling/dollar pool in the sterling area became increasingly difficult to solve and were symptomatic of loosening Commonwealth ties.

Britain was becoming, with great reluctance, more concerned with the affairs of Europe, often to the detriment of the Commonwealth. NATO, the Council of Europe, and the Schumann Plan linked Britain closer to Europe and the United States. Similarly, Canada, Australia, and New Zealand made their own security arrangements with the United States. Eire and South Africa were straining at the leash.

As long as Smuts was premier, relations with South Africa were relatively cordial, although he demanded a great deal in return for his friendship. He wanted control over the High Commission territories of Bechuanaland (Botswana), Basutoland (Lesotho), and Swaziland as well as a decisive influence in East Africa and Northern and Southern Rhodesia. Early in 1946 the British Labour government agreed that the Union of South Africa should absorb German South-West Africa (Namibia). This unfortunate decision was to cause endless difficulties and bloodshed.

Because Britain did not want to offend South Africa in the High Commission territories, it refused to allow the chief of the Bamangwato tribe, Seretse Khama, to return to Bechuanaland until 1956. Khama had married a white Englishwoman while he was a law student at the Inner Temple, and the British government feared that his presence might upset racists in South Africa. He became the first prime minister of Bechuanaland in 1965 and, having received a knighthood, president of Botswana in the following year. Another scandalous incident occurred when the South African government secured the dismissal of the undersecretary at the Commonwealth Office, John Parker, for his forceful pursuit of a Boer murderer and his attempts to help the starving Basutos.

Matters became considerably worse in May 1948 when Dr. Daniel Malan became prime minister. A racist religious fundamentalist, Malan was a bitterly anti-British, pro-Nazi republican, and he was supported by even more sinister elements in the extremist Broederbond. He was determined to cut the ties to the British Crown and to establish absolute white supremacy through apartheid, a policy of institutionalized racism that he had invented.

The British government was appalled at this turn of events. It could do nothing to interfere in the internal affairs of South Africa, but it was determined that apartheid should not be allowed to spread to Bechuanaland, Basutoland, or Swaziland. An even greater danger was presented by the Rhodesias (which even the moderate Smuts had wanted to annex), where many of the white settlers sympathized with Malan.

105

A solution to this problem was offered by Andrew Cohen, the forceful head of the Africa Department in the Colonial Office who was known as the "King of Africa." He proposed a federation of the Rhodesias, arguing against tremendous opposition that Southern Rhodesian whites could be weaned away from South African white supremacist ideas and might be convinced that the wealth of Northern Rhodesia could be shared with the Africans. But when Creech Jones went to the Rhodesias, he discovered that the Africans in the North were strongly opposed to federation and that the southern whites were incorrigibly racist.

When Creech Jones lost his seat, Cohen set to work on his successor, James Griffiths, a highly principled Welsh miner with no experience of colonial affairs. Cohen was determined that a Central African Federation should be created to halt the advancement of apartheid and further the cause of African advancement and decolonization, to which he was totally committed. He needed all his diplomatic skills, intelligence, and vision to convince Attlee's government to try to get the white Rhodesians to agree. He proposed a federation of the Rhodesias and Nyasaland in which defence, economic policy, and education would be federal concerns while each component retained its own constitution and was responsible for law and order, African affairs, agriculture, labour, mining, health, and relations with the British government.

From the outset the proposed federation was beset by problems. The African leaders, Hastings Banda in Nyasaland and Harry Nkumbula in Northern Rhodesia, complained that the system perpetuated the enslavement of Africans and made only token concessions. In Southern Rhodesia, the leading spokesman, Joshua Nkomo, did not agree. He and others saw the federation as a means of getting out from under the domination of the white settlers, who objected to the scheme for the same reason.

In 1951, Oliver Lyttleton, the colonial secretary when the Conservatives regained power, enthusiastically favoured federation and discounted the views of Banda and Nkumbula as unrepresentative, arguing disingenuously that they obviously did not know what the word federation meant. He also pointed out that Northern Rhodesia and Nyasaland would have to do what they were told since they were under the direct rule of the Colonial Office. The Labour Party, now the Opposition, was not so sure, many feeling that the needs of the Africans had not been sufficiently weighed. Lyttleton also lacked the support of Andrew Cohen, who had been appointed governor of Uganda.

The main problem was the attitude of the whites in Southern Rhodesia. Lyttleton was prepared to compromise, reducing both African representation in the proposed legislature and Britain's rights to interfere to uphold African rights. He made these concessions because he wanted to avoid running the risk of Southern Rhodesia declaring independence or joining South Africa. The prime minister of Southern Rhodesia, Sir Godfrey Huggins, accepted the compromise, pointing out to his fellow whites that given the "unctuous rectitude and apparent hypocrisy" of the British, the much vaunted word "partnership" could well mean the relationship between a rider and his horse. Lyttleton steered the measure through Parliament, and the new state was formally recognized on 1 August 1953. Few of its citizens, however, were enthusiastic. Africans and liberal whites were appalled at Sir Godfrey's remarks and knew that they were in for a bitter struggle. Since each of the three component parts of the federation was free to deal with "native policy" in its own way, there was bound to be trouble.

Immediately after the war, the Gold Coast (now Ghana) was given a new constitution that gave twenty-two of the thirty-one seats in the legislature to Africans. This concession was not enough to satisfy the African leadership, and they used the crisis provoked by widespread unemployment, high inflation, and a stagnant economy to form a new political party, the United Gold Coast Convention (UGCC), which the British considered to be a communist organization. The party brought a handsome, articulate young lawyer, Kwame Nkrumah, who was also a communist, from London to become UGCC secretary.

British authorities blamed widespread rioting in 1948 on the UGCC, and the party leader, Dr. Joseph Danquah, Nkrumah, and four other senior party officials were banished to the north even though there was no evidence against them. Overnight they became national heroes and martyrs.

Creech Jones and Andrew Cohen immediately appointed a commission to investigate the riots. The commission, headed by a Scottish judge and former Labour candidate, Aiken Watson, recommended major constitutional changes as the only possible remedy. Cohen and Creech Jones endorsed these proposals, agreeing that if major concessions were not made, there might be a revolution. Danquah and the moderates had to be strengthened and the radicals around Nkrumah isolated. Nkrumah had already made a decisive move. Denouncing Danquah and his friends as reactionaries, he left the party and founded the Convention People's Party (CPP) with himself as its leader and "Self-government Now" as its slogan.

Nkrumah called for "Positive Action" to protest the constitutional proposals. Outbursts of violence soon became alarmingly frequent. Nkrumah was arrested and sentenced to three years' imprisonment. Like his banishment, this action only served to enhance his popularity. The elections went ahead, the first with a universal adult franchise in Black Africa. The result was a stunning victory for CPP. The governor, Sir Charles Arden-Clarke, felt he had to release Nkrumah, a man he had recently compared to Hitler, from jail. Nkrumah soon became Arden-Clarke's close friend and associate. The governor relied on Nkrumah to keep political peace, and thus he was obliged to follow him on the road to full independence. The momentum was such that even the Conservative government was unable to stop the process.

In 1949 the Colonial Office was relieved of one burden when Eire declared itself a republic and severed its Commonwealth links. The break was made with little rancour, and Eire was given favourable terms in those matters of most importance to the country—trade and immigration. Northern Ireland was largely ignored at this time, but it came back to haunt British and Irish politicians with a vengeance in the years to come.

During the Labour government's administration, Creech Jones had set about applying the principles of Fabian socialism to the Empire. To this end the Colonial Office established two giant corporations—the Overseas Food Corporation, which bought staple crops in bulk, and the Colonial Development Corporation with a capital of £100 million. The latter had some spectacular failures, the most notorious of which were a ground-nut scheme in Tanganyika and an egg project in Gambia. Right-wing critics of socialist waste and state planning had a field day, and the scandal was a major reason why Creech Jones lost his seat in the 1950 election. Criticism of the ground-nut scheme was amply justified. No proper analyses of the soil and climatic conditions were carried out, and the project was grossly misman-aged. The CDC did have some successes elsewhere in Africa and made a significant contribution to economic growth in the colonies, but these aspects were largely forgotten in the uproar over the ground-nut fiasco.

The Colombo conference of January 1950, at which Bevin represented the government, resulted in the Colombo Plan for India, Pakistan, Ceylon, Malaya, and British North Borneo (now part of Malaysia). A total of £1,868 million was to be invested by the Commonwealth over a six-year period to stimulate economic growth. The success of this and other such plans was somewhat mitigated by the British government's determination to protect sterling. Those Commonwealth countries that had dollar surpluses had to contribute them to the "dollar pool" so that it could be spent by Britain and other members of the sterling area. For countries that had dollar surpluses, like Malaya, Ceylon, the Rhodesias, and the Gold Coast, this was a distinct disadvantage.

Creech Jones, who enthusiastically supported the idea of federation in Central Africa, also tried to further the federal principle elsewhere. He began planning for a West Indian federation but achieved little during his term of office.

His greatest success was the Union of Malaya, which was by far and away Britain's most valuable colony, producing one-third of the world's rubber and earning huge dollar surpluses. The British returned to Malaya two weeks after Japan capitulated. They were welcomed by the Malay ruling class and pushed aside the communist guerrillas they had armed, giving them a campaign medal and a miserable gratuity of 250 Malayan dollars. The communists hung on to as many of their weapons as they could and were determined to drive the British out and wrest the country from the hands of its traditionally powerful elites: the Malay sultans, Chinese merchants, and the landlord class.

Malaya had a small communist party, the MCP, made up largely of poor immigrant Chinese workers. The secretary general of the party from 1936 to 1947, Lai Tek, had been in the pay of the British and the Japanese, depending on who was in power at the time. He vanished when the central committee began investigating his increasingly suspicious activities.

The British were astonishingly naive about the communist threat. They regarded the communists as good patriots who had fought bravely for the common cause and lifted the ban on the party. The Labour Party also wished to encourage trades unions throughout the Empire as the first stage in educating colonial peoples for democracy. In Malaya, these unions were soon dominated by the communist party, and they set about disrupting the economy as much as they could. In the summer of 1948 the British decided to ban the communist party once again. The communists, in turn, had already decided to take to the jungle in order to wage a guerrilla war.

During the Second World War Attlee had chaired a committee that suggested that the three colonies known as the Straits Settlements and nine protectorates run by the sultans should be federated with Singapore because of its strategic importance. The proposal by the Labour government to create a Malayan Union was opposed by the sultans, who feared, correctly, that they would lose much of their power.

The sultans were able to mobilize the Malays against the British, and the majority of the long docile and acquiescent Malay population suddenly became politically active in the United Malays National Organization (UMNO). Their demands were simple—the Union proposals should be dropped, and the Chinese should not be given full citizenship. Faced with this united opposition the British capitulated.

In place of a union, the British now suggested the creation of a federation in which the sultans would retain their powers and virtually only the Malays would be citizens. UMNO and the sultans accepted these proposals and were not at all concerned that self-government remained a distant prospect. The communists made much of the fact that the Chinese had not been given citizenship, and they were able to recruit members from the labouring classes along with a handful of urban intellectuals. Arm-chair strategists from European communist parties encouraged them to begin an armed revolt.

The Federation of Malaya was formally created in February 1948. That summer, communists murdered three of their leading Chinese opponents and also three European rubber planters. The British declared a state of emergency and a twelve-year war began. A few thousand communist guerrillas hid in the jungle and made raids on rubber plantations, police stations, and government offices. Under the circumstances it was probably the only strategy that they could adopt, but it had serious weaknesses. Living in the jungle was impossibly hard, and the guerrillas were utterly dependent on supplies of food and ammunition from the small squatter communities on the fringes of the jungle, which they terrorized into absolute submission.

The British had no idea how to deal with terrorists. They undertook sweeps through the jungle, in accordance with Boer War tactics, but they came up with nothing. The terrorists were now murdering an average of one hundred people per month, and many planters packed their bags and left. Frustration led to brutality on the British side, the worst instance of which was the murder of twenty-four villagers at Batang Kali in December 1948. At the beginning of the election campaign in 1951, the terrorists shot and killed the British high commissioner, Sir Henry Gurney. Altogether in 1951 they killed 504 members of the security forces and 533 civilians.

Churchill, returned as prime minister, sent General Sir Gerald Templer as Gurney's successor. He had virtually dictatorial powers, which he used to the full. British and Commonwealth troops outnumbered the guerrillas by fifty to one at the height of the emergency, but Templer argued that "The answer lies not in pouring more troops into the jungle, but in the hearts and minds of the people." He saw to it that the concentration camps, where the villagers on whom the terrorists preyed were resettled, were transformed into pleasant villages with modern amenities and local elected councils.

There was no independence movement in Malaya, and thus the communist appeal for a crusade against the British fell on deaf ears. Democracy was granted in stages before it was demanded by the native population. In 1952 local elections were held, in 1955 a majority of the seats on the legislative council were made elective, and in 1957 independence was granted.

The main problem facing the commissioner-general in south-east Asia, Malcolm MacDonald, was to establish a degree of harmony between the principal ethnic communities in Malaya, particularly between the Malays and the Chinese.

The leading Malay politician, Dato Onn bin Ja'afar, had tried to make UMNO into a multi-racial party, but he failed. The Malays insisted on "Malaya for the Malays." This racially exclusive party was then taken over by Tunku (Prince) Abdul Rahman, a playboy who had taken twenty-five years to qualify as a barrister. A poor public speaker and an even worse administrator, he appeared to be a highly improbable character to lead Malaya to independence.

The Tunku soon realized that Malaya had to be a multi-racial state, and he shrewdly decided to form an electoral alliance between UMNO and the Malayan Chinese Association (MCA), an organization of rich, anti-communist Chinese businessmen. This alliance worked admirably at the local level, and at the first federal election in July 1955 the Tunku allotted fifteen of the fifty-two seats to the MCA and two to the Indian National Congress.

In December 1955 the communist leader, Chin Peng, offered to disband his guerrillas if Tunku Abdul Rahman would agree to allow the communist party to take part in the political process. The Tunku turned down the offer, and Chin Peng returned to the jungle to continue a sporadic campaign that went on until the mid-1980s. Chin Peng, who was aided neither by China nor by the Soviet Union and who had no popular support, was a defeated man.

The Tunku was not only determined to keep Malaya free from communism, he also insisted that Malay should be the official language of the new state and that Islam should be the state religion. The British wanted equal citizenship for all races. The Malays, although they accounted for 85 per cent of the population, feared that the Chinese with their higher birth rate would eventually swamp them and insisted on the preservation of their privileges. The Chinese and Indians, convinced that they would fare best under the electoral alliance, agreed to continue their support. The British therefore had no alternative but to concede to the Tunku.

A far more taxing problem than Malaya was Palestine. Ernest Bevin had been sympathetic to the Zionist cause, but as foreign secretary he changed his mind. Having discussed the problem with Foreign Office officials, Bevin thought that not more than fifteen hundred Jewish refugees per month should be allowed into Palestine. President Truman, however, insisted that a hundred thousand European Jews should be given permission to travel to the mandate and leaked Attlee's negative reply to the press. Attlee and Bevin were understandably furious, and the moderate Jewish leaders saw their hopes that the Labour government would be more favourably disposed towards them dashed. David Ben Gurion now decided to join forces with the Stern Gang and the Irgun to fight the British.

Bevin reacted to the outbreak of violence in Palestine by trying to involve the United States. The Americans accepted a proposal to establish an Anglo-American committee on Palestine, and it recommended that a hundred thousand refugees be admitted. But it added that Palestine alone could not possibly solve the problem of the European Jews. Truman made life exceedingly difficult for Bevin by making a series of pro-Zionist statements designed to win over the Jewish vote. When the State Department warned him of the effects of such statements in the Arab world, he blandly replied that he did not have hundreds of thousands of Arabs among his constituents. Bevin was equally tactless, claiming that Truman wanted to send a hundred thousand Jews to Palestine because he did not want to have them in New York.

The Jewish terrorist campaign was skilfully conducted and remarkably effective. Despite its hundred thousand men, the British security force had little success. On 22 July 1946 Menachem Begin's Irgun blew up a wing of the luxurious King David Hotel, which contained the headquarters of the British government and forces in Palestine. Ninety-one people were killed—twenty-eight British, forty-one Arabs, seventeen Jews, and five others. The Zionist leaders were shocked at this outrage, for it was the first time that the victims had been given no warning. The British commander-in-chief, General Sir Evelyn Barker, promptly ordered his troops to punish the Jews "in a way the race dislikes . . . by striking at their pockets and showing our contempt for them." When the Zionists made this order public, it did much to counter the sympathy felt for the British after the explosion.

Truman again torpedoed British negotiations with the Zionist leaders when, despite urgent pleas not to, he delivered a speech aimed at the Jewish voters of New York in which he demanded a viable Jewish state.

The Hagannah, Irgun, and Stern Gang stepped up their terrorist campaign, reaching a new height when they hanged two British sergeants, Clifford Martin and Mervyn Paice, in retribution for the execution of three Irgun terrorists. The British security forces in Palestine ran amok, killing five Jews, beating up numerous others, and destroying property. There were also anti-Semitic riots in a number of British cities.

The Zionists had another propaganda triumph with the way Britain handled the refugee ship *Exodus*. The refugees were refused entry to Palestine, there was no space available in the camps in Cyprus where illegal immigrants were kept, and they refused to settle in France, which had offered asylum. Bevin then ordered them back to Germany, where they were put in a camp at Poppendorf near Lübeck. World Jewish opinion now saw the British as the heirs of Nazi Germany.

Shortly after the *Exodus* affair, the United Nations Special Committee on Palestine (UNSCOP) published a report calling for an end to the British mandate and for the partitioning of Palestine. Although the British government thought that the proposal was unfair to the Arabs, it was delighted to be able to get out of Palestine. In order to win favour in the Arab world, the British announced that they would not impose the United Nations' partition plan upon the Arabs even if got the necessary two-thirds majority in the General Assembly.

In fact, it was generally assumed that the proposal would fail to pass, but once again Truman's obsession with capturing the Jewish vote was the decisive factor. Although Secretary of State George Marshall and the State Department hoped that the plan would fail, Truman announced that the United States favoured partition. Chaim Weizmann also persuaded the president that the Jewish state needed an access to the sea in the Gulf of Aqaba and, therefore, that the Negev Desert would have to be Jewish rather than Arab. The American government exerted massive pressure to ensure that the measure would pass, as it did on 29 November 1947. The British government, washing its hands of the whole issue, abstained.

The British began to withdraw from Palestine amid a civil war between Jews and Arabs. Almost as soon as they had gone, the new state of Israel was attacked by its Arab neighbours, beginning a war that despite recent positive negotiations, has yet to end. British policy in Palestine was widely and fiercely criticized, but it is difficult to see what else Bevin could have done. He was correct in insisting that an imposed settlement would lead to endless strife. Unable to find a solution, the British simply abdicated from responsibility for their least successful colonial experience. It was certainly not a glorious end to the mandate, but it seemed then, and it seems now, the best policy.

Egyptian nationalists, on the other hand, had high hopes for the Labour government, and their optimism was well founded. Attlee and many others wanted to withdraw from the Middle East entirely after the war, and even Bevin wanted to evacuate British troops from Egypt to Cyrenaica, or to Palestine, Cyprus, Aden, Transjordan, almost anywhere that would get them out of Egypt. The military and Churchill resisted, but after prolonged arguments, Bevin got his way. In the Anglo-Egyptian accord, Britain agreed to leave the towns first and then to evacuate the Canal Zone by September 1949. For its part, Egypt agreed to consult with Britain on security matters in the region.

Both sides were satisfied except for a single issue. The British insisted that the Sudanese would have to be consulted about their future. The Egyptian prime minister, Sidki Pasha, agreed, but when he got home, the Egyptian parliament, the

Wafd, demanded that Britain withdraw from the Sudan and that Farouk be named king. Having only just signed the accord, Sidki refused. The Wafd voted not to ratify the treaty, and Sidki resigned. The British moved out of the towns but kept a substantial force in the Canal Zone.

While Egyptian nationalists felt that Britain had tricked them once again, the British were in a truly awkward situation. They could now no longer move their troops to Palestine, and in Cairo the Mufti of Jerusalem was stirring up the Muslim League and calling for a Jihad to free the Palestinians from the Jews. As a fundamentalist, the Mufti was also sharply critical of King Farouk, who enjoyed the seamier offerings of Western civilization. In part to counter such criticism, Farouk's government entered the war against Israel. When the Egyptian Army was soundly defeated, Egyptians promptly blamed the British for failing to train and equip it. It is hardly surprising that they had not. If they had, it would almost certainly have joined forces with the Germans.

After the Egyptian elections of 1950, the prime minister, Nahas Pasha, demanded that the British reduce their forces in the Canal Zone from some eighty thousand men to the ten thousand specified in the Anglo-Egyptian treaty of 1936. When the British refused, the Egyptians cut off supplies of fresh food and removed the forty thousand Egyptian workers in the Zone. The Americans attempted to create a Middle East Command that would include the Egyptians, but the British foreign secretary, Herbert Morrison, felt a purely British base in Egypt was essential, and he also objected vigorously to the American proposal that the Sudan should become part of Egypt.

Suddenly, in October 1951, Nahas Pasha, enthusiastically supported by the Egyptian parliament, unilaterally abrogated the both the 1936 treaty and the 1899 treaty that had created a condominium in the Sudan. With some forty thousand troops still in the Canal Zone (which could be instantly strengthened by the parachute brigade stationed in Cyprus and the Guards Brigade in Tripoli), the British position was strong. Field Marshal Slim argued that they should strike immediately to demonstrate to the Egyptians and the rest of the world that Britain was not "spineless." Morrison agreed, but Attlee, in his last few days as prime minister, would not approve the use of force.

The Egyptian crisis happened in the middle of the election campaign that returned the Conservatives. Anthony Eden, who had signed the Anglo-Egyptian treaty, was back in the Foreign Office. He knew that the treaty was binding in international law and that Nahas was making a desperate bid for popularity. His government and his own wife were under suspicion of large-scale corruption, the

114

army was disaffected after its humiliation by the Jews, and the king was generally unpopular. Eden was much less truculent than Morrison, and he hoped to call Nahas's bluff. However, the Egyptians unleashed a guerrilla campaign that reduced the British troops in the Canal Zone to virtual prisoners.

The argument that Egypt was essential for the defence of India was no longer valid, for India had become independent. Attlee had been determined that India should achieve independence as soon as possible after the war. The India Committee, with Attlee in the chair, was made up of the highly respected but elderly F. W. Pethick-Lawrence, the secretary of state for India, Stafford Cripps, Ellen Wilkinson, and the Labour peers Listowel and Stansgate. The committee recommended elections to legitimize the assembly that would make the necessary arrangements after independence.

The elections were a triumph for Congress, and the League swept the board in the Muslim seats, making Jinnah even more overbearing. The problem now was to get Congress and the League to agree on a formula for an independent India, whether divided or united. Wavell was obviously not the man to bring the two sides together, for his relations with Congress were strained and he regarded Gandhi as a "malignant old man." Attlee therefore appointed a cabinet mission made up of Cripps, who was the leading figure in the team, Pethick-Lawrence, and the affable First Lord of the Admiralty, A. V. Alexander, who had little sympathy for Indians.

The problems facing the mission were enormous. Jinnah listened politely, but no one knew what he wanted. Gandhi announced that he was no longer a member of Congress and thus had nothing to say. Maulana Azad, the Congress president, spoke for the party, but he had little power. It was uncertain whether Nehru or Vithalbhai Patel was actually the leading figure in Congress, but it was doubtful whether either of them, or indeed anyone else, could persuade the party to concede enough territory to Pakistan to satisfy Jinnah. Then there were the sixty million in the "scheduled castes," a euphemism for the untouchables, whom their leader, Dr. B. R. Ambedkar, felt should be allotted their own seats. The Sikhs, fearful that they would be oppressed by the Muslims, demanded a separate Sikh state or, failing that, a guarantee of protection.

After endless wrangles, Jinnah accepted the mission's proposals for a three-tiered system of government. Foreign affairs, defence, communications, and some aspects of finance would be controlled by an all-India federal government. The eleven provinces, which formed the bottom tier, were allowed to form groups so that a non-sovereign Pakistan could exist in the middle tier. Jinnah felt that this arrangement would guarantee the rights of Muslims in areas where they were a minority, areas where his influence was greatest, and that it would give the League a disproportionate influence in a united India. He feared that in a separate Muslim state there would be endless problems with political leaders in the Punjab and Bengal.

Congress, quickly realizing that Jinnah stood to benefit the most, began to quibble over the details of the interim government and reneged on their agreement to the three-tiered plan. Nehru, who was now president of Congress, announced that in the constituent assembly his party would not feel bound by any previous agreements, even though the Muslim League had only accepted the mission's proposals on the grounds that they would be considered binding on the constituent assembly. The League, feeling tricked by Congress and betrayed by the British, announced that 16 August 1946 would be "Direct Action Day."

The violence began in Calcutta where Muslims murdered some Hindus, provoking appalling retaliatory action by Hindus and Sikhs. In three days of slaughter, an estimated four to five thousand people died. In an attempt to stop the spread of violence, Wavell urged Congress to agree to a coalition government, but Gandhi and Nehru rejected this proposal, saying that they would not give way to threats. Wavell believed that the compromise, which had been accepted by both Congress and the League, should be respected; but the British government ordered him not to alienate Congress and to accept an all-India government led by Nehru with no League representation.

Attlee regretted the breach with the League, but he felt a break with Congress would be a total disaster. Congress had a majority, and Attlee believed that the will of the majority had to be respected. With the League excluded from the interim government and likely to be excluded from the constituent assembly, tensions ran high. Violence spread from Calcutta to East Bengal and then to Bihar. Fearing that the police and army would not be able to restore order, Wavell proposed that the British abandon India. Attlee, who was determined that a political solution be found before Britain withdrew, fired Wavell and appointed Lord Louis Mountbatten as his successor.

Mountbatten's handling of the political situation in Burma when he was Supreme Commander SEAC had impressed Attlee, who decided he had the energy and skills necessary for the task in India. Mountbatten insisted that he would have to be able to take action without having to consult the secretary of state for India or even the Cabinet. Furthermore, so that the Indians had to make up their minds quickly, he demanded that it be announced that British rule in India would end by June 1948. The consequence of this rigid timetable was that if Congress and the League could not agree, the British would hand power over to the provinces, which, in turn, would make the creation of Pakistan an inevitability.

116

When Mountbatten arrived in Delhi at the end of March 1947, he found Congress and the League locked in battle. The League minister of finance, Abdul Kalam Azad, did everything he could to sabotage the work of the Congress ministers, and his fellow Muslim, Abdur Rab Nishtar, used his powers as minister of communications to wiretap their phones. Realizing that the Muslim League could not be beaten, Congress finally decided that Bengal and the Punjab would have to be partitioned.

Mountbatten used his great social skills and considerable charm to establish a relationship of trust with Gandhi, Nehru, Jinnah, Liaqat Ali Khan, and the Congress home minister, Patel. His relationship with the rich, patrician, Harrovian widower Nehru was one of mutual trust and admiration. Mountbatten disliked Jinnah, whom he described as "psychopathic," but he was able to win the trust of this most suspicious man. Although he did not think that Gandhi was any longer a key player, the viceroy was also to establish a friendly relationship with the man who could do more than anyone else to stop the bloodshed.

Jinnah continued to press for a greater Pakistan and rejected the idea of partitioning the Punjab and Bengal. He argued that all provinces with a Muslim majority should be included in Pakistan, regardless of the size of the Hindu minority. But he knew that Mountbatten's deadline for withdrawal weakened his position and that his direct action campaign put the Muslims in Hindu-dominated areas at considerable risk. Jinnah's demands for a greater Pakistan soon turned to pleas that Pakistan not be too small. Mountbatten continued to argue that the Muslims would be better off with the cabinet mission's scheme, for they would then control the whole of the Punjab and Bengal within the "middle tier." However, Jinnah replied that Congress wanted a Hindu Raj and that the Muslims would only be safe in an independent Pakistan.

Dividing India meant dividing the army, a prospect that appalled both the commander-in-chief, Field Marshal Auchinleck, and Baldev Singh, the Sikh minister of defence. Mountbatten and General Ismay, his military adviser, also opposed the idea. All agreed that the disintegration of the Indian Army would be a disaster at a time when it was needed to maintain law and order. The Muslims felt that this reluctance to divide the army showed typical British favouritism towards Congress. The British replied that since most of the officers were Hindus, the Muslims would be without an effective army. Mountbatten then tried to persuade Jinnah to accept a supreme defence council in which the Indian Army would remain united.

The army problem was soon overshadowed by Nehru's emphatic rejection of Mountbatten's plan for independence, which had been accepted by the British government. Mountbatten's weakest suit was detailed and methodical work, and he had simply assumed that the provinces would opt for either India or Pakistan. Nehru pointed out that the opting-out clause opened the way to the balkanization of the country because some provinces, notably Bengal, might well wish to become completely independent. Without a strong central authority, Nehru argued, the country would fall apart and a civil war would probably ensue.

Mountbatten reacted promptly to Nehru's objections and asked the British government to drop the plan. He was recalled to London for consultation, and some ministers felt he should be replaced. Attlee, however, continued to support Mountbatten and welcomed his suggestion that it might be possible to persuade both India and Pakistan to become members of the Commonwealth.

At first sight it seemed impossible that the Commonwealth idea would succeed. Nehru had specifically ruled it out, saying that it would spell political ruin to anyone who proposed it. Jinnah did not share this view. He saw distinct advantages in the Commonwealth connection, particularly in the military sphere. Mountbatten then artfully suggested to the Congress leaders that Jinnah would enjoy distinct advantages as a Commonwealth leader. The viceroy's constitutional adviser, V. P. Menon, who had always favoured a Commonwealth link, worked out a deal with his friend Patel. If Britain would immediately transfer power to the governments of India and Pakistan as Dominions, then Congress would do everything possible to keep India within the Commonwealth. Mountbatten leaped at this suggestion and asked Menon to draw up a plan. It was ready within a few hours, quickly accepted by both Congress and the League, and then Mountbatten took it to London for cabinet approval, which was immediately granted. On 4 June 1947 Mountbatten gave a press conference in Delhi to announce that independence would be granted at midnight on 14–15 August.

The major remaining difficulty was to reach an agreement on the division of Bengal and the Punjab. Bengal would have preferred to be an independent "second-tier" state in a united India, but it no longer had such an option. The coalition government of Hindus and Muslims now had to decide whether to join either India or Pakistan or to agree to partition. They opted for division.

The Punjab proved more difficult. Given the divisions in its population of Muslims, Hindus, and Sikhs, no party was able to form a government, and the province had been ruled under emergency powers granted to the governor. Beginning in early 1947 there were endless riots in which thousands were killed, and the situation became even worse, particularly in Lahore and Amritsar, when the partition plan was announced. A special force of fifty thousand men was sent to the Punjab, but it could not stop the endless murders and arsons.

At this point Sir Cyril Radcliffe, a distinguished lawyer, arrived at the head of a commission to draw up the boundaries in the Punjab and Bengal as well as Assam. This was his first visit to India, and he was completely ignorant of Indian affairs. He decided to try to preserve his impartiality by staying in Delhi and relying on the reports his commissioners from Lahore and Calcutta submitted to him. Unfortunately, the commissioners, who came from rival groups, could not agree among themselves. Among the major problems that had to be solved were whether Calcutta, which had a Hindu majority, should go to Pakistan because East Bengal's jute was processed in the city's mills and whether the tribespeople around Chittagong, who distrusted the Muslims, should be included in Pakistan. Calcutta went to India; the Chittagong hills to Pakistan (initially East Pakistan, now the independent state of Bangladesh).

The Punjab was even more difficult to divide. Mountbatten insisted that the awards should only be announced after independence so that the celebrations would not be marred by communal violence. Thus, on August 15th many Punjabis did not know which citizenship they had been allotted. When the frontiers were announced, Pakistanis accused Radcliffe of favouring India by granting it the district of Gurdaspur, which gave the Indians access to Kashmir.

The army was divided, and although there were some violent incidents as units travelled across the subcontinent to their new states, Hindu, Sikh, and Muslim officers parted amicably, not imagining that they would ever be called upon to fight one another. India got the bulk of the equipment, and none of the ordnance factories were in Pakistan. Much the same held true in the division of the civil service. Most Muslims went to Pakistan, but they left their office equipment behind in Delhi. The government in Karachi had to start from scratch, and India inherited the government machinery in Delhi.

What about the 565 princely states, most of which were in what was to become Indian territory? It had been assumed that, unable to exercise full sovereignty on their own, they would opt for India or Pakistan, and Jinnah tried to win over the fourteen that were contiguous to Pakistan. Sir Conrad Corfield, head of the political service that advised the princes, held the view that paramountcy, the system whereby Britain recognized the princes' independence but took care of their defence and foreign policy, could not simply be transferred to the successor states. He also argued that accession should not be negotiated until after independence.

Mountbatten, however, mindful of Nehru's concerns about the balkanization of the subcontinent, wanted all such arrangements to be made before independence. He warned the princes that if they did not accede before 15 August, the terms would be markedly less favourable. Once again V. P. Menon and Patel worked out a compromise solution. The princes would hand over responsibility for defence, foreign policy, and communications to India or Pakistan, but they would retain full authority for internal affairs. The political service was disbanded, and Corfield retired to Britain, having burned a number of compromising documents that had been prudently kept in case blackmail had been required. A new States Department of the Government of India was established with Patel as its capable head and with the invaluable V. P. Menon as his chief adviser. Most princes had no alternative but to accept, and in the end only Hyderabad, Kashmir, and Junagadh refused.

As Dominions, India and Pakistan would need governors general. Nehru suggested that because British assets would have to be divided equitably after independence, there should be one governor general for the two states. He believed that Mountbatten was the best man for the job. Jinnah, however, insisted that he should be made governor general of Pakistan with Liaqat Ali Khan as prime minister. Mountbatten, much flattered by the prospect of being governor general twice over, was furious, and Jinnah did not tell him his reasons for this strange demand. Jinnah knew he was dying of tuberculosis, and he wanted to secure Liaqat Ali Khan's position while he still held on to executive power. This was the only way he could control his political rivals in the new state. Mountbatten thus became governor general of India alone, and his hopes of creating a common defence council and other co-operative mechanisms were dashed.

The independence celebrations were exhilarating. Nehru gave a brilliant address: "Long years ago," he said, "we made a tryst with destiny, and now the time comes when we shall redeem, our pledge. . . . At the stroke of the midnight hour, while the world sleeps, India will awake to life and freedom. A moment comes, which comes but rarely in history, when we step out from the old to the new, when an age ends and when the soul of a nation, long suppressed, finds utterance." Mountbatten had pulled off a tremendous diplomatic feat, but there were widespread feelings that, even though there was no viable alternative, the creation of Pakistan had been a mistake. And then the killing reached new levels of brutality.

In the divided Punjab there was no effective police force. Policemen had fled to safety on either side of the border. Sikh leaders incited their followers to murder Muslims, and they eagerly answered the call. Liaqat Ali Khan and Nehru met to do what they could to stop the appalling bloodshed. They convinced the Sikh leaders to try to stop the campaign of terror; but it was too late. Columns of Hindu and Sikh refugees trudged eastwards, and Muslims struggled in the opposite direction. Sikhs and Hindus murdered and mutilated Muslims, who retaliated in kind whenever they got the chance. Initially, the Muslims suffered the most, particularly in the eastern Punjab where the Sikhs indulged in an orgy of indiscriminate killing, but in Lahore, which had a Muslim majority, Sikh and Hindu merchants lived in fear of their lives. Units of the Punjab Boundary Force usually arrived on the scenes of massacres when the killing was over. When the killings at last began to peter out towards the end of November, official estimates of deaths were a quarter of a million. Most observers feel this number is a gross underestimation; probably about a million men, women, and children were murdered in the Punjab.

The killings also spread eastward. In Delhi, where the mostly Muslim police had left for Pakistan, Hindus and Sikhs murdered Muslim shopkeepers and then moved into the poorer districts and slaughtered their co-religionists. Nehru and Patel pleaded with Mountbatten to accept emergency powers to deal with the crisis. He prudently refused, but he did agree to chair an Indian cabinet committee with Nehru and Patel as members. That the former viceroy had these extraordinary powers almost immediately after independence was kept secret for many years, although some have suggested that Mountbatten exaggerated his importance.

Gradually the carnage abated. That the transfer of power was so bloody was in no small part the result of Churchill's intransigence in the 1930s and 1940s, which enabled Jinnah to hold out and made Congress impatient. If India had been allowed a more effect form of representative government at almost any time in the decade after 1935, much of this terrible tragedy could have been avoided.

If Churchill is the villain of the piece, Attlee is its hero. He set a precise date for British withdrawal and decided to send Mountbatten to India. His energetic support for constructive proposals and his passionate commitment to finding as fair and equitable solution as was humanly possible were major reasons why the situation did not get completely out of hand. Mountbatten got most of the credit, but Attlee made all the really important decisions. In Britain, people were so concerned with the crisis over sterling convertibility and the nationalization of the steel industry that few worried about events in distant India.

That both India and Pakistan chose to remain within the Commonwealth was seen as something of a vote of thanks to the British. Dr. Rajendra Prasad, who became India's first president, described the transfer of power as "the consummation and fulfillment of the historic traditions and democratic ideals of the British"; but India and Pakistan soon developed in quite different directions. Jinnah died just over a year after independence, and after Liaqat Ali Khan was assassinated in 1951, the country degenerated into a corrupt military dictatorship. Divisions between West and East Pakistan became increasingly acute, with the Bengalis accusing the westerners of seizing the profits of their jute exports and investing them in West Pakistan. In 1971 East Bengal broke away to form the independent state of Bangladesh.

In India, less than a year after independence Gandhi was assassinated by a religious fanatic. Although he was devastated by the death of a dear friend and great leader, Nehru had strongly opposed Gandhi's philosophy of communalism and rejection of Western technology. Nehru was personally autocratic, but he was also a modernizer determined to uphold those aspects of the British tradition that he admired—the rule of law, parliamentary democracy, a highly trained civil service, and religious toleration. During the sixteen years Nehru remained in office, he fought off the proponents of the "panchayati raj" based on village communes as well as the supporters of the idea of a Hindu Raj. His legacy was an India that remains, in spite of endless problems, secular, democratic, and officially tolerant.

The transfer of power in India and Pakistan was the outstanding achievement of the Labour government. It stands in marked contrast to the retreat from empire by the French, Dutch, Belgians, and Portuguese. It was the single most important step in the creation of a multi-racial Commonwealth that had Jawaharlal Nehru as its outstanding champion. Labour inherited an Empire with 457 million inhabitants in 1945. By 1951 it had only 70 million. Curiously enough, Labour devoted little attention to Commonwealth or colonial policy during its term in office. The left wing of the party indulged in bouts of knee-jerk anti-imperialism, and Creech Jones, as Bevin complained, resolutely hid his light under a bushel. Overshadowed at the time by ground nuts and Gambian eggs, Indian independence now appears as the Labour Party's greatest and most lasting contribution to the cause of freedom and economic advancement.

Of course, the story is not one of pure selflessness and enlightenment. Self-interest, both economic and strategic, determined policy towards Ceylon, Malaya, and East Africa and the proposals for a Central African Federation. The white settlers in Rhodesia and Kenya were able to ruin some of Labour's more enlightened schemes, and the manipulations of the dollar pool were singularly disadvantageous to a number of Commonwealth countries. Britain was still trying to play the role of a great power. Many of the Conservatives who were returned to power in October 1951 were determined to hang on to what was left of the Empire, unwilling to accede to nationalist clamours for independence that were growing increasingly persistent. Ironically, it was a Conservative administration that finally brought the Empire to its end.

7 The End of the Empire

The most pressing problem facing the Conservatives when they regained office in 1951 was the tense situation in Egypt, which was soon to enter a new, more violent phase. In January 1952, the Egyptian guerrillas launched a foolhardy attack on the British base at Tel-el-Kebir. The British occupied Ismailia in retribution, and when they attacked the police headquarters there, fifty Egyptians were killed and another one hundred injured. On the following "Black Saturday," mobs in Cairo went on the rampage in an orgy of murder, arson, and looting. King Farouk delayed before sending the army in to restore order, and lacking American support, the British decided not to intervene. Within a few months the king and the Wafd (the Egyptian Nationalist Party) were sent packing by the "free officers" led by Colonel Gamal Abdel Nasser, the real power behind Egypt's new ruler, General Mohammed Neguib.

British Conservative foreign secretary Anthony Eden, who became prime minister three years later, wanted to negotiate a phased withdrawal from the Canal Zone, but Churchill wanted to hang on. At first, Nasser simply wanted the British out. Then he refused to become involved in the defence of the so-called "northern tier," an arrangement aimed at the containment of the Soviet Union that was formalized in the Baghdad Pact, signed by Britain, Iraq, and Turkey in February 1955 and soon acceded to by Pakistan and Iran. Nasser then became fired with ambition to gain a major role on the world stage as a leader of the non-aligned nations. He hoped to play the West off against the Soviets and at the same time become leader of the Arab world. He was determined to stop other Arab nations from joining the Baghdad Pact, which he denounced as a reactionary, imperialist alliance.

In April 1955, Nasser attended the Afro-Asian Bandung conference called by President Sukharno of Indonesia and attended by the great figures of the non-aligned world. Nehru, Chou En-lai, and Tito encouraged Nasser to buy arms from the Russians and told him that he need not fear the consequences. Not only was Nasser flattered by such illustrious attention, he was also completely taken in by the heady mixture of Marxist, liberal, and religious clichés of which Nehru had become a past master. The Soviets were eager to leap across the northern tier and sent arms to Egypt via Czechoslovakia. Alarmed by growing Soviet influence in the Middle East, the British were determined to win Nasser back into the fold.

Nasser seized the opportunity to find financing for his pet project, the building of a gigantic dam on the Nile at Aswan. Because the prime minister, Eden, feared that this might become a Soviet-sponsored project, he proposed to the United States that the two countries form a consortium with the World Bank to finance the scheme. At this point, however (in March 1956), King Hussein of Jordan dismissed the British commander of his army, Sir John Glubb. Eden, obsessed with the idea that Nasser had inspired the king's action, decided to teach him a lesson. He ordered the Aswan project dropped, which pleased John Foster Dulles, the American secretary of state, who felt Nasser was too closely involved with the Soviets.

Nasser reacted by nationalizing the Suez Canal in July and announcing that the dam would be built with the revenues it produced. Eden ordered preparations for the invasion of Egypt. When the service chiefs told him that an invasion force could not be ready for six weeks, the affair should have ended. Britain had to act immediately or not at all. It would have been best to have done nothing, since the nationalization of foreign assets with due compensation, as Nasser had promised, was not illegal. But Eden was now convinced that Nasser was another Mussolini who could not be appeased. He was goaded by backbench Conservatives who felt that he had been far too conciliatory towards Egypt in the past. He was also seriously ill with bile duct problems during the Suez crisis and at one point was delivered into hospital with a temperature of 106. Part of his erratic behaviour can be explained by the effects of amphetamines and tranquillizers, which caused him to have outbursts of violent temper followed by periods of serene detachment.

Dulles played for time, and Nehru exerted his influence on Nasser to compromise since he wished to avoid a war between a Commonwealth and a Bandung (non-aligned) state. As the weeks slipped by, a settlement seemed possible. Then the French, smarting under a series of defeats in Indochina, Tunisia, and Morocco and fighting a war against nationalists in Algeria, whom Nasser was openly supporting, came up with a plan to teach the Egyptian dictator a lesson. Israel would seize the Sinai; an Anglo-French force would occupy the Canal, Port Said, and Suez. Eden was delighted at this suggestion, despite the fact that Britain was obliged by treaty to defend Egypt if it was attacked. The Israelis demanded that the RAF make a pre-emptive strike against Egyptian airfields before they began their attack, but Eden and the French persuaded them that it was impossible, promising instead that the Egyptian air force would be destroyed twelve hours after the Israeli invasion. The Israelis reluctantly accepted this assurance since Nasser had unified the commands of the Egyptian, Syrian, and Jordanian armies and clearly intended to try to destroy Israel at the earliest opportunity.

The Israelis attacked on 29 October 1956. As predicted, Egypt refused to accept the ultimatum, the RAF began their bombing campaign, and the first units of the Anglo-French force were landed. By the time they arrived, however, the Israelis had agreed with Egypt to a ceasefire, and since the two fronts were well separated, there was no excuse for them to be there at all. The situation rapidly collapsed into a tragi-comedy. The Americans were completely in the dark because the British had conveniently not found a replacement for their ambassador.

The United States immediately placed a resolution before the Security Council of the United Nations condemning Israeli aggression. In the General Assembly, only Australia and New Zealand supported the invasion. The House of Commons was in an uproar, and Eden was unable to answer the probing questions of the Opposition. The Cabinet, most of whom had also been kept in the dark, was badly divided, and some members, notably R. A. Butler and Harold Macmillan, thought their turn to be prime minister had come. The Egyptians sank ships to block the canal, doing exactly what the Anglo-French invasion was supposed to stop. Britain now had to import oil from the Americas, which caused a run on the pound and a rapid drain on gold and dollar reserves. The British thus had to go cap in hand to the Americans, who made their loan conditional on a ceasefire in Egypt, as did the International Monetary Fund. Harold Macmillan, the chancellor of the Exchequer, who had been an enthusiastic supporter of the Suez adventure, now abandoned Eden. He told the Cabinet that Britain had to withdraw or face financial ruin. On 6 November, Eden announced that all was over, and a few weeks later, sick and his career in ruins, he resigned. He had tried to act like the leader of a great power, but Britain was now a member of the medium ranks. This was a lesson that Macmillan learned during the Suez crisis. Britain could no longer wield the big stick; she had to rely on cunning, diplomacy, and public relations. The new prime minister was a skilled practitioner of these arts.

Having lost their airfields in Iraq and London as well as being forced out of Suez, the British desperately needed a new secure base in the area, and Aden, at this time the second busiest port in the world and a British colony since 1839, seemed the best choice. Aden had been strengthened in the nineteenth century to meet the challenge of the French in Egypt. When the French left, Aden lost its strategic importance, but it continued to thrive as a coaling station and trade centre. Britain paid protection money under the guise of treaties to the emirs (chieftains) who ruled the region around the port of Aden rather than lead punitive expeditions against them across the desert. Some ninety such protection treaties were signed.

After the collapse of the Ottoman Empire at the end of World War I, the ruler of Aden's neighbour, Yemen, began to nibble away at these British protectorates, but when he advanced on Aden, he was bombed into submission by the RAF, and under the treaty of Sana (1934), Yemen because the last territorial acquisition of the British Empire.

Aden's commercial importance grew rapidly after World War II, especially after British Petroleum, expelled from Iran in 1954, built a huge refinery in Aden.

The population prospered, and the British felt secure. Then the "Voice of the Arabs" was heard on transistor radios in remote tents and villages, and Nasser's image began to appear on shops and walls. The emirs in the Aden protectorate became alarmed. Arab nationalists fired by Nasser's rhetoric and Yemeni ambitions both threatened them, and their position deteriorated further when the Crown Prince of Yemen announced that he had joined Nasser's pan-Arabic camp.

The emir's fear at this development enabled the British to persuade them—although they were mostly locked into ancient blood feuds—to unite, as the Federation of Arab Emirates of the South, in February 1959. It was a curious and anarchic state in which tribesmen continued to shoot at one another and at the Federation's army. The RAF made occasional disciplinary raids, there would be brief moments of quiet, and then this traditional sport would be renewed.

In Aden the main threats to the British were the Federation tribesmen and the Yemenis organized in the Aden Trades Union Congress (ATUC), which was strongly influenced by Nasserite pan-Arabism, anti-imperialism, and socialism. Its aim was to create an independent socialist state made up of Aden, the Federation of the Arab Emirates of the South, and Yemen. The British, no longer able to arrange the elections to the Aden legislative council, which was clearly going to have a Nasserite Arab majority, forced Aden to join the Federation in September 1962 so that a coalition of pro-British businessmen and federal rulers could ward off the pan-Arabs.

The day after this vote, the royalist imam of Yemen was deposed, and a pro-Egyptian, but unstable, revolutionary government took over, opposed by the royalist forces, strongly supported by Saudi Arabia, who started a civil war. The British government wanted to improve its relations with Saudi Arabia, but it also wanted to recognize the new régime in Yemen in the hope of arriving at some modus vivendi with the pan-Arabs in Aden, a hope encouraged by a noticeable moderation of the anti-British tone of Egyptian propaganda.

Although the American president, John F. Kennedy, recognized the Yemeni republican government and many senior British officials argued that Britain should follow suit, Harold Macmillan decided to support the royalist mercenaries in their efforts to overthrow the régime. These forces were trained and equipped by the British army. Nasser replied in kind by sending seventy thousand Egyptian troops to support the Yemen government. Most of the population of Aden enthusiastically supported Nasser and the Yemen régime. The tribesmen in the Federation might also be won over, and the British could not, anyway, rely on these unruly types. The emirs were incompetent, and the businessmen in Aden were interested in profit, not government. The British position was, in short, extremely precarious, but Macmillan felt that Arab nationalism was a temporary nuisance rather than a wind of change. The governor, Sir Kennedy Trevaskis, hoped that if the Federation were granted independence from Britain under the emirs and the Aden businessmen, all would be well.

At this point, in 1964, however, Labour was returned to office in Britain. The new government had no sympathy at all for reactionary emirs and greedy businessmen and a great deal for the Aden Trades Union Congress (ATUC). Labour felt that the best solution was to grant independence with power in the hands of ATUC's competent and popular leader, Abdullah al Asnag. This scheme came to nothing, partly because President Lyndon Johnson did not want Britain to abandon the base at Aden at a time when the Americans were increasingly engaged in Vietnam and also because of the emergence of a new armed faction in Yemen, the National Liberation Front (NLF), which was dedicated to the overthrow of the imperialists and the creation of a proletarian state. The NLF were not the familiar wild and undisciplined tribesmen, they were a highly proficient guerrilla force, trained by the Egyptian army and PLO terrorists, who had a network of contacts throughout the Federation, including inside the Federal army.

When the terrorist campaign began in earnest in Aden in 1964, the trade unionist leader Al Asnag feared that he was about to be overtaken on the left, and he organized his own guerrilla force, the Front for the Liberation of Occupied South Yemen (FLOSY) and gained Nasser's support. The half-baked Marxism-Leninism of the NLF was too much even for him to swallow. The NLF promptly denounced FLOSY as counterrevolutionary agents of the Egyptian bourgeoisie. The Egyptians, stung by this accusation, encouraged the violence in the Federation, announcing that it was the only way to achieve true independence.

In February 1968, despite President Johnson's pleas and the need for American support to avoid the devaluation of the pound, Britain's Labour government decided they could not hang onto Aden and announced that independence would be granted that year. The beleaguered emirs and Aden businessmen regarded the decision as a craven betrayal. In their view, when the British withdrew their troops, they would be deserting those whose safety they had guaranteed to the mercy of assorted communists, trigger-happy tribesmen, ineffectual idealist nationalists, and urban thugs. Al Asnag was also in a awkward situation. He had to prove that he was even more anti-imperialist and anti-Zionist than the NLF. Nasser enthusiastically supported Al Asnag, putting the head of the NLF under virtual house arrest and announcing that he, Nasser, intended to continue to play a role in Yemeni affairs. His position only served to strengthen the NLF's case that FLOSY were Egyptian stooges and that the Egyptians were as much imperialists as the British. Nasser wanted to take over control of Yemen, Aden, and the protectorates, and, as he told a startled Dennis Healey, Labour's minister of defence, he intended to play the role Lord Lugard had played in West Africa in his region.

The new foreign secretary appointed in 1966, George Brown, was determined to strike a deal with this Egyptian Lugard in order to stop the terrorism in Aden and secure a peaceful withdrawal. This was easier said than done. Nasser might be willing to co-operate, but the NLF would not stop the killings for fear that they would look like appeasers of the imperialists; and as long as the NLF went on killing, FLOSY had to keep up the slaughter for fear of similar accusations. The situation was further complicated by a mutiny in the Federal army as a result of which a number of British soldiers were killed.

Then Nasser suffered a humiliating defeat when he attacked Israel in 1967. He had to withdraw all his troops from Yemen and could no longer afford to support FLOSY. With a useless Federal army, with FLOSY without a backer, and the British determined to leave, the NLF were the clear winners. The emirs fled to Saudi Arabia or London, and the Federal government collapsed. The NLF and FLOSY continued to kill one another, and in the final stages the NLF won the support of the Federal army. No one would talk to the British for fear of being branded a traitor. The unfortunate governor of Aden, Sir Humphrey Trevelyan, had no one to whom he could hand the keys when he left, but in a gentlemanly fashion he had Government House repainted for the new occupant.

The NLF leader Qahtan Asshabi inherited a ruined economy. The British base had gone, the Suez Canal was closed, the refinery idle. The emirs had taken their money with them. He established a Marxist dictatorship called the People's Democratic Republic of Yemen, and Soviet naval vessels now anchored where once the Royal Navy rode. Soviet imperialism had replaced British. For the British, it was an unseemly scuttling, but they could comfort themselves that this now worthless port was the only colony to end up in the clutches of the Soviet Empire.

Britain's other great strategic base in the area was Cyprus. The island had been captured by Richard I during the Third Crusade, in the 12th century, but it was quickly sold off. In 1878 Disraeli had persuaded the Turks to give Britain a lease on Cyprus in return for protection against Russia, and he announced to his Queen that he had thereby won the "key to India." After World War I, the British annexed Cyprus outright as the Ottoman Empire was divided up. Cyprus was eclipsed when Britain established bases in Egypt, but it became correspondingly significant as the British withdrew from Egypt and Palestine.

The population of Cyprus was largely Greek, but there was a significant Turkish Muslim minority. The majority of Greek Cypriots wanted union with

128

Greece (enosis). British officials seriously considered granting this wish in the early 1920s, but the idea was rejected under the influence of imperial enthusiasts like Milner and Churchill. After World War II, the Labour government also toyed with Greek hopes, but then rejected enosis on strategic grounds. Britain needed a secure base from which to protect its huge Middle Eastern oil interests. Proposed constitutional reforms would have given the Greeks a greater say in the running of the island, but since enosis was ruled out, these were unacceptable to them.

In 1950 a new Greek Orthodox archbishop of Cyprus was appointed— Archbishop Makarios III, a thirty-seven-year-old of exceptional political skill. Two years later he made a pact with Colonel George Grivas, a fanatical right-wing thug of Greek Cypriot origin. It was a curious alliance and distinctly embarrassing to the Greek government, which did not want to alienate the British. The movement for enosis might well have been contained had it not been for Eden's tactless remark to the Greek prime minister in 1953 that Greece might as well lay claim to New York as to Cyprus since there were more Greeks living there, adding that there would never be a Cyprus question. These infuriating remarks were followed by statements in the House of Commons in July 1954 by a junior minister at the Colonial Office, Henry Hopkinson, to the effect that Cyprus would never be granted independence. This was the last straw for the Greek government, which now brought Cyprus to the attention of the United Nations and began to regard Grivas and his National Organization of Cypriot Fighters (EOKA) in a more favourable light.

The terrorist campaign began in earnest in 1955, and it rapidly won support. The British reacted by sending the chief of imperial general staff, Field Marshal Sir John Harding, as governor. He met Makarios shortly after his arrival and asked him to disown EOKA violence. In return, Makarios demanded that the British government disavow Hopkinson's statement. A saving formula was worked out, but Makarios broke off the talks, hoping for better terms. Pushed by the Greek government, Makarios did resume talks with Harding, but now he demanded that there should be an amnesty for EOKA terrorists, that the police force should be run by Cypriots rather than the British, and that there should be a guaranteed Greek Cypriot majority in the assembly, which the British had agreed was to be elected and would exercise partial self-government. The colonial secretary, Alan Lennox-Boyd, travelled to the island and agreed to virtually all these conditions. Once again Makarios, the eternal haggler, broke off the talks, hoping to get an even better deal.

The British lost patience. They deported Makarios to an island in the Seychelles and mounted a campaign to crush EOKA. Grivas and his men were soon on the run, but British troops, maddened by the murder of many of their comrades, often used brutal methods in their search for and interrogation of suspected terrorists. The courts, nevertheless, acted with scrupulous fairness. Harding was winning the war, and in August 1956, Grivas called a truce. But as soon as British troops were withdrawn to go to Suez, he reopened his campaign.

Macmillan, who took over as prime minister in early 1957, after the 1956 Suez débacle, was determined to cut defence costs, end the unpopular National Service (2 years conscripted military service for British men), and roughly halve the size of the armed forces. That thirty thousand troops should be tied down in Cyprus chasing some three hundred guerrillas was clearly absurd, especially since, after Suez, there was no question of Cyprus being used as a base from which to launch a major offensive. Keeping a couple of bases on the island would be sufficient. To make these proposals acceptable to the Greeks, Macmillan ordered the release of Archbishop Makarios.

The British had found part of Colonel Grivas's diary and knew that he had been acting under Makarios's orders. Now they hoped to persuade the archbishop to end the violence. The Greek government also wanted EOKA to lay down its arms since they feared that the Turks would unleash their guerrillas (VOLKAN) and plunge Cyprus into a civil war. Since the police force was now largely manned by Turkish Cypriots, even though they were a small minority in the island, the Turks were in a powerful position. They also had the full support of the Turkish government. Makarios asked Grivas for his opinion on this proposal, and Grivas rejected it out of hand. He wanted self-determination for Cyprus, something that was promised by the Labour Party, which was confidently expected to win the next election. Macmillan then appointed a new governor, Sir Hugh Foot, who was clearly sympathetic to the Greek Cypriot cause. Makarios and Grivas were impressed and called a temporary truce. The Turks, however, thought this was the first step towards enosis, and they immediately unleashed a wave of violence. Cyprus was rapidly descending into chaos. Greeks killed Turks, and Turks killed Greeks; both killed the British, and Grivas, an ascetic clerico-fascist, let EOKA loose on the Cypriot communists (AKEL).

The claims of the Turkish Cypriots could no longer be ignored. Turkey was far stronger than Greece and would certainly win a war over the island, a war that seemed increasingly likely. Makarios had also lost the Labour Party's support for enosis, and so he suddenly announced that he had abandoned the idea and wanted an independent Cyprus with links to neither Greece nor Turkey. Greece reluctantly backed independence in order to stop Macmillan's plan for Cyprus, which would have given the Turks a say in its government. In negotiations between the Greek and Turkish foreign ministers an agreement was eventually reached whereby the Turks were to have a small military base on the island, the president would be Greek and the vice-president Turkish, and the rights of both factions would be carefully guaranteed by intricate constitutional mechanisms. Makarios nearly vetoed the deal at the London conference in February 1959, but he realized that doing so would almost certainly mean war with Turkey. With great reluctance, he signed the agreement.

Cyprus officially became a quasi-independent republic in August 1960 with Makarios as president. Its sovereignty was limited, for it could not form a political or economic union with any other country, the fundamental articles of the constitution could not be changed, and no Cypriots, Greeks, Turks, or Britons could serve on the Supreme Constitutional Court, the president of which was a German. None of these items was of much concern to the British. They had got out of Cyprus, and they still had their bases. Cyprus after independence was even more unhappy and violent than it was before. Civil war broke out, and the island was partitioned and policed by UN troops, as it still is. In July 1974 Makarios was overthrown by EOKA and replaced by Nikos Sampson, a murderous bully who had only escaped the hangman's noose because the British judge thought that his confession had been obtained by force. Makarios fled to the protection of the British. Turkey invaded Cyprus and extended the Turkish enclave well beyond the existing limits. Makarios returned as president of a rump Cyprus in the south.

British rule in Cyprus had no positive features. The island was obviously not the key to India, it never served a useful purpose as a base in the Mediterranean, and it even remained untouched during World War II. It merely provided a bloody and unfortunate footnote to the story of the end of the British Empire and left a legacy of hatred, bloodshed, and fanaticism.

In the other parts of the Empire, there were also many changes taking place in the 1950s and 1960s. In West Africa, for example, Churchill and his colonial secretary, Oliver Lyttleton, had agreed that the Gold Coast (Ghana) was moving too rapidly towards independence, but it was too late to halt the process. Nkrumah's victory at the polls in 1954 horrified the Ashanti, who denounced his party as a gang of corrupt, incompetent, half-baked Marxists. They organized the National Liberation Movement (NLM) in response, and Danquah and other middle-class elements joined it. Violence soon erupted between the para-military organizations of the CPP and the NLM.

The rapid growth of support for the NLM made it difficult for the British to go forward on the basis of the 1954 election results, in spite of Sir Charles Arden-Clarke's continued support for Nkrumah and the CPP. In new elections held in July 1956, Nkrumah was once again victorious overall, but the NLM won the Ashanti vote, and their allies the NPP won the Northern Territories. Arden-Clarke and

Lennox-Boyd would have liked to have seen independence delayed, but the CPP, despite the NLM's success, had won more than 40 per cent of the votes in Ashanti and the Northern Territories and thus had a clear mandate in the country as a whole. Lennox-Boyd visited the Gold Coast and got Nkrumah to agree to a degree of regional autonomy to satisfy the Ashanti and those in the north who were demonstrating against independence and Nkrumah's "black raj." Nkrumah had no intention of honouring this commitment or any other constitutional provision, but he agreed for the sake of independence. The Gold Coast became an independent Ghana in 1957, power firmly in the hands of Nkrumah's party. The chiefs with whom the British had traditionally dealt felt bitter and betrayed.

Elsewhere in Africa the whites in the Central African Federation (Northern and Southern Rhodesia and Nyasaland) were confident that they enjoyed the support of a large number of Conservatives and that the federation would not degenerate into what its prime minister, Sir Geoffrey Huggins, was pleased to call a "native benefit society." Britain's Labour party, now in Opposition, had serious misgivings about the federation on the grounds that its organization ignored the wishes of the African majorities in the northern protectorates. This view was shared by *The Times* and the liberal press as well as the churches. Huggins brushed aside all such objections saying: "We want to indicate to Africans that provision is made for them to have a place in the sun as things go along. But we have not the slightest intention of letting them control things until they have proved themselves, and perhaps not even then. That will depend on our grandchildren." His successor as prime minister of the Central African Federation, Sir Roy Welensky, insisted that the whole idea of adult suffrage was "rubbish and completely unsuitable for Africa." The existing franchise had such high income and property qualifications that few Africans were on the electoral rolls. Northern Rhodesia, for example, had an electorate of 15,447 settlers and 3 Africans.

The Africans had a somewhat unlikely champion in the prime minister of Southern Rhodesia, Garfield Todd. He was a liberal minded New Zealander, a brilliant public speaker, and a rancher with a ninety-thousand-acre spread who appealed to Huggins both because of his unquestionable talent and because he had a proclivity for making such remarks as: "We're taking the African people by the scruff of the neck and saying, 'come with us into the twentieth century.'" But Todd, a sincere Christian, also held the heretical view that all men are born equal; he suggested that the whites had nothing to lose and much to gain by conceding to African demands for equality of opportunity.

Todd moved cautiously, gradually introducing important reforms that improved the lot of the Africans. The problem was that these reforms, although in themselves acceptable to the white settlers, raised African expectations, and Todd's colleagues began to mutter about the "thin end of the wedge." Two specific issues brought about his downfall. The first was his violent reaction to a proposal that sexual intercourse outside marriage between white men and black women be made a punishable offence. Todd announced that he thought this proposal was absurd and impossible to police, and he added that the 1903 law forbidding unmarried black men from having sexual intercourse with white women should be repealed. Many whites considered Todd an apologist for black rapists, and the new law passed with Todd voting against the measure.

The other issue was even more serious. Todd had the temerity to suggest that the six thousand Africans with ten-years' schooling (many of them professionals) should be given the vote. At the time there were more than fifty thousand whites on the electoral rolls in Southern Rhodesia and about five hundred Africans, amply demonstrating the hypocrisy of the claim that the whites would give Africans the vote "when they were ready." At first it seemed that Todd had called their bluff. The measure to amend the franchise was accepted, but then his cabinet colleagues, fearful for their political futures, refused to serve under him, and his party replaced him. Any hope for modest liberal reform in Rhodesia was now dashed.

Huggins hoped that he would be able to achieve full independence for the federation before his imminent retirement and thus assure white supremacy, He had therefore found Todd's moderate liberalism useful because it could be used as evidence to the British government that the federation was sincere in its policy of partnership.

The British government insisted that the African franchise would have to be extended before independence. Doing so proved to be an extraordinarily complex problem. Not even the Africans wanted universal suffrage because they were afraid that it would lead to a mass exodus of the hugely outnumbered whites and to consequent economic ruin. As a result, a different franchise requirement was needed in Northern and Southern Rhodesia, in Nyasaland, and in the federation.

One proposal was to extend the indirect African vote, as it existed in Nyasaland, to the federation. Under this system a white MP had to win a significant proportion of the African vote and vice versa. Thus, perceived extremists, such as the African nationalist Joshua Nkomo, could be defeated. A proposal to amend the federal electoral system in 1957 to allow six additional African seats, but making four of them subject to the white cross-vote, was ruled discriminatory by the African Affairs Board, which monitored African rights. The Conservative British government promptly overruled these objections, Commonwealth Secretary Lord Home later explaining that their main concern was to keep the federal government on their side and that, after all, the number of African MPs had been increased. To the Africans this episode proved that the African Affairs Board was a sham, and when Garfield Todd was deposed, it seemed that the federation was rapidly becoming an apartheid state.

The Nyasas were determined to resist. They persuaded their most distinguished expatriate, Dr. Hastings Banda, who was practising medicine in Ghana, to return after an absence of forty-three years. Banda hesitated, but when federation Prime Minister Welensky got the British government to agree not to amend or repeal any federal act, he decided he could wait no longer. He returned in 1958 to an explosive situation. While the British government had announced that it would review the federal constitution in 1960, African political leaders in Nyasaland were demanding that the country leave the federation. Banda found himself leader of a movement he could not control. He was a profoundly conservative man with a great admiration for the British way of life, having (or perhaps in spite of having) taken his second medical degree in Edinburgh and having practised in London. He could no longer speak his native language, and although he became president of the Nyasaland branch of the African National Congress, he could not control the irresponsible radicals in its ranks.

The radicals opposed agricultural regulations, such as the requirement to inoculate cattle and to take certain steps to prevent soil erosion, measures that Banda knew were essential. They also objected to Banda socializing with whites, including the governor, Sir Robert Armitage. The crowds that followed Banda often became unruly, although he always opposed violence.

Sir Roy Welensky described himself as "50 per cent Jewish, 50 per cent Polish and 100 per cent British." He was a rough and tough union boss from a poverty-stricken home. He regarded African nationalism as a communist plot that had to be crushed. Banda and the Northern Rhodesian leaders Kenneth Kaunda and Harry Nkumbula attended the first Pan-African Congress hosted by Kwame Nkrumah in Accra in 1958. When the Congress signed a declaration calling for the break-up of the Central African Federation, Welensky saw his worst fears confirmed.

On his return, Banda was greeted at Salisbury airport by enthusiastic crowds, which convinced Welensky that he and his followers had to be stopped. Since the police in Nyasaland were under the control of the governor, he decided to pressure Armitage by mobilizing the Southern Rhodesian armed forces. The governor, however, remained cool, waiting for Whitehall to come up with constitutional proposals that would calm the Africans. Banda decided to keep up the pressure, hoping that he and some of his followers might be arrested and thus cause a political scandal in Britain. Some Congress members went much further, calling for violence and the murder of whites and their African sympathizers.

There was some violence in the following months, but none of it was directed against whites. Arrests were made, and Welensky demanded that the governor declare a state of emergency so he could send in the troops. Armitage kept his nerve, and the British government at last agreed to send a minister with concrete constitutional proposals. Armed with this welcome news, the governor begged Banda to condemn the violence, but Banda hesitated, possibly because the situation was out of his control. Armitage called in the Southern Rhodesian troops. Banda then refused to condemn the violence, which spread throughout the country. He was arrested and dragged off to Southern Rhodesia. Soldiers fired on demonstrators protesting his arrest, and some fifty Africans were killed. Dr. Hastings Banda had got the scandal he wanted.

In Britain the colonial secretary, Alan Lennox-Boyd, announced, on the basis of lurid accounts from the white settlers, that Congress was planning to massacre the whites and their sympathizers. Sir Robert Armitage was appalled when he read the text of Lennox-Boyd's speech, for he knew that the violence had been directed not against whites but against African civil servants. Harold Macmillan decided that a commission of inquiry should be sent out to examine the facts and recommend changes.

The commission was headed by Britain's most brilliant judge, Sir Patrick Devlin, and his report was a bombshell. He insisted that Sir Robert had acted quite properly in declaring a state of emergency but that during the emergency many government officials had broken the law and alienated even the most loyal Africans by their behaviour. He suggested that Banda was indeed a man of compromise and concluded that not a single African supported the federation.

The government and prime minister rallied in defence of Lennox-Boyd and enlisted the unfortunate but loyal Armitage in their dubious cause. In the House of Commons the attorney-general publicly poured scorn on the Devlin Report, but Macmillan had decided that there had to be a fundamental change in colonial policy. Could the British government support the killing of Africans for the sole good of white settlers? Had African nationalism reached the point that it could no longer be stopped? The year 1959 proved to be a true turning point.

Macmillan was convinced that Banda had to be released from jail and that the federation had to be split up without Welensky declaring independence unilaterally. Were he to do so, his government would have to be forcibly removed. Fortunately for Macmillan, Lennox-Boyd decided to retire from Parliament to become managing director of his wife's family firm, Guinness. His successor, Iain Macleod, was a spellbinding orator, able to convince his opponents with his incise logic and burning conviction. He presided over Britain's retreat from Africa, where by 1968 only a single colony, Southern Rhodesia, remained. The affable Macmillan and the mercurial Macleod presided over a revolution in British colonial policy. To Lord Home, still Commonwealth secretary and much alarmed at his chief's conversion, it appeared that "Macmillan was a wind of change man and Macleod was a gale of change man." Macmillan took great trouble to appear considerably less radical than he was. He liked to quote Thomas Babington Macaulay to the effect that waiting for a people to be ready to govern themselves is similar to the attitude of the old fool who would not go into the water until he had learnt to swim. He was also much taken by the remark of a colonial governor who said that if one were to wait fifteen years it would make no difference since the native leadership would revolt and he would have to lock them up in prison where they would gain no administrative experience.

Sir Robert Armitage continued to insist that Banda should not be released, on the grounds that federal troops would have to be called in to keep the peace. He put this case to Macmillan when he toured Africa in 1960, the first British prime minister to do so. Armitage was strongly supported by Welensky in Salisbury and by Lord Home, who, mindful that the Belgians had just abandoned the Congo, argued that Banda's release would lead to widespread violence.

Macmillan found himself in a precarious situation. If he released Banda, Lord Home was likely to resign; if he did not, Macleod would probably go. If he released him and his followers went on the rampage in Nyasaland, as many predicted, Macmillan's government could well fall. Macleod decided to discuss the future of Nyasaland with Banda at Government House. A deal was made quickly and amicably. Macleod promised majority rule, and Banda promised that there would be no violence. This decision spelt the end of the federation, for Banda's African majority government could not possibly share power with Welensky's white majority federal government.

Welensky was determined to fight to the last ditch to keep the two Rhodesias together, but it was a hopeless cause. Macleod supported Kenneth Kaunda's struggle for independence in Northern Rhodesia, while Welensky stirred up backbench Conservative support to oust Macleod. Most serious of all, Lord Salisbury, Conservative grandee and former Commonwealth secretary, delivered a vicious attack on Macleod in the House of Lords. Such was Salisbury's influence in the party that Macmillan, although he supported Macleod's policies, felt that he had to remove him from the Colonial Office. In the long run, this action did not save Macmillan's skin. Many in his party were out to get him, in no small part because of his progressive policies towards the colonial question, and they seized the opportunity of the Profumo scandal to depose him in 1963.

Dr. Hastings Banda led Nyasaland to independence, renaming the country Malawi. Under Kaunda, Northern Rhodesia became independent as Zambia. In Southern Rhodesia the white minority was still in power, but they were bitter that they were not independent and that the British government would not give them dominion status on the grounds that it would be unacceptable to most other Commonwealth countries. The friendless white Rhodesians were desperate and feared that their country would fall prey to mass slaughter as was the case in Kenya, the institutionalized witchcraft of Malawi, the corrupt pseudo-Marxism of Ghana, or the brutal anarchy of the Congo. The only solution seemed to be a unilateral declaration of independence (UDI).

Welensky had rejected UDI for fear that the Southern Rhodesian officers, judges, and civil servants might take their oaths to the Queen seriously and also because a British blockade would be an economic disaster. The new prime minister, Ian Smith, was a man of quite a different type. He was stubborn, inflexible, and incorrigibly petit bourgeois, a man who made Welensky seem like a liberal. The governments of both Lord Home (Conservative), who had resigned his peerage to become Sir Alec Douglas-Home, and of Harold Wilson, who became Labour prime minister in 1964, were determined to resist UDI. Wilson had such a slender majority that he ruled out the use of force. Knowing this, Smith declared independence on the symbolic day of 11 November in 1965. The governor, a charming old-Etonian Rhodesian farmer, was trapped in Government House, his telephone cut and his salary blocked, but he continued to hold formal dinner parties with loyal toasts in an ineffectual display of defiance of Smith's illegal move. The United Nations security council called on all nations to refuse recognition and aid to the white Rhodesian régime.

There was precious little that Wilson could do. He had ruled out force since he knew that attacking whites, many of whom (including Ian Smith) had fought gallantly in the war, would provoke a strong reaction that might well bring down his government. Sanctions could not be expected to work because goods would continue to enter Rhodesia via South Africa and the Portuguese colony of Mozambique, but Wilson, having no alternative, apparently persuaded himself that they would, even if only half-heartedly applied. Pressure could not be brought to bear on South Africa to enforce sanctions because Britain was in the middle of a severe balance of payments crisis, and South Africa was one of its most important trading partners. Sanctions would hurt not only Rhodesia but also land-locked Zambia, which needed Rhodesian coal as well as imported oil. As a result, Rhodesia had some oil shortages and difficulties selling its tobacco crop, but a successful programme of import substitution resulted in a minor boom.

Faced with the failure of sanctions, Wilson turned to negotiations, but his offer to Smith of complete autonomy with only a feeble clause about progress towards majority rule was a virtual admission of defeat. Smith and his government, however, became obsessed with some of the irrelevant details of the proposals and felt that Wilson was trying to pull a fast one. They therefore rejected the offer and left Wilson stuck with sanctions that not only did not work but that were also denounced by most Commonwealth countries as fraudulent. His desperate attempt to get off the hook had failed.

The African guerrilla campaign in Rhodesia began to gain momentum, but the immediate result was to make the South Africans and the Portuguese even more determined to help the white Rhodesians. The guerrillas were an intense embarrassment to the British government, for if they complained to the Zambians that their country was being used as a guerrilla base, it would seem as if they were attempting to prop up the Smith régime. Wilson hoped to resume negotiations, but the Rhodesians were successfully acting as a fully independent government and saw no reason for further talks unless they were to be offered even better terms. When talks were resumed, Smith refused to make any concessions at all. In June 1969 Smith called a referendum for a new constitution that would guarantee permanent white supremacy. Wilson, however, was relieved of the responsibility of dealing with this impossible situation when he lost an election to Edward Heath's Conservatives in 1970.

Sir Alec Douglas-Home, now foreign secretary, met Smith, who agreed to accept a royal commission to test African opinion because he was confident that it would confirm his assertion that Rhodesian's were "the happiest Africans in the world." The commission, headed by a highly respected judge, Lord Pearce, found, on the contrary, that the overwhelming majority of the Africans rejected the Smith-Home proposals for "unimpeded progress to majority rule," which would in fact be so slow that it would guarantee white domination for years to come, and Sir Alec felt obliged to withdraw the offer.

When Smith failed to negotiate independence on his white supremacist terms, the African nationalist guerrillas stepped up their campaign. They were divided into two hostile camps: Joshua Nkomo's Zimbabwe African People's Union (ZAPU) and the younger and more radical Robert Mugabe's Zimbabwe African National Union (ZANU). Pressure was exerted on Rhodesia by an improbable coalition of Kenneth Kaunda of Zambia and John Vorster of South Africa. Kaunda was determined to achieve majority rule in Rhodesia, and he was now supported by Mozambique as well as by Tanzania and Botswana, states around Rhodesia that were ready to host guerrillas and exiles. Vorster wanted to end the guerrilla war because it threatened to spill across his border. The stubborn Smith continued to ignore all advice and refused to make any concessions to the Africans. Finally, after Rhodesian troops invaded Mozambique, in spite of Vorster's warning that this would be a disastrous move, and killed twelve hundred ZANU supporters in a camp at Pungwe, South Africa began to apply crippling sanctions. In addition, South Africa announced in the United Nations that it favoured majority rule in Rhodesia, provided that there were adequate safeguards for the white minority. Smith was finally forced to concede by American Secretary of State Henry Kissinger, who was determined to reach a settlement that would avoid a disaster similar to the fiasco in Angola, where Cuban communist forces had beaten American-backed anti-communist forces.

Smith now set about making majority rule acceptable to the whites. To him doing so meant ensuring that the doctrinaire Marxist Robert Mugabe did not get to power and that the moderate Bishop Abel Muzorewa would form a government instead. Smith's proposal was to reserve twenty-eight parliamentary seats in Parliament for whites and to allow the remaining seventy-two to be chosen by universal suffrage. Mugabe and the leaders of the front-line states would not accept this solution, and the guerrilla war continued. In the ensuing elections, which appear to have been reasonably fair and which had an acceptably high turn-out despite guerrilla attempts to stop people from voting, Bishop Muzorewa won an impressive victory, and he became prime minister in April 1979.

Margaret Thatcher, who won the British general election a few days after Muzorewa won Rhodesia's, was keen to recognize the new government, but she was persuaded that recognition would leave Britain isolated and opposed by most of the Commonwealth. At a lengthy conference at Lancaster House in London chaired by the new Conservative foreign secretary, Lord Carrington, all parties trying to work out an acceptable constitutional arrangement that would end Britain's responsibilities for Rhodesia were represented. After endless problems, new elections were held in February 1980. This time Mugabe's party won fifty-seven of the eighty African seats. Since only twenty seats were now reserved for whites, this Marxist revolutionary terrorist had an absolute majority. The British were horrified; the Rhodesian army commander, General Walls, planned a coup. The governor, Lord Soames, did much to calm nerves, and Mugabe, fearful that skilled whites would flee the country, called for moderation, tolerance, and compromise. The British did not get what they wanted, but they got what they needed. Had a coalition government of Muzorewa, Nkomo, and Smith emerged from the election, the guerrilla war would have continued.

Mugabe was the only man who could stop the fighting. Zimbabwe was thus created because Britain could not impose her will but also because her leaders recognized their powerlessness and were willing to learn from their own and others' mistakes.

East Africa also had educated nationalist leaders. Jomo Kenyatta had returned to Kenya from London as early as September 1946, and he rapidly became the spokesman for the Africans, especially for his own tribe, the Kikuyu. He was a curious figure, a fervent nationalist who nevertheless berated his people for their indolence, ignorance, and proclivity for petty crime while supporting features of traditional Kenyan society—such as female circumcision—criticized by many outsiders. He was determined to achieve independence, but he was convinced it would be a long haul.

Other younger and more impatient Kikuyu felt that independence could only be achieved by violence. They organized a secret organization called Mau Mau to murder whites. Their early recruits came from the landless and often jobless urban proletariat, many of whom had been driven from the land by Kikuyu chiefs as well as by white landowners, but soon the rural poor joined the "wild boys" of the cities. Their violence was at first directed against fellow Kikuyu who served in the police force or who were otherwise thought to be traitors. Kenyatta was ambivalent towards Mau Mau, but in August 1952 he denounced the organization at a huge rally and poured a vivid Kikuyu curse on their heads. Mau Mau reacted immediately by warning Kenyatta that if he repeated this performance he would be dead. The murder of a number of chiefs showed that this was no empty threat, and Kenyatta took it to heart.

In the same summer Kenya was given a new governor, Sir Evelyn Baring. Sir Philip Mitchell, the outgoing governor, had not taken the Mau Mau threat seriously. In fact, Princess Elizabeth and Prince Philip had been on holiday in Kenya in February 1952 when King George VI died, and the new queen had to return to England at once. Baring, however, realized that the situation was extremely serious. He believed that Kenyatta was involved with Mau Mau and that his denunciations of their violence were insincere. The British government permitted him to declare a state of emergency and to arrest nationalist leaders, including Kenyatta.

Baring's hope that a leaderless movement would soon collapse proved vain. A further series of murders, including those of an entire white family, occurred during Kenyatta's trial, making the atmosphere even more tense. Although there was virtually no evidence against him, Kenyatta was sentenced to seven years in prison, after which he was to be banished to a remote area. Mau Mau was soon crushed by the internment of seventeen thousand suspects and the creation of concentration camps that were euphemistically called "new villages." Soon there were eighty thousand detainees in the camps, ten thousand Kikuyu had been killed, and one thousand hanged. Although a total of about seventy Europeans were murdered, many with exceptional savagery, the Mau Mau were, in terms of numbers of deaths, less dangerous than Nairobi traffic. The whites, nevertheless, were in a state of hysterical anxiety, which led them to indulge in indiscriminate and savage reprisals.

Baring was convinced that in order to stop a revival of Mau Mau, it was essential to carry out a massive programme of land reform and to give the Africans a say in the government. The Kikuyu's rich farm lands, by tradition, were divided up into uneconomical strips. Baring set about consolidating these holdings into viable modern farms producing for the export market. It was an enormously ambitious and expensive undertaking, but it was largely successful, both economically and politically.

At first Africans were appointed to the legislative assembly; then eight were elected. Their leader was Tom Mboya, a member of the Luo tribe and a trade union leader from Nairobi, who, inspired by the example of Ghana, pressed for majority African representation. Baring and the colonial secretary, Alan Lennox-Boyd, were sympathetic, and although they thought Mboya was too impatient, they tried to persuade the whites that major concessions would have to be made to maintain peace. They proposed "power-sharing" between the fifty thousand whites and the five million Africans. Mboya wanted majority rule, as did his fellow Luo, Oginga Odinga. They both refused to take office and campaigned for independence and Kenyatta's release.

Suddenly, in March 1959, Kenya became a central concern for the British government. At the detention camp at Hola, African warders savagely beat eighty-eight prisoners who had shown some reluctance to work. Twenty were seriously injured, and eleven died of their injuries. Harold Macmillan, about to face a general election, was genuinely outraged by the massacre and was convinced that giving Kenya independence was the only possible way to atone. His new colonial secretary, Iain Macleod, fully agreed and argued that if independence was not granted soon, there would be widespread bloodshed. Macleod's brother was a farmer in Kenya who held unusually progressive views. He felt that the case against Kenyatta had not been proven, and he was dedicated to the idea of a multi-racial Kenya. He also knew that African majority rule was required. As Iain Macleod wrote later: "The situation in autumn, 1959, was grim. . . . Perhaps the tragedy of Hola Camp, even more than the 'murder plot' emergency in Nyasaland was decisive."

A conference at Lancaster House in early 1960 agreed upon a new constitution that gave the Africans a majority of one in the legislature. Mboya and Odinga still refused to join the new government and campaigned for the Kenya African National Union (KANU), a powerful alliance of the Kikuyu and the Luo that had Kenyatta as its absent president. In order to placate the whites, who were threatening to pack their bags and leave Kenya, taking along their capital and their expertise, Macleod decided not to release Kenyatta yet. The settlers quietened down and share prices ceased to fall, but everyone realized that Kenyatta would have to be set free before long.

When that day came in 1961, Jomo Kenyatta, with his spell-binding and deliberately ambiguous oratory, rapidly became a national figurehead who transcended his Kikuyu origins. In May 1963 KANU won a decisive victory at the polls, and Kenyatta became prime minister. Shortly afterwards, in August, he delivered a remarkable address to three hundred white farmers in what used to be called the White Highlands. His call for mutual forgiveness and future co-operation completely won over the audience, most of whom had previously thought of him as the devil incarnate. When independence was granted in December 1963, Kenyatta proved as good as his word. He even chose as acting chief justice the man who had turned down his appeal and sent him to prison.

Independent Kenya, however, was riven by tribal jealousies and resentment against the corruption of the Kikuyu élite. Mob action against the Indian minority who had decided to keep their British passports diverted some tensions for a brief time. About twenty thousand Indians lost their property and had to flee the country. Then, Tom Mboya, Kenya's outstanding politician, was gunned down in July 1969. His murder made many of the Luo tribe deeply suspicious of Kenyatta and the Kikuyu. Kenyatta, in turn, was increasingly fearful of Oginga Odinga (Luo), who had resigned as vice- president in 1966 and now led the socialist Opposition, the Kenya People's Union Party. In October 1969 the Kenya People's Union was banned, and Kenya became a one-party state. Kenyatta thus remained in power, his position never seriously challenged, preserving a semblance of harmony and stability while the economy expanded impressively.

After Kenyatta died in 1978, the country continued in relative prosperity in spite of many difficulties. Compared with most other African states, which seemed to be full of corruption and tribalism, Kenya was something of a success story. But since then, widespread repression, torture, and the violation of human rights have pushed Kenya down to near the bottom of the pile.

8 The Commonwealth Today

The Commonwealth began with the recognition of the sovereign independence and equality of the Dominions (Australia, New Zealand, South Africa, and Canada) in the Statute of Westminster, 1931, with certain residual and largely formal rights remaining in Britain. The most important event in the creation of the modern Commonwealth was India's decision to join it as an independent republic. As they gained independence, almost all the other colonies followed the Indian lead, but the Commonwealth soon seemed on the point of breaking up because of passionate political differences. The main problem was the British attitude towards the racist policies of South Africa, which alienated most of the African states. Britain, in turn, was beginning to feel that the Commonwealth was something of a liability.

Member states began to reappraise the role of the Commonwealth, and in 1965 it was completely transformed with the creation of a Commonwealth Secretariat. The Commonwealth became a genuinely international body, its administration no longer in British hands. The British monarch, however, has been Head of the Commonwealth since 1949 and is also head of state in Britain as well as in thirteen of the seventeen Commonwealth monarchies.

The old Imperial Conferences had been tremendously formal affairs, and it was not until 1944 that a more informal gathering of prime ministers was held. No formal administrative structure for the Commonwealth existed. The British Cabinet Office organized prime ministers' meetings, and other business was conducted by the Commonwealth Relations Office, which superseded the Dominions Office in 1947. As the process of decolonization gathered momentum, British government departments were reorganized. The Commonwealth Relations Office (CRO) and the Colonial Office had a common secretary of state from 1962. At that time, the Colonial Office was renamed the Dependent Territories Division, and it was absorbed by the CRO. In 1968, as a result of the recommendations of the Plowden Committee, the CRO joined the Foreign Office, which became the Foreign and Commonwealth Office (FCO).

The proposal to establish a Commonwealth Secretariat was put forward by Ghana, Nigeria, Trinidad, and Uganda at the 1964 prime ministers' meeting. The following year Commonwealth officials met in London to work out the details.

The Commonwealth is a remarkably loose and informal alliance that has no constitution or binding rules. The heads of government meeting in Singapore in

1971 published a Declaration of Commonwealth Principles in which this voluntary nature and the equality of the member states were stressed. The Declaration further denounced racial prejudice, colonial domination, and great disparities of wealth. The member states promised that they would work together to maintain the peace and to ensure material and social progress through consultation, discussion, and co-operation. The Commonwealth thus stands for basic human rights and freedoms that are central to the liberal tradition but that are unfortunately often trampled upon by many of its members. The determination to combat racism was further stressed in the Lusaka Declaration of the Commonwealth on Racism and Racial Prejudice in 1979.

Although it is understood that the internal affairs of a member country cannot be discussed without its agreement, certain minimum standards are expected if a country is to remain a member. South Africa's policy of apartheid was such a clear violation of Commonwealth principles that the country could not remain a member. Similarly, the outrageous conduct of Idi Amin in Uganda in the 1970s could not be tolerated.

The Commonwealth can expel members, but it has no coercive powers. The heads of government meetings held every two years last for about a week. They are informal gatherings at which common problems and concerns can be discussed with considerable frankness. They also provide a good opportunity for Commonwealth leaders to get to know one another that is particularly valuable for small states, such as Tuvalu or Nauru, which are unlikely to get much of a hearing at any other international gathering. It also provides a forum for medium powers like Canada and Australia to play an important role in international affairs. The Commonwealth is not a decision-making body; it simply provides a framework for discussion, for bargaining, and for establishing principles and priorities.

High-minded declarations on basic human rights are backed by strictly practical measures of economic aid. At the Singapore meeting in 1971, for example, members agreed to establish a Commonwealth Fund for Technical Co-operation (CFTC). As the principal funding arm of the Secretariat, it is designed to provide technical assistance to member countries, and it offers special training programmes.

The first Commonwealth secretary general was a highly regarded Canadian diplomat, Arnold Smith. His headquarters were at Marlborough House in London, which the Queen had allowed to be used for Commonwealth meetings since 1962. Under the Agreed Memorandum, the Secretariat was not permitted to "arrogate to itself executive functions," but it was supposed to provide the setting for member countries "to exchange opinions in a friendly, informal and intimate atmosphere." The Secretariat was given a modest budget, member countries paying according to their size and wealth. In 1988–89 30 per cent of the costs were paid by Britain, 16.3 per cent by Canada, and 8.31 by Australia. Some of the smaller of the 48 Commonwealth countries could make no contribution at all. The total budget was a mere £6,792,610. Member countries also contribute modest amounts to the Commonwealth Science Council (CSC) and the Commonwealth Youth Programme (CYP). The Commonwealth Fund for Technical Co-operation (CFTC), with a budget of £22,864,619, which is funded by voluntary contributions from governments, remains by far the most important department of the Secretariat.

The secretary general is appointed by the heads of government and serves for five years. There are two deputy secretaries general, one responsible for political affairs, the other for economics. Two assistant secretaries general look after the CFTC and social affairs. The Commonwealth has been fortunate in having outstanding secretaries general. Arnold Smith showed great diplomatic skill in keeping the Commonwealth together in spite of the serious disagreements over South Africa and Rhodesia. He was also remarkably successful in fostering the Commonwealth's economic programmes. His successor, Shridath S. Ramphal, who served three five-year terms, had been minister of foreign affairs and of justice in Guyana and was a persuasive representative of the Third World. He further enhanced the influence and distinction of the office of secretary general by his statesmanship.

The heads of government meeting is a diverse and often divisive forum, a kind of mini-United Nations for one-quarter of the world, which frequently finds it difficult to agree on a common set of principles to steer its deliberations towards practical conclusions. The old Imperial Conferences had no such problems. They were dominated by Britain and attended only by the white Dominions, which shared a common heritage and had a similar political culture. As the Commonwealth grew, so did the differences between its members, to the point that it seemed as if it might well fall apart. Many saw Britain and the white Dominions as paternalistic and patronizing, the African states seemed to be obsessed with the question of race, the Indians and their followers were thought to be playing one side in the cold war off against the other to their own advantage, their self-interest dressed in the verbiage of moral superiority.

Discussions at heads of government meetings became increasingly acrimonious, and attacks on the British became more outspoken and strident. Both sides were finding it difficult to adapt to the post-colonial situation. Britain had lost her Empire but still clung to the illusion that she was a great power. She sought to find within the Commonwealth a surrogate to the old Empire, a means of asserting her status as a world power. Both the major parties shared this attitude. Conservatives with their Disraelian paternalism and Labour with their emphasis on the moral role of the Commonwealth were not very far apart; if anything, the Conservatives were more realistic and pragmatic.

Naturally, the developing countries resented this attitude, even though it was essentially well-meaning and commonsensical. They mouthed slogans about neo-colonialism and denounced Britain's pride at the remarkable speed, general amicability, and relative bloodlessness with which she had surrendered the Empire, calling it a hypocritical cover for continued domination and exploitation. There was much talk of a shared tradition, but many pointed out that this was a British, not an African or Asian tradition. Macaulay had argued "that by good government we may educate our subjects into a capacity for better government [until] having become instructed in European knowledge they may, in some future age, demand European institutions." That Marxist socialism was part of the European tradition was not acknowledged, and good government did not seem to have done much to overcome tribal rivalries and caste divisions.

Such Eurocentrism as Macaulay's or that of those who argued that the Westminster model was the ideal form of government was unacceptable to Third World leaders, who were often more attracted to Bandung and Moscow than to London. The British did not take kindly to such complaints and, faced with mounting problems at home, began to lose patience, particularly when a close association with Europe seemed, for a brief moment, to be a more attractive alternative. The Commonwealth did not seem to be particularly useful. Britain had to listen to lectures from Indians on the wickedness of her Suez adventure, and there was not much sign of Westminster-style democracy in some countries that had seemed so promising. Pakistan was under corrupt military rule, Ghana had a brutal dictatorship and preventive detention, and Nigeria was riven with tribal strife. India seemed to find the Soviets more agreeable than the British, the Africans took Pan-Africanism more seriously than Commonwealth ties, Canada has always been more concerned about its relationship with the United States than with Britain.

Many questioned whether Commonwealth membership mattered very much. When South Africa left the Commonwealth in 1961, there was no effect on trade or emigration, and Simonstown remained a British base. A Britain that had to go cap in hand to the Americans to update its antiquated nuclear forces was hardly in a position to afford the luxury of a Commonwealth that brought no strategic benefits and accounted for increasingly less of Britain's overseas trade. Immigration from the Commonwealth was also causing problems at home, and in 1958 there was the first of a series of race riots in London's Notting Hill. The Americans mocked the Commonwealth as an institution that "has no political structure or unity or strength" and said that Britain's claim for special consideration based on its leading role in this amorphous structure was absurd.

Although no leading British politician actually wanted to abandon the Commonwealth and there was never a serious danger of Britain opting for Europe rather than the Commonwealth, an increasing number of Commonwealth leaders began to fear that it could actually disintegrate. The prospect of Britain joining the EEC made the New Zealanders worry about their butter, the West Indians about their sugar and bananas, the Canadians about wheat, the Indians about textiles, the Australians about wool and defence. It made many countries realize that the Commonwealth was, after all, an institution from which they drew considerable benefit, in spite of their complaints. Gradually the feeling grew that compromise was needed, on both sides; the problem was how to achieve it.

In a speech given at the opening of the Commonwealth Institute in London in 1962, the Queen suggested that "It is the thread of personal concern and understanding between individual peoples that weaves a strong fabric of the modern Commonwealth." The emphasis should thus be less on relations between governments, which are easily upset over political differences, and more on contacts between other representatives of the member nations. Students, engineers, doctors, and lawyers, along with artists, writers, and cricketers, would form the weft and warp of the new Commonwealth of peoples rather than statesmen.

The problem with this sensible approach was that politics cannot be ignored. Sport could become highly political when touring teams went to South Africa, and technical experts often tackled problems that had significant political overtones.

At the centre of these political altercations was the sensitive issue of race. Racial differences and tensions were a constant reminder that the Commonwealth was an association of erstwhile subject peoples. British aspirations to use the Commonwealth to make its status as a world power legitimate, coupled with its continued paternalism, served to drive the point home. Thus, the often acrimonious discussions at Singapore in 1971 centred on the British decision to send arms to South Africa as part of a global strategy to contain the Soviet Union and to make a profit doing so. Many member states violently opposed this action and called upon the British to reconsider. Julius Nyerere argued that no Commonwealth country should pursue policies that threatened the fundamental interests of another member country. He added that it was particularly incumbent on Britain to heed this requirement since her actions were of the most consequence. A heated debate followed that was finally ended by Pierre Elliot Trudeau's proposal that while member states had a solemn duty to respect the requirements of others, they also had to be free to define their own vital interests. This solution was accepted because, as Milton Obote of Uganda said, it would be a pity if the Commonwealth were to disintegrate because of the racist régime in South Africa. It is hardly surprising that the Declaration of Commonwealth Principles was such an unexceptional document. Few could argue with the desire to maintain peace and liberty, to combat racism and oppression, and to promote co-operation between peoples. Some may mock such a high-minded statement of principles and point out the blatant hypocrisy of some of those who supported it, but it is important in other ways. The Declaration was not merely one of principles but of the Commonwealth's desire to survive. That at least was genuine and was a triumph for the moderate member states who had successfully mediated between the warring factions over the sale of arms to South Africa.

The functions of the Secretariat are basically twofold. It is concerned with political questions, and it is also a service agency. There is the political Commonwealth of issues and the functional Commonwealth of skills, resources, and services. Obviously, these two aspects of the Secretariat's work cannot be divided into two watertight compartments, and the Commonwealth is most successful when the political and the service aspects are in harmony and work together in genuine partnership as its founders intended.

The divisions supervised by the deputy secretary general (political) facilitate consultations between the member countries and organize the meetings of heads of government and senior officials. The Commonwealth has had observer status at the United Nations since 1975, and the International Affairs Division provides the link to the UN as it does to a host of other international organizations that affect the Commonwealth, such as the United Nations Conference on Trade and Development (UNCTAD), the General Agreement on Tariffs and Trade (GATT), the Organization for Economic Co-operation and Development (OECD), the Organization for African Unity (OAU), the European Community, and the Caribbean Community (CARICOM).

The Legal Division provides expert assistance in legislative drafting, arranges for the exchange of technical information on law reform, and attempts to resolve problems over extradition and law enforcement. The division also hosts biennial meetings of ministers of law and attorneys-general. The Commonwealth Legal Education Association, founded in 1981, supports legal education and research. The Commonwealth Legal Bureau, founded in 1969, encourages the formation of law societies in developing countries and organizes meetings of Commonwealth lawyers. The Commonwealth Magistrates' Association, dating from 1970, provides training for magistrates and does what it can to improve the administration of justice in countries that fall below acceptable standards. The Legal Division also publishes a quarterly journal, the *Commonwealth Law Bulletin.*

In the early years there was little information or detailed analysis available to the heads of government. Moreover, smaller countries did not have the resources to maintain many overseas missions or to finance a sizeable research staff. The Commonwealth is able to provide an extremely valuable service in this regard. An important example of its service occurred when the Secretariat instructed the Economic Affairs Division to collect the information necessary for negotiations between the developing countries and the European Community. The division also provides a series of technical studies on such matters as economic development, international trade, finance, and a host of social issues.

Matters of a more general and less technical nature are handled by the Information Division, which provides press releases, produces television and radio programmes, and publishes pamphlets and periodicals on a wide range of subjects. The division also organizes training courses through the Commonwealth Media Development Fund (CMDF).

The main political concern of the International Affairs Division has always been racial discrimination. Events in Southern Africa have, therefore, always been a central issue for the Secretariat, which was established shortly after South Africa's Nationalist government announced it intended to introduce a policy of apartheid. As the African colonies became independent and joined the Commonwealth, this issue became even more pressing.

Although there was general agreement that apartheid was unacceptable, there were serious differences about how to combat it. These disputes frequently placed the secretary general in a delicate position. Britain favoured a moderate and gradual approach, while the African states mostly refused to make any compromises. These differences became especially acute over Rhodesia, and many African states were sharply critical of Britain's behaviour. Tanzania actually broke off diplomatic relations with Britain and yet remained in the Commonwealth. In such situations, the secretary general has to be seen to be impartial, although as the office becomes more secure and the power and influence of Britain lessens, his influence is greater. Even the Queen, in her capacity as head of the Commonwealth, criticized the policies of her prime minister, Margaret Thatcher, towards South Africa. Shridath Ramphal has also been outspoken in his condemnation of any compromise on apartheid, which, he rightly says, would be a betrayal of the basic principles of the Commonwealth.

In the Nassau Accord of 1985 the Commonwealth agreed on initial economic sanctions against South Africa. This policy was confirmed and strengthened, in spite of British dissent, at the Vancouver meeting of Commonwealth leaders in 1987 and set out in the Okanagan Statement of the Commonwealth Committee of Foreign Ministers on Southern Africa. The Commonwealth has made detailed studies of the impact of sanctions, countered the South African government's propaganda, and lent assistance to the front-line states. Although Britain consistently disagreed with the rest of the Commonwealth over sanctions, there was general agreement that a negotiated settlement must be reached so that further violence could be avoided. There can be little doubt that the Commonwealth has played an important role in combating the evils of apartheid. It has pressured and embarrassed the British, and to some extent the American, government into making suitable noises about apartheid. While they did very little about it and did not really see the need to do much, the question was kept before the conscience of the world. Moral outrage against racism was, in the long run, more powerful than weary reiterations about the ineffectiveness of sanctions.

The Commonwealth was also able to provide some practical assistance to Mozambique, which suffered directly as a result of the guerrilla war in Rhodesia and from South African support for rebels opposed to its Marxist government, but the funding for this programme did not reach the target. Help has also been given to other front-line states but also on a very modest scale. The Commonwealth also supported the implementation of UN resolution 435 on Namibian independence, but in this matter it has followed the lead of the United Nations, whose actions were, in turn, prompted by the superpowers.

The most important and successful activities of the Secretariat are those undertaken by the Commonwealth Fund for Technical Co-operation (CFTC). Its purpose is to put the expertise developed in one part of the Commonwealth at the disposal of those countries where it is lacking. Such functional co-operation is central to the Commonwealth's efforts to be a genuine partnership.

The CFTC's General Technical Assistance Division (GTA) provides the mechanism for sending experts, either as short-term consultants or on long-term assignments, to meet the needs of member countries. Many of these are contracted for specific tasks, but the Secretariat has a Technical Assistance Group (TAG) on the permanent staff that can be sent at short notice to deal with immediate problems. These experts are most frequently needed for assistance in economic and financial affairs, usually at the highest levels of government, or in areas of high technology. There is less and less demand for people from the basic professions since most Commonwealth countries are by now self-sufficient in this regard. The GTA have, for example, provided experts to reorganize central banks and finance ministries and to provide assistance in macro-economic policy and the collection and analysis of statistical data. Law reform, which provides the essential legislative framework without which economic progress is scarcely possible, is also an important aspect of the division's work. It also helps developing countries in devising legal and financial safeguards when they are dealing with large international corporations

Transport infrastructure, a particularly pressing problem for countries made up of small islands, has also been tackled by CFTC specialists. In other countries the division provides advice on road building or harbour construction. There is an increasing demand for assistance in computerization, robotics, and artificial intelligence, even in countries as advanced as Singapore.

Education and training are a major concern of the Secretariat and are supervised by the Human Resource Development Group (HRDG). Improved access to higher education is the focus of the Commonwealth of Learning, the first new Commonwealth organization to be founded in the last ten years. With its headquarters in Vancouver, it is also the first to be located outside London. Its main purpose is to encourage and co-ordinate distance education throughout the Commonwealth. The Commonwealth Scholarship and Fellowship Plan provides some thirty-six hundred awards for study at universities overseas.

HRDG also provides teacher training and assistance in curriculum development and the collection of teaching materials. Its Management Development Programme is designed to improve managerial skills in public enterprises. The Commonwealth Youth Plan (CYP) devotes much of its energies to developing strategies to promote youth employment and entrepreneurship. HRDG also emphasizes the dissemination of information on the new technologies, particularly computers. Its principal concern is to help countries with fewer than two million inhabitants, which face a host of problems inherent in their smallness.

Human resources covers more than education; it also includes combating social evils, providing preventive medicine, and helping to deal with the consequences of natural disasters. Drug abuse and trafficking are major concerns of the HMDG. So also is AIDS; efforts so far have concentrated on Africa, where it is most widespread. The Science Division of HMDG has provided assistance in predicting natural disasters and training in crisis management.

The Vancouver meeting of heads of government adopted a Plan of Action to improve the status of women in the Commonwealth. The plan was directed at enhancing the participation of women in the activities of the Secretariat and at encouraging member countries to develop policies on women. The Women and

Development Programme is responsible for the implementation of the plan. It conducts research into the effects of economic and structural adjustment programmes and of recurrent economic crises on the many roles of women as workers, mothers, managers of domestic consumption, and social organizers. It also does what it can to ensure the implementation of the United Nations Convention on the Elimination of All Forms of Discrimination against Women (CEDAW). In many countries there is considerable resistance to such efforts, and the Secretariat lacks enforcement powers, but there has been modest improvement, particularly in the number of women receiving awards from the Fellowships and Training Plan and training sponsored by the Commonwealth Youth Plan.

It is impossible to say how near the Commonwealth was to collapse at Singapore, but there can be no doubt that in the years following Pierre Trudeau played an important part in strengthening the Commonwealth. Canada has always been strongly supportive of the Commonwealth. Both Conservative and Liberal governments have seen the Commonwealth as a forum where Canada, as a medium power, can play an important role and shake herself loose from the influence of her superpower neighbour. Canadian foreign policy has always been liberal, and Canada has contributed generously to the Commonwealth and done much to assist developing countries. The country has always been the most outspoken of the white countries in its condemnation of racism in South Africa.

Trudeau was at first understandably critical of the Commonwealth with its petty wrangling over procedures and joint communiqués and its bitter and unresolved divisions. However, he soon made close political friendships with Commonwealth leaders like Indira Gandhi, Kenneth Kaunda, and Julius Nyerere. He also saw the advantages of strengthening Canada's ties with the Caribbean. Trudeau believed, as did a number of other prominent figures in the Commonwealth (among them Lee Kuan Yew of Singapore, Michael Manley of Jamaica, and even the more radical Nyerere and Kaunda), that the areas of general agreement should be widened and strengthened and that this could best be achieved if the heads of government meetings were less formal.

Trudeau hosted the Ottawa meeting in 1973 where this new approach proved most successful. There were only two plenary sessions, at the beginning and the end of the conference; the other meetings were much smaller, involving only the leaders and a handful of their senior advisers. An informal weekend retreat for the heads of government was a further successful innovation. A session on "comparative techniques of government" enabled leaders to discuss policy making, administrative reform, and practical difficulties of government. It proved to be far more constructive than yet another slanging match over racial policy or neo-colonialism.

As a result, the discussion of the worsening terms of trade for developing countries and the implications of Britain's entry into the EEC was conducted without the usual emotional outbursts and recriminations.

The question of Rhodesia was likely to cause difficulties and disrupt the new found harmony. The African states no longer demanded that the British should intervene militarily, but they wanted recognition of the guerrillas. The British insisted that the solution had to be peaceful. The Africans, confident that the Zimbabwean guerrillas would soon be victorious, agreed to disagree, and a confrontation was avoided.

The next CHOGM was held in Kingston, Jamaica, in 1975. The main topic for discussion was the worsening terms of trade for the primary producers. It was a topic that threatened to be highly divisive. The reason it was not was that most of the developing countries realized that they were in an extremely weak bargaining position and that they had to accept less than they wanted. Guyana and Mauritius were thus on their own with their unrealistic demands for massive redistribution of wealth in favour of the poor nations.

At the CHOGM held in London in 1977 on the occasion of the Queen's silver jubilee, the report of a committee struck at Kingston to discuss problems of energy policy, import restrictions, Third World debt, and international finance was debated at length. The committee's recommendations were far too radical, and so little was done about them. This awkward issue was passed over by the appointment of another committee to examine the proposal that a fund should be established to maintain commodity prices. The Commonwealth's habit, typical of any such body, of referring controversial issues to a committee was not particularly courageous, but at least it meant that serious confrontations over irreconcilable differences were avoided.

A major issue at the London meeting was Uganda. The British prime minister, James Callaghan, had told Idi Amin that he was not welcome and that his country's delegation should be headed by someone else. Callaghan's decision placed some African leaders in an awkward position. They were concerned about this breach of the Commonwealth's policy of non-interference, and they were reluctant to expose a man who not long before had been president of the OAU. Still, having taken a high moral position for so long, they had to make some protest against an obviously unacceptable régime. Even the extremely loose definitions in the Singapore Declaration of the ideals of the Commonwealth could, some members feared, be used to justify a witch hunt against countries that clearly fell well below the standards. The newly appointed Secretary General, Shridath S. Ramphal, skilfully avoided unpleasantness by insisting that: "There will be times when one member or another will provoke the wrath of others beyond the limits of silence. Any other relationship would be so sterile as to be effete."

At the CHOGM in Lusaka in 1979, at which Mrs. Thatcher made her debut, Rhodesia was the main topic of discussion. The British, eager to reach a settlement, were prepared to make concessions and agreed to new elections, a constitutional conference, and a monitoring role for the Commonwealth. The breakthrough in the negotiations came during an informal weekend session, showing once again the value of such meetings. Yet another declaration on racism and racial prejudice was published, and the Commonwealth defined itself once more as "an international organization with a fundamental and deep-rooted attachment to principles of freedom and equality," a statement that may well have caused some embarrassment in certain quarters.

At Melbourne in 1981 New Zealand was accused of breaching the Gleneagles Agreement of 1977 on apartheid in sport by maintaining sporting links with South Africa. New Zealand's prime minister, Robert Muldoon, truculently defended his reading of the ambiguous document and made a number of unfortunate remarks that made the situation exceptionally tense. Because he had alienated all the other members by his undiplomatic behaviour, the conference could afford to ignore him and get on with its business. There was a useful discussion of economic disparities and Third World indebtedness as well as global political changes. These resulted in the Melbourne Declaration, in which the Commonwealth expressed its resolve to do what it could to overcome the "gross inequality of wealth and opportunity currently existing in the world."

The Declaration was an admission that there was precious little that the Commonwealth could do on its own to tackle this fundamental problem, but it was an admirable context within which to discuss such issues openly and frankly and to adopt positions that would lead to constructive debate in a wider forum. In this instance the Melbourne Declaration was intended as an expression of determination that the next round of North-South discussions at Cancún would produce some practical results. It was obvious that the Commonwealth was not, and never had been, a decision-making body, but when its members could rehearse the arguments and agree on a common position, a concerted effort could be made in other international meetings that would greatly enhance the chances of success.

The pattern of subsequent CHOGMs at New Delhi in 1983, Nassau in 1985, Vancouver in 1987, and Kuala Lumpur in 1989 was broadly similar. The two issues of race and the plight of the poorer nations continued to dominate discussions. There was nothing much that the Commonwealth could do about either except accuse Britain of failing to do all that it could for the African majority in Rhodesia, for continuing to be South Africa's main trading partner, and for joining the rich club of the EEC and ignoring the needs of the developing countries to maintain commodity prices and be relieved of the burden of debt.

Commonwealth preference had gone, but as a member of the EEC, Britain did what it could to help the sugar cane producing countries against the challenge of increased production by the European beet growers and the banana producers of the Caribbean against non-Commonwealth competition by means of special protocols in the Lomé Convention. But by and large the Convention did more to secure sources of raw materials for the EEC than it did to open the European market to the Third World countries. There was also very little that Britain could do to assist the newly industrializing nations, such as India, Singapore, Hong Kong, and Malaysia. The only practical steps taken were to increase the contributions to the Fund for Technical Co-operation and to publish a series of intelligent and well-researched studies on Third World poverty and the North-South dialogue. Still, none of these efforts reversed the trend for the wealthy nations to get richer, the poorer to sink further into misery.

The issue of South Africa combined the explosive problems of economics and race. No one could support apartheid, though some might silently question whether the South African régime was really more immoral than the Uganda of Idi Amin and then of Milton Obote, not to mention some of the other appalling dictatorships that disgraced the Commonwealth. Apartheid was bad, but how was it best to be combated? Sanctions were widely felt to be the best solution, but they presented a number of problems. Some Commonwealth countries had no interests involved, and sanctions would make no difference to them. Most countries that would not be affected by sanctions were, predictably, outspoken supporters of them. Some members, particularly the former Dominions, stood to gain from sanctions because they would knock out a powerful competitor. The front-line states wanted sanctions, but they also wanted compensation, whereas Botswana argued that sanctions would hurt them more than South Africa. Britain, South Africa's major trading partner and the principal source of investment, stood to lose a great deal if mandatory sanctions were imposed.

These issues were up for discussion at the Nassau meeting in 1985, and Britain's Margaret Thatcher was hardly the person to back down. Moreover, the new boys, particularly Rajiv Gandhi, Brian Mulroney, and Bob Hawke, wanted to make a big splash. Once again a vague and imprecise compromise was worked out. The heads of government agreed that a committee of "Eminent Persons," made up of Malcolm Fraser from Australia, Lord Braber from Britain, Sardar Swaran Singh from India, Bishop Edward Scott from Canada, General Olusegun Obasanjo of Nigeria, Dame Nita Barrow from Barbados, and John Malecela from Tanzania, should be sent to South Africa to examine the possibility of dialogue between the whites and the Africans.

The Commonwealth Group of Eminent Persons' Report was discussed at a meeting of seven Commonwealth leaders at Marlborough House in August 1986. The meeting soon developed into one (Margaret Thatcher) against six (Rajiv Gandhi, Bob Hawke, Brian Mulroney, Kenneth Kaunda, Lynden Pindling from the Bahamas, the host of the Nassau meeting, and Robert Mugabe). The six expressed their deep regret at the British government's attitude and stated their intention to implement the full range of sanctions suggested at Nassau along with some additional measures. They also announced that they would do everything possible to mobilize the international community against South Africa.

South Africa was again the main item on the agenda at the Vancouver conference in 1987. Margaret Thatcher was called upon to support sanctions, and once again she refused with the familiar arguments that they would hurt Africans as much, or even more, than they would hurt the whites and that fellow EC countries and the United States would simply take over Britain's share of South African trade. After some acrimonious debates, the meeting issued the Okanagan Statement on Southern Africa. It stated that: "With the exception of Britain, the leaders believed sanctions had had significant effect. Wider, tighter and more intensified application must remain part of the international response to apartheid. With the exception of Britain, the leaders believed genuine efforts should be made to secure universal adoption of measures adopted by Commonwealth and other countries." Since Britain was the only country in a position to do anything positive, this declaration amounted to little. The signatories could feel suitably self-righteous, and the British could point out that they, along with the Canadians, had at least taken the practical step of increasing their aid to the South African Development Coordination Conference (SADCC) and to Mozambique, which had been admitted to the Vancouver conference as an observer.

In political terms, the Commonwealth has not been a decision-making body but a forum for argument, usually over race in general and South Africa in particular. In economic terms it might seem to be somewhat more concrete and positive. On 31 September 1931, shortly before the Statute of Westminster was given parliamentary approval, Britain abandoned the gold standard. In the 1930s the "sterling bloc" of countries that pegged their currencies against sterling was formed. At the Ottawa conference in 1932, and at a number of subsequent meetings, the British fought off attempts to internationalize the management of sterling. It remained firmly in British hands, but at a considerable cost. Members of the sterling bloc had to be given easy credit and favourable interest rates to keep them in line.

When war broke out in 1939, the sterling bloc was transformed into the sterling area, with rigorous exchange controls to stop the drain on reserves. Capital flow within the area was not restricted, but gold and monetary reserves were held in London.

Parallel to the sterling bloc was the system of imperial preference, established at the Ottawa Imperial Economic Conference of 1932. Here too Britain tried to keep a tight control over trade within the Commonwealth and Empire. It was a system that was to remain in force, in spite of drastic modifications, until the Lomé Convention of 1975 between the EEC and the African, Caribbean, and Pacific countries (ACP). In the postwar years Britain's trade with countries outside the Commonwealth, particularly with the European countries, expanded more rapidly than with those within it. The liberalization of world trade by the GATT also served to undermine the system of Commonwealth preference.

Britain emerged from the war heavily indebted to the United States, and she was unable to resist the American demand that sterling should be made convertible since it was made the precondition for further loans. The sterling area continued to operate, but it was regarded both in Britain and abroad as a burdensome constraint. The financial crisis of 1971 delivered the death blow to the sterling area, and its demise went unmourned.

As the sterling area and Commonwealth preference collapsed, the Commonwealth was gradually converted into a service organization in which the rich were to lend assistance to the poor. It took a long time for economics to take precedence over politics, and in part this change was the result of the different interests of the secretaries general. Although he did not neglect economics, Arnold Smith was primarily concerned to give the Commonwealth a distinct political image. Shridath Ramphal, however, has been deeply concerned with Third World development. He served on the Brandt Commission and played an important role at Cancún in 1981. For him the Commonwealth is an admirable institution to help bridge the gap between "North" and "South."

Most of the Commonwealth's economic programmes are organized by the CFTC (established 1971), whose activities have been somewhat restricted by lack of funding. This is largely because Britain has been reluctant to pay its fair share because it prefers to channel aid into programmes that bring at least some benefits to the donor (generally, direct bilateral agreements). The CFTC is designed to provide training and technical advice, so it does not necessarily give any advantages to British industry and commerce. Canada, by contrast, has always been extremely generous in its contributions towards CFTC, which it sees as a suitable agency for North-South transfers and which provides a mechanism for countries to get high marks for good conduct on the cheap.

The Export Market Development Division of the Secretariat (EMD) tries to bring buyers and sellers together and thus to encourage exports in line with the Brandt Report's emphasis on export-led growth and with the stipulations of the World Bank. The Division organizes regional ventures for countries too small to be competitive. It also encourages the export of high quality finished products rather than raw materials, since processing creates jobs and increases profits. Some considerable successes have been achieved by the EMD, including millions of dollars worth of Sri Lankan and Tanzanian exports to the United States and a major export drive for Malaysian products, mainly to Indonesia and the Philippines.

That many of these export drives are directed outside the Commonwealth is not a matter of great concern since they reduce the clamour for the protection of home markets. In any case, the Commonwealth has long since ceased to be a trading area. Britain joined the EEC, and other Commonwealth states entered regional agreements such as ACP or the Associated African States and Madagascar (AASM), which then dealt directly with the community's headquarters at Brussels. The Commonwealth has done much to encourage regional co-operation and has convinced the developing countries of the need for non-reciprocal trade agreements with the industrial world. Non-reciprocity at Lomé thus enabled industrial expansion in the CARICOM countries to go ahead without undue fear of European competition. They already have enough difficulties with the domination of their markets by American and Canadian industry and finance, the price they pay for preferential treatment in these valuable markets. But Britain imposes quotas on Commonwealth countries that are not associated with the EC when their exports are thought to threaten British or EC interests.

As British power has declined and the Commonwealth has expanded, there has been a tendency for the formation of regional groups, and they have been actively encouraged, at least since the Ottawa CHOGM in 1973. The fact that CHOGMs were for many years preoccupied with South Africa and Rhodesia was extremely frustrating to countries that have other pressing concerns. As a result, a series of Commonwealth Heads of Government Regional Meetings (CHOGRMs) have been held to discuss questions of mutual interest.

Commonwealth countries are also members of non-exclusive formal groups, among them NATO, ANZUS, OAU, OAS, and ASEAN. In the case of the Organization for African Unity (OAU), Commonwealth countries have been less active and enthusiastic members than the former French and Belgian colonies, which form a powerful bloc within the organization. On a number of issues the Commonwealth OAU states have been more conservative and restrained than the francophone countries, but on South Africa, Rhodesia, and Namibia, they have been in the forefront. They also led the movement to overthrow Idi Amin in Uganda, but this effort, unfortunately, only led to an even bloodier régime. Because of its size and its considerable petroleum assets, Nigeria has been the most active of the Commonwealth states within the OAU and in the Economic Community of West African States (ECOWAS), which has its headquarters in Lagos.

Although heavily outnumbered, Commonwealth countries play an important role in the Organization of American States (OAS). Canada has only recently become a member, but most of the Commonwealth Caribbean states have used the opportunities of membership to forge close links with their Latin American neighbours. The Commonwealth Caribbean states gave considerable support to Belize in its struggle against territorial claims from Guatemala, and they also endorsed British actions in the Falklands. Such policies have led to severe differences between the black Caribbean and white Latin America, which have sometimes taken on racist overtones.

The Association of South-East Asian Nations (ASEAN) was established in 1967 as a loose, informal arrangement to discuss political questions of common interest. In large part as the result of vigorous encouragement from Lee Kuan Yew of Singapore, economic questions have become increasingly important, and member states have made a number of major agreements, even though some ASEAN countries have resisted agreeing to common policies and to establishing a preferential trading area. In this process Commonwealth countries, particularly Singapore and Malayasia, have played a very important role, and they have been actively supported in their endeavours by the Commonwealth Secretariat.

Informal organizations, such as the African Caribbean Pacific (ACP) group, which negotiated with the EEC and signed the Lomé Convention, are also strongly encouraged by the Commonwealth Secretariat. It gave the ACP expert advice and assistance that would not have been available had not a large number of the member countries also been members of the Commonwealth. It is precisely in such instances that the Commonwealth can be of enormous benefit to its members, not only on the practical level but also in enhancing their prestige. In the ACP-EEC negotiations, for example, Commonwealth countries took the lead, and the francophone states tagged on behind.

The Caribbean Community (CARICOM) is an exclusive group of Commonwealth countries that links these scattered territories in place of the failed federation. Much of its effort has been economic, and one of its major achievements has been the creation of the Caribbean Free Trade Area (CARIFTA). There is little trade between the CARICOM countries, but CARIFTA negotiated with the EEC on behalf of its members and associated countries when Britain decided to join the Community. Here again the Secretariat was able to give valuable assistance in helping to bring the negotiations to a satisfactory conclusion. The Caribbean Development Bank, with its headquarters in Barbados, supported by Britain, Canada, and the United States and with close links to the IMF, plays an important role in long-term economic planning and does what it can to overcome the divisive tendencies of the region, be they economic, political, or personal.

The South Pacific Forum, founded in 1971, was far more political in its origins, formed in part to create a common front against atomic testing by the United States and France and against their unrestricted fishing practices. Economics were by no means ignored, and in 1973 the South Pacific Bureau for Economic Cooperation (SPEC) was created, funded largely by Australia and New Zealand. The Forum and SPEC are typical examples of the Commonwealth at work. Both are flexible and informal institutions in which matters of common concern can be debated, a consensus reached, and practical results achieved. Both can count on the full support of the Commonwealth Secretariat.

The are times when it is tempting to apply de Tocqueville's remark about the British constitution—that "it does not exist"—to the Commonwealth. It is not a close alliance with a set a specific tasks. It is not inspired by lofty ideals, and the principles it professes to uphold are honoured more in the breach than in the observance. It has no common ideology or symbolism that might forge links between a host of disparate countries. The Crown has symbolic value to only a handful of countries, although the Queen is universally admired for her exemplary statesmanship as Head of the Commonwealth. There are no inspiring visions of the Commonwealth from intellectuals and writers as there were of the Empire. The Secretariat has greatly enlarged its field of operations, and Secretary General Ramphal has spoken of "a necessary growth, necessary both to dissolve the residual film of Anglo-centricity that was distorting its image and to support its increasingly functional dynamism." This growth has led to a number of problems, particularly in the political field, when the Secretariat seemed to want to become the instrument for executive action. It was not only the issue of sanctions against South Africa that led to difficulties between Britain and the Secretariat. When Britain plays too strong a hand, there are always murmurings about neo-colonialism. When Britain shows little interest in Commonwealth affairs, there are accusations of selfishness and suggestions of racism.

Britain can never be coequal within the Commonwealth. Britain has successfully got rid of her Empire, but she cannot shake herself free from the imperial legacy. To the British the Commonwealth may often seem tiresome and expensive, its immigrant citizens the cause of strife, but it is still a kind of consolation prize. The Commonwealth exists because the British Empire existed, and such cohesion as it has is a result of a shared historical experience.

At first sight the Commonwealth sometimes appears to be a loose, quarrelsome, and often hypocritical collection of self-seeking states. Its critics insist that its achievements are modest and that its main purposes are to provide a world stage for second-rate politicians to mouth their clichés and to offer enticing travel opportunities for civil servants and experts. Its real value may well be unspectacular, but nonetheless it is considerable. It has resulted in the formation of a series of networks that get on with the business at hand in a sensible, pragmatic fashion without playing to the political gallery or providing a forum for personal advantage. These networks run the full gamut from heads of government to students and apprentices. They provide invaluable expert assistance to the developing countries and help enhance the international prestige of the developed countries. Above all, the Commonwealth provides a framework within which one-third of the world's nation states get on with one another remarkably amicably, in spite of frequent family squabbles. That quality alone makes it an institution that deserves to be cherished and strengthened.

9 The Commonwealth: Problems and Perspectives

Most of the leaders of the newly independent states that were to form the new Commonwealth believed that under the imperialist system, Britain had grown rich at the expense of her colonies. They were certain that with independence their economies, organized on broadly socialist lines, would prosper. Bold five-year plans and foreign policies based on non-alignment and international co-operation would lead to social and economic justice and rapid and relatively painless development.

This rosy vision was soon shown to be a cruel deception. Grandiose and expensive schemes for economic development often failed, leaving countries destitute. A handful of corrupt officials grew immensely rich whilst their populations sank to the depths of misery. Political freedoms were eroded and civil liberties denied. The disparity between rich and poor nations grew ever wider, and indebtedness reached astronomic proportions.

Rapid population growth greatly exacerbated these economic problems. On average, populations in Third World countries grew at about three times the rate in the industrial nations. Since the labour force does not grow at anything like the same rate, poverty increased alarmingly. Urban growth is rapid in spite of the lack of jobs, and the chronic social problems of slums plague most Third World countries. Almost the only checks on this population explosion are terribly high infant mortality rates and appalling famines in places like Ethiopia, the Sahel, and Bangladesh. Even in countries like India, which has been relatively successful in famine relief, malnutrition is disproportionately high, particularly among women.

One reason for the failure of the newly independent countries to realize their visions of socialism or developmentalism was that successor governments made exotic claims that progress would necessarily follow the ending of colonial ties. Because independence was won from Britain through negotiation, not revolutionary struggle, the leaders did not have the legitimacy that comes from a successful armed conflict. As a result, they sought support by promising a bright future.

Commonwealth planners, American liberals, and Soviet strategists all encouraged Third World governments in their optimistic assessments of the possible growth. The Americans thought financial aid would help achieve political stability and so immunize the Third World against communism. Politicians and their advisers assumed that economic development would go hand-in-hand with political development and that economic growth would strengthen democratic institutions.

Walt Rostow's *The Stages of Economic Growth: A Non-Communist Manifesto* expounded the new wisdom in an easily comprehensible form. Foreign aid would provide the capital necessary to enable Third World economies to reach the stage of "take-off" into self-sustained economic growth. The Kennedy administration's considerable aid to the non-aligned countries meant that funds poured in from both the United States and the Soviet Union, which squandered its capital in an attempt to win the Third World over to its camp. For example, India, which has a mixed economy, received hand-outs from both sides and had a private sector boosted by American capital and a public sector, principally the steel industry, financed by the Soviet Union.

It soon became clear, however, that existing international institutions, such as GATT and the IMF, served the interests of the industrialized nations rather than the needs of the Third World. Dependency theorists insisted that Third World countries were trapped in a system of unequal exchange whereby their terms of trade as primary producers constantly deteriorated, multinational corporations transferred their surpluses from South to North, and the Third World was starved of capital and modern technology. The structural restraints of the world economy condemned Third World economies to everlasting backwardness.

Few argued that the Third World would have to sever all ties with the industrialized world, for it was difficult to see how this could be possible. The only hope of breaking the ties of dependency, which the new orthodoxy insisted were inherent within the capitalist system, was to urge the developed nations to correct these imbalances. Although industrialized nations refused to accept the gloomy prognostications of the dependency theorists, they generally agreed that the Third World countries should be given better access to Western markets for their manufactured and semi-manufactured goods. A great deal of time and effort was spent developing a new scheme of preferences, but it did little to help improve the situation. Since most Third World countries were primary producers of raw materials and foodstuffs and had few manufactured goods to offer for export, the effect was minimal.

The Third World was encouraged in 1973-74 when OPEC managed to quadruple the price of oil. In addition, in 1974 a severe frost wrecked the Brazilian coffee crop, and coffee prices also quadrupled. As a result, other commodity prices were rising, and the industrialized world began to discuss measures to counter this trend. Negotiations between the Western powers and the Group of 77 (non-aligned states) began in UNCTAD to work out an agreement on commodities, but they soon ran into difficulties since there was no consensus on how an accommodation could best be achieved. The Commonwealth then took the lead, with the secretary general optimistically announcing that although the Commonwealth could not negotiate for the world, it could help the world to negotiate. Once again, discussions came to nothing, and world markets continued as they had before.

For most of the developing countries the oil crisis had disastrous effects. Even Nigeria, where oil revenues were substantial, neglected the agricultural sector and believed that money would continue to pour in. Countries that had no oil resources experienced an alarming increase in indebtedness. They imagined that this disorder was temporary and would be overcome when they succeeded in following the example of OPEC and forced up the price of their commodities. Michael Manley of Jamaica, a prominent radical who had swallowed the dependency theory whole, played a leading role in establishing the International Bauxite Association, and Zambia negotiated with the Latin American copper producers to form a similar organization.

UNCTAD's New International Economic Order (NIEO), proclaimed in 1974, soon proved to be yet another empty acronym. The oil producers began to pursue their own national interests and ceased to act as a cohesive group. Their aid programmes for the developing world were every bit as politically motivated as those of the industrialized world, and there was no enthusiasm for a multinational programme for Third World development. The industrialized countries took countermeasures by exploiting the natural resources of safe areas like North America and Australia in order not to depend on supplies from countries they deemed to be politically unreliable. Investment and exploration in the Third World was cut back, Jamaica's bauxite industry was ruined, and the price of strategic minerals fell.

In 1981 an international commission under the chairmanship of Willy Brandt published the "North/South Report: A Programme for Survival" in an attempt to rekindle interest in the chronic problems of the developing countries, which were largely ignored by world leaders like Ronald Reagan and Margaret Thatcher, whose neo-classicist economic advisers warned them of the naiveté of such concerns. The report suggested that if Western technology, Arab money, and Third World manpower could be brought together, both North and South would prosper. Although "North/South" entered the vocabulary of politicians and journalists and even became a cliché, Western politicians basically ignored the report. Its prescriptions were essentially Keynesian, and Keynes was now regarded as an evil genius whose misguided theories had led to inflation and massive government debt.

The failure of schemes like the NIEO has led to a mood of resigned realism. The dreams of rapid development have been shattered; the emphasis is now on saving what it is possible to save, on survival. Old radicals have abandoned Marxist rhetoric and now announce in the best Thatcherite terms that countries cannot spend what they have not earned. Some still cling to the theories of dependency or threaten the world's banking system with a gigantic default, but most realize that they must set their houses in order by often painful structural adjustments.

More modest regional agreements have replaced old ambitious and unrealistic schemes for reforming the world economy. In these the Commonwealth has played an important and constructive role. Third World countries now acknowledge that they cannot blame all their misfortunes on the capitalist system, on unequal exchange, on the imperialist legacy, or on neo-colonialism. The most important result of the United Nations Emergency Session on Africa in 1986 was the admission by African governments that their own mismanagement and misguided policies caused many of their problems. It is likely that institutions like the World Bank and the IMF will support their determination not to repeat the mistakes of the past and to implement necessary changes.

For many Third World countries the remedies are painful. If they want assistance from international financial institutions, they have to accept their prescriptions, and it still remains to be seen whether they are effective. In the absence of any other practical solution, one can do little but devoutly hope that they will be.

Plans to redistribute wealth and create welfare states were highly desirable in countries with widespread poverty and gross inequalities of income, but they presupposed sufficient wealth to redistribute and to finance extensive social programmes. Such schemes, it is generally accepted, have to be postponed until sufficient income is generated to support them.

The dangerous illusion that the problems of development could be solved by aid programmes or by restructuring the world economy has been shattered. The Soviet Union no longer provides an alternative model to the capitalist market economy. The difficulties of the Third World can no longer be blamed on the greed, rapacity, and immense wealth of the industrialized nations. Given this new mood of sombre realism, the Commonwealth may be able to play an important role as mediator, adviser, and facilitator. The prospects are not bright, but they are probably no worse than at any other time since World War II.

Many Commonwealth states are plagued by ethnic, regional, and religious divisions that were largely overlooked at the time of independence. United in the struggle against the imperial power of Britain, leaders had no time for serious consideration of the consequences of future rivalries. Once this sense of common purpose was dissipated, tensions rose to the surface and were aggravated by poverty, exploitation, the weakness of the liberal élite, and the authoritarian traditions of the colonial past.

It was hoped that by waving the macro-economic Keynesian wand, problems of economic growth and income distribution could soon be solved. By the early 1970s there were grounds for believing that the promised land would soon be in sight. Growth rates were remarkably high, higher indeed than in the great industrial nations during the nineteenth century. Standards of living were rising from the intolerable almost to the level of an acceptable minimum.

No matter how much they rejected the colonial legacy, the politicians who led the newly independent Commonwealth countries were generally attracted to British traditions and institutions and sought to emulate the achievements of the Labour government of 1945-51. They mostly subscribed to some version of social democracy. Belief in economic development, fair shares, and a welfare state was part of the credo as was a commitment to fundamental human rights and freedoms.

Economic development and civil liberties are interrelated. The "full belly thesis," which was bandied about during the discussions about the New International Economic Order, asserts that political rights can only be granted once basic economic rights have been achieved. Although it was certainly not the intention of the original proponents of this thesis, it was all too often used as an excuse for the violation of political rights in the Third World.

Even more dangerous was the assertion that the doctrine of universal human rights was a form of cultural imperialism, an attempt to force a Western worldview on societies that had quite different traditions and moral values. Julius Nyerere of Tanzania thus announced: "We have no more need of being 'converted' to socialism than we have of being 'taught' democracy. Both are rooted in our past, in the traditional society that produced us." In a similar vein, Kenneth Kaunda of Zambia argued that: "The tribal community was a mutual society. It was organized to satisfy the basic human needs of all its members and, therefore, individualism was discouraged."

Such assertions were based on a highly romanticized view of traditional African societies, and the idea that one-party dictatorships fulfil the traditional commitment to communitarian ideas is absurd. Even those African states that claim to be socialist have done little to redistribute wealth or to ensure social harmony, despite their claims that these aims are inherent in African society. The problem with the once fashionable theories of cultural relativism is that they can excuse the most frightful despotism on the grounds that it arises from a specific cultural context that must be respected. Human rights must be considered universal; even when making due allowance for cultural differences, it is imperative to avoid the fallacy that all cultures produce equally acceptable moral values.

Freedom is difficult to quantify, but it is possible to hand out marks to different countries on their human rights performance. The best known such attempt is the 1986 Comparative Survey of Freedom published by Freedom House. According to its findings in forty-five Commonwealth countries, only twenty-one rated as "free," with Barbados, Belize, St. Kitts-Nevis, and Tuvalu getting full marks. Nineteen states were rated as "partly free." Ghana, Malawi, Nigeria, the Seychelles, and Tanzania were rated as "not free," but they at least received slightly better marks than the states of the then Soviet bloc.

Freedom House's criteria have been the subject of considerable criticism on the grounds that they were too narrowly ideological and placed too much emphasis on "freedom to" rather than "freedom from." The World Human Right's Guide is more broadly based and uses a similar weighting to that used by Amnesty International. Its 1986 ratings placed Papua New Guinea well ahead of the rest, with Trinidad and Tobago, Botswana, and Jamaica following behind. At the bottom come Bangladesh, Zimbabwe, Ghana, Tanzania, and Kenya. Commonwealth Third World states, however, do mostly rank above the average for developing countries.

These ratings can also be criticized for their Western liberal bias, but even by more objective criteria, such as those used by the Overseas Development Council in Washington, which are based on expectation of life, infant mortality, and literacy, the Commonwealth scores above average, and many countries rank almost as highly as the developed world. Under another system, the Index of Social Progress calculated by Richard Estes, the Commonwealth developing countries do less well in comparison to other states at the same stage. Common to all of these rating systems is an agreement that the Caribbean countries score best, followed by those in the Pacific. African states score lowest.

These findings are hardly surprising. African Commonwealth states have, on the whole, had a dismal record on human rights. Most are single-party or military dictatorships, opposition parties are forbidden, the press is muzzled, torture and the death penalty are widespread. Most of their unfortunate citizens live in squalor, child labour is exploited to the full, and vicious discrimination against women is condoned. Female circumcision and infibulation are widespread practices. Demagogic appeals to racism and tribalism have had gruesome results. No criticism can be voiced for, as Julius Nyerere insisted: "Until our war against poverty, ignorance and disease has been won, we should not let our unity be destroyed by someone else's book of rules." Everyone, except for a few devout Western liberals who curiously admire behaviour in African leaders that they would find outrageous at home, knows perfectly well that such wars can never be won.

The most frightful of these régimes was General Idi Amin's in Uganda. It made Evelyn Waugh's grim satire "Black Magic" seem rather small beer. Even Nyerere said that Amin was worse than Vorster of South Africa or Smith of Rhodesia, but when his own Tanzanian army liberated Kampala, they looted and raped, rigged the elections, and brought back the grossly incompetent Milton Obote. The country had to endure horrific tribal warfare and terrorism that resulted in even more deaths than Amin was responsible for.

Ghana seemed to be well set on the way to democracy and prosperity until it was ruined by the megalomaniac pretensions of Nkrumah and by military dictatorship. But the situation is now somewhat curious. The alarmingly erratic Flight-Lieutenant Jerry Rawlings ordered the public execution of three former heads of state. He is certainly no democrat, but by radical methods he has done much to improve the economy so that Ghana is able to manage its debt and is now regarded by the IMF and the World Bank as an exemplary country.

Ghana is also somewhat untypical in that the idea of a unitary state has never been seriously challenged. On the other hand, Nigeria, once economically secure and a model of constitutionalism, suffered a ferocious civil war when Biafra seceded. The enormous loss of life was compounded by famine. In Zimbabwe the Ndele of Matabeleland were massacred, and similar atrocities have occurred elsewhere throughout Africa. Some of the one-party states, such as Tanzania, are reasonably benign, though hardly the models of democracy that their Western admirers claim; others, such as Kenya, have degenerated into viciously repressive régimes. States like Botswana and Gambia are praised for tolerating more than one party, but such democracies are insecure and provide little inspiration for others.

In Asia, India is touted as the world's largest democracy, and, indeed, it has been able to preserve a degree of democracy in very adverse circumstances. Ethnic, religious, and caste violence is a constant problem, and the measures successive governments have instituted to combat it have often violated basic human rights. Yet in spite of grinding poverty, caste prejudice, and widespread discrimination on the basis of sex, particularly in the lower classes, India has always returned to constitutional government after bouts of presidential rule and emergency decrees. There is much corruption and staggering improvidence in ruling circles, but at least the élite aspires to include the hundreds of millions of the dispossessed in the open, secular, and free society whose benefits they enjoy.

Bangladesh, which declared itself independent from Pakistan in 1971, joined the Commonwealth the following year. It is the poorest of all the Commonwealth countries, with a per capita GNP less than half of that of Tanzania. Where there is such poverty, political rights are inevitably of secondary concern, but a series of military régimes has been guilty of murder and torture, particularly of the hill people in Chittagong.

At independence in 1948, Sri Lanka had a classic Westminster-style constitution that functioned effectively; governing parties regularly went down to defeat in general elections. In 1970, Mrs. S. Bandaranaike announced that she intended far-reaching constitutional reforms, and the country became a republic. After her defeat in the 1977 elections, J. R. Jayewardene introduced an executive presidency along Gaullist lines. In recent years, communal tension between Tamils and Sinhalese have escalated to the point of civil war, with the Tamils calling for a separate state in the north of the island. Tamil Tigers terrorists have consistently abused human rights, and government forces have retaliated with the murder and arbitrary arrest of Tamils.

Malaysia and Singapore have been economically successful, but both countries place restrictions on basic freedoms. Malaysia's obsession with the threat of communism has resulted in the outlawing of the party and the arbitrary arrest of a number of people suspected of communist sympathies. Singapore is a far more authoritarian régime in which the rights of the opposition are severely restricted, the press is heavily censored, and traditional Confucian strictures deny the rights of women .

The Caribbean, in spite of many social problems, enjoys the highest degree of freedom within the Third World Commonwealth. In most Caribbean states democracy has worked well; the military and police have remained neutral, and the judiciary and administration have been relatively free from corruption and outside influence. The major problems have been violence, particularly in Jamaica, and the corruption involved with drug trafficking, which is glaring in the Bahamas. In Guyana, the government of Forbes Burnham was corrupt and violent and exploited the bitter racial tensions between Africans and Indians. By his brutality and incompetence, Eric Geary paved the way for a radical coup and counter-coup in Grenada.

The Commonwealth countries of the Pacific have not excited much attention from political analysts, and the region has, on the whole, been peaceful, comfortable, and relatively content. Fiji is a major exception. In 1987 the army, dominated by Melanesians, seized power and ousted the democratically elected Fiji Labour Party, which the army considered to be dominated by Indians. Under a ferocious internal security decree, basic political rights were suspended and the Indian population was terrorized. Many Indians felt obliged to emigrate, mainly to other, more peaceful parts of the Commonwealth where their rights are respected.

The Commonwealth's record on human rights is not impressive. It may be a little better than that of other countries, but it falls far short of the ideals it professes to espouse. At Singapore in 1971 the heads of government announced that they believed in: "the liberty of the individual, in equal rights for all citizens regardless of race, colour, creed or political belief, and in their inalienable right to participate by means of free and democratic political processes in framing the society in which they live." Very few of the politicians present can have put their names to this document in good faith.

At the 1979 conference in Lusaka, Sir Dawda Jawara of Gambia proposed a Commonwealth Commission on Human Rights. Nothing came of the proposal, largely because a number of members of the working party established to set up the commission were overthrown in coups and there were too many villains who did not wish to have their behaviour scrutinized. Everyone could agree to denounce racism, wag fingers at South Africa, and even to express certain misgivings about the gerrymandering of the Ugandan elections in 1980—the first for eighteen years. They were, after all, confident that their own conduct would not be subjected to similar close inspection.

Shridath Ramphal was well aware of this erosion of civil rights, but he could see no way out of the dilemma it posed. In his 1977 report, he asked the Commonwealth "to work for an ethic which constrains meddling but . . . also inhibits excesses of the kind that demand and justify protest from without." How excesses could be stopped without meddling was difficult to understand, and the secretary general certainly supported the idea of meddling in the affairs of South Africa. He was highly critical of those who did not. It may be that the hypocrisy shown in dealings with South Africa will become a thing of the past now that apartheid has begun to be dismantled. Perhaps the Commonwealth will confront its own problems, not constantly avoid them by denouncing the evils of Pretoria. The Commonwealth should revive the Gambian proposal and set up a Human Rights Commission, which must be prepared, in the manner of Amnesty International, to chastise member states that fail to maintain minimum standards of civil rights.

For liberals at home and abroad the dissolution of the British Empire was an occasion for optimistic rejoicing. Britain could retire in reasonable comfort, if in somewhat reduced circumstances, from the ranks of the imperial powers. The British felt that they had done a reasonably good job and that they had abandoned pretensions to world power with good grace. Now they could watch with amuse-

170

ment and despair the antics of the Americans and Soviets as they tried their hand at the imperial game. The legacy the British had left to their erstwhile colonies was one of which they were proud. It included the belief in the sovereignty of the people enshrined in the principle of national independence, respect for the rights of the individual, and the social democratic commitment to social justice, welfare, and economic progress. The inspiring vision gave rise to hopes for continued economic development and the protection and extension of civil rights.

Regrettably, these aspirations proved to be unfounded. Many newly independent states had money in the bank and seemed committed to democracy; yet, within a few years, they were buried under mountains of debt, political power was being scandalously abused, and the new nations were falling apart as a result of ethnic, religious, linguistic, class, and caste struggles. But there was still reason for hope. In the Caribbean, with the unfortunate exception of Guyana and Grenada, and in India and Sri Lanka, elections continued to be held, governments changed, and the democratic process took root. However dubious the practice, parliamentary democracy remains an ideal and universal suffrage an accepted principle. Moreover, no alternative ideology has been able to replace these established liberal values. Indeed, throughout much of the Commonwealth there is agreement about what fundamental human rights are, even if they are seldom enjoyed.

In his memoirs, published in 1981, Arnold Smith suggested that one hundred years hence people would regard the Commonwealth as Britain's greatest contribution to man's social and political history. Although the creation of the Commonwealth was a remarkable piece of statesmanship, not only by Britain but also by the newly independent nations, and although Arnold Smith's enthusiasm is perfectly understandable, it is doubtful whether this will indeed be the case. As the years go by, the specifically British nature of the Commonwealth fades into the background. The Empire is a thing of the distant and romantic past, lacking any political immediacy. Even the fact that the member states were once British colonies becomes increasingly less significant as can be seen in the precise status of the Queen as Head of the Commonwealth. It is the Queen as an individual who exercises this essentially ceremonial function, not the Crown. It is not in her capacity as the constitutional head of state of the United Kingdom that she attends the Heads of Government meetings but as an individual. The Queen of the United Kingdom and the Head of the Commonwealth are, constitutionally speaking, two persons. This status is symbolized by the Queen's use of a special personal standard for Commonwealth meetings. (It is made up of an "E" surrounded by a garland and surmounted by a crown and is quite different from the personal standard she uses in her capacity as the British monarch.) It is for this reason that the Queen properly

171

refused to allow Margaret Thatcher to influence her addresses to Heads of Government meetings. The Queen's commitment to the Commonwealth is unquestioned, and she has been an exemplary head of this unique institution.

These constitutional niceties are lost on most people, but in both her roles, the Queen appears impartial, and she scrupulously keeps them separate. A far more important reason for the dwindling role of Britain within the Commonwealth is the enormous enhancement of the role of the secretary general. Sir Shridath Ramphal, who has held the post since 1972, is an ambitious activist determined to increase the power of the office. He has achieved his aims without alienating the member states. He made a bid for the United Nations' Secretary-Generalship on the retirement of Kurt Waldheim, but since he lacked support outside the Commonwealth, (either because he was unknown or more likely because many felt he might actually do something), he was defeated by the colourless Perez de Cuellar. Ramphal refused a lesser position as Commissioner for Refugees and soldiered on in the Commonwealth.

Ramphal's assessment of what can and should be done determines the activities of the Commonwealth, building on foundations laid by Arnold Smith, who had been far more forceful and innovative than most governments expected. A career diplomat, Smith also turned out to have exceptional political and entrepreneurial flair. He built up an office with a permanent staff of three hundred from twenty-five countries, but he had little patience for administration, bureaucratic procedure, or endless wrangling with civil servants. He preferred to deal directly with heads of governments.

Ramphal was determined to use the power and authority passed on to him to change the world. In his first report to the Heads of Government, he clearly stated his ambitious objectives. They were to secure the liberation of Southern Africa, to restructure the world economy, to serve the world community, and to make practical contributions to the improvement of the economic and social conditions of Commonwealth states. Restructuring the world economy has proved to be an intractable problem, and the well-meaning but facile prescriptions of the Brandt Report of 1981 were rejected by all but a few remaining idealists and ideologues who refused to face bitter realities. Subsequently, Ramphal has had to place greater emphasis on more modest and practical issues, and he has had a number of successes.

The Commonwealth is no longer the British Empire in modern dress. It has been no more successful in changing the world than has any other international body. As an organization concerned with the interests of small states, it has not proved particularly effective. The American invasion of Grenada, a Commonwealth country, is a case in point. When Maurice Bishop and the leading members of his government were assassinated, the United States invaded. Reactions in the Commonwealth were very mixed. African and Asian members saw the invasion as a typical example of American imperialism. Even Margaret Thatcher was concerned about the implications of the Americans invading an independent country that had not been attacked from abroad, and the British refused to support the U.S. action in the United Nations. On the other hand, the view of the conservative Caribbean nations was forcefully articulated by Eugenia Charles of Dominica, who supported the United States. After all, she said, the Americans had been invited to invade the country by the Organization of East Caribbean States (OECS). Most Caribbean countries rejected even the suggestion that Commonwealth troops might replace the U.S. Marines, although a small West Indian contingent accompanied the invasion force.

Ramphal deplored the invasion and did everything he could to stop it from happening. When this proved impossible, he tried to defuse the situation by ensuring that the interim government was genuinely representative of Grenadan opinion and by discussing the issue with Commonwealth representatives at the United Nations. Unpleasantness was avoided at the CHOGM in Delhi in November, and a rather anodyne communiqué issued from Goa carefully avoided naming names. It expressed alarm at the "disregard for the moral and legal principles which should govern the conduct of states" and at the "readiness of nations to resort to illegal use of force."

The case of Grenada exemplifies the limitations of the Commonwealth as an international organization. It has no foreign policy because the international interests of member states are often very distinct. Commonwealth countries belong to different international and regional alliances and organizations whose interests are not always those of other member nations. The Commonwealth can act to smooth over differences and to relieve tensions, but it cannot engage in concerted supranational effort. It does not vote on specific issues but relies on consensus. When there is no consensus, a minority view is tolerated with varying degrees of reluctance.

Britain, for example, has refused to be tied down by Commonwealth policy on South Africa. Bob Hawke of Australia argued in 1986 that Commonwealth sanctions would not work unless they were supported by sanctions from the United States and the European Community. Brian Mulroney of Canada, a country that stood to gain from sanctions, felt that the Commonwealth should lead the way by setting a lofty moral example. Britain found herself isolated at the Commonwealth mini-summit in August 1986, but this policy difference underscored rather than caused the transfer of power away from Britain. It also served to remind people that a Commonwealth that was no longer centred on Britain had gained nothing in international influence and prestige. That it also had not lost any was cold comfort.

As the Commonwealth looks less and less like the Empire in a new guise, it becomes increasingly difficult to find the basis for a new consensus. Endless chest beating over Third World poverty is pointless without any suggestions for a practical solution. A Commonwealth without Britain is no longer necessarily a contradiction in terms, but with the passage of time its uses become increasingly questionable. All Commonwealth countries were once British colonies, the use of the English language is a common heritage, cricket is widely enjoyed, and some Commonwealth countries have adopted the Westminster style of government. None of this, however, has much immediate significance.

When Britain joined the European Economic Community, its action was widely felt to be in part a rejection of a neo-imperialist vision of Commonwealth. As the country continues to dither on the brink of European political and monetary union, some still cling to a paternalistic vision of Commonwealth culture, and others fall back into a defensive rhetoric of isolationist superiority. Refusing to adjust to the diversity of Europe, they cannot accept the even greater cultural diversity of a Commonwealth of self-determining nations.

If Britain enjoys a certain prestige in the Commonwealth, it does so on the cheap. In 1988-89 Britain's per capita contribution to the secretariat and to CSC, CYP, and CFTC was 18 pence. The Australians committed 30p, the Canadians 40p, and the subjects of the Sultan of Brunei a staggering £4.58. The richest members of the Commonwealth pay lip service to the ideals of international co-operation and repeatedly profess their determination to grapple with world poverty, but they do not seem prepared to back their words up with hard cash.

At Commonwealth meetings there is much talk of the "common endeavour," but there is silence when it comes to talking about what the Commonwealth actually does. At a speech at Exeter University in November 1986, Ramphal asked, with a hint of weary desperation, whether the Commonwealth was ready to take a step beyond merely speaking with a more-or-less common voice.

Everyone likes the Commonwealth; no sensible person could possibly be against it. As the German president, Richard von Weizsäcker said, it is against no one. For Ramphal that is not enough. The Commonwealth must, he says, help to alleviate poverty, to ensure world peace, and to end all forms of racial discrimination. But he too is disconcertingly vague when it comes to practical suggestions. The resolve to dismantle apartheid cannot of itself justify the existence of the Commonwealth; nor can the resolve of some ministers of justice to combine efforts to combat drug-trafficking be seen as a triumphant vindication of the common effort. Its real achievements are at a much less exalted level than its ambitious claims for the Commonwealth as an example of international understanding and co-operation.

In 1970 Lord Beloff said the Commonwealth was "a good idea—a pity it failed." Similar views are held by many other members of the British establishment.

The Commonwealth has certainly been beset with difficulties since World War II. The Dominions have been determined to assert their independent status, an understandable concern, but one that has also given rise to such remarkable incidents as the Pommy-bashing outburst of the Australian prime minister in February 1992, and his suggestion in the 1993 election campaign that Australia become a republic. Australia and New Zealand had looked to the Commonwealth for defence and saw the British base in Singapore as a guarantee of their security. This proved to be a cruel illusion in 1942, and Australia was saved from the Japanese not by the Royal Navy but by the American victory in the Coral Sea. India had hardly taken the remarkable step of choosing to remain within the Commonwealth when it was locked in a bitter dispute with another Commonwealth country, Pakistan, over Kashmir. In 1956 the Commonwealth was seriously divided over the Suez adventure, and that crisis had barely been overcome when issues related to Rhodesia and then South Africa caused further disruptions.

Some of Britain's disillusionment with the Commonwealth results from its declining status as a world power. The "special relationship" with the United States, for which Churchill pleaded in 1946, became over the years an empty cliché. The Falklands War did not cause a split within the Commonwealth, in part because the British position was enthusiastically supported by Ramphal. Still, it was a humiliating reminder of Britain's standing when, during the United Nations debate on the issue in 1985, the British were only able to gain the support of Belize, Oman, and the Solomon Islands. In the European Community Britain is often seen as endlessly hesitating to make a commitment.

Britain was eager to create a large Commonwealth as a consolation prize for the loss of empire. It welcomed India and the newly independent African states with open arms, and there was bitter disappointment when Burma refused to join the club. Britain was now head of a vast multiracial Commonwealth and as such could play a major role in world affairs. But its position soon soured under the constant attacks by Commonwealth members. Even Canada joined India in the chorus of disapproval over Suez and in 1961 supported the move to oust South Africa despite the British prime minister's expressed wishes. Subsequent British governments have been denounced by Commonwealth members as racist and holding fundamental human rights in contempt.

British reactions to these attacks and accusations have been equally strident. African politicians who the British hoped would learn the ways of the Westminster model of government were called a bunch of bloody dictators, pseudo-socialists, and corrupt specialists in violent coups. Even the white Dominions, which really ought to have known better, joined in with Africans and the duplicitous Asians in making endless trouble over Rhodesia and South Africa and loosened their ties with Britain.

From the outset the Commonwealth Secretariat fiercely defended its independence. Arnold Smith kept the British at bay, and Sonny Ramphal has always been able to rely on Third World support to ensure that the Commonwealth has its own independent voice. British prime ministers have to put up with high-minded lectures from outraged Commonwealth leaders instead of presiding over exclusive and respectful gatherings of dominion prime ministers. Moreover, Britain's poor economy, coupled with a scandalous degree of parsimony, has meant that aid to Commonwealth countries has been minimal.

For most member countries the Commonwealth is of secondary importance. Asian countries look to ASEAN or prefer to play the non-aligned game. Similar regional organizations in the Pacific, Africa, and the Caribbean are smaller in scale than the Commonwealth but are of more immediate concern.

Nevertheless, it would be a great mistake to dismiss the Commonwealth. It is surprising how many Commonwealth leaders, among them Indira Gandhi, Bob Hawke, Pierre Trudeau, Dr. Mahathir of Malaysia, started out as at best agnostic towards the institution and yet came to appreciate its usefulness. The fact that most Commonwealth leaders attend the CHOGMs is clear indication that they serve a real purpose. For Canada, Commonwealth membership underlines its independence from the United States. Australia, excluded from ASEAN, finds it a useful setting for a medium power. African states have used the Commonwealth to stop Britain caving in to Ian Smith's régime in Rhodesia. Lee Kuan Yew of Singapore found among the Commonwealth leaders people of influence who were prepared to listen to his extraordinary ideas. The Commonwealth is the only international gathering where states like Vanuatu, Tuvalu, Kiribati, or Nauru are at all likely to get a hearing. But the Commonwealth's utility goes beyond allowing heads of government to meet in a relatively congenial atmosphere to discuss matters of common concern. The Commonwealth provides, as we have seen, all manner of technical, educational and professional assistance. It has done a great deal of good and precious little harm.

Parallel to the "official" is the enormously important and vital "unofficial" Commonwealth made up of a large number of non-government organizations

(NGOs) concerned with every imaginable topic from forestry to literature, scouting to town planning, Methodism to the press. There are 328 universities in the Association of Commonwealth Universities, which provides a network of higher learning stretching across twenty-nine countries. At this unofficial level the Commonwealth provides the setting for invaluable work in practical co-operation that is not hampered by ideological grandstanding or petty politicking.

Above all, the Commonwealth is a going concern that offers many opportunities for its members, whatever their wealth or size, to advance their interests and enhance their status. It may be unspectacular and at times a trifle quaint, but if cynicism and misplaced idealism can both be avoided, it will continue to play its unique role as an instrument of genuine international co-operation and it could even become both a challenge and an inspiration.

Selected Bibliography

Albertini, R. von, *Decolonization: The Administration and Future of the Colonies 1919-1960,* New York, 1971.

Ansprenger, F., *The Dissolution of Colonial Empires,* London 1989.

Anstey, R., *The Atlantic Slave Trade and British Abolition, 1760-1810,* London 1975.

Austin, D., *Politics in Ghana, 1946-1960,* Oxford 1966.

Bailyn, B., *The Ideological Origins of the American Revolution,* Cambridge, Mass., 1967.

Baumgart, W., *Imperialism: The Idea and Reality of British and French Colonial Expansion, 1880-1914,* Oxford 1982.

Bayly, C.A., *Imperial Meridian: The British Empire and the World, 1780-1830,* London and New York 1989.

Blackburn, Robin, *The Overthrow of Colonial Slavery, 1776-1848,* London 1988.

Blake, R., *A History of Rhodesia,* London 1977.

Bolt, C., *Victorian Attitudes to Race,* London 1971.

Braithwaite, E., *The Development of Creole Society in Jamaica, 1770-1820,* Oxford 1971.

Bullock, A., *Ernest Bevin, Foreign Secretary,* London 1983.

Canny, N. and Pagden, A., *Colonial Elites, 1500-1800,* Princeton 1987.

Craig, G.M., *Upper Canada, 1784-1841,* Toronto 1963.

Cross, C., *The Fall of the British Empire,* London 1968.

Crouzet, F., *Le Conflit de Chypre,* Brussels 1973.

Cumpston, I.M.(ed), *The Growth of the British Commonwealth, 1880-1932,* London 1973.

Curtin, P.D., *Cross Cultural Trade in World History,* Cambridge 1984.

Eldridge, C.C., *Victorian Imperialism,* London 1978.

Elphick, P. and Giliomee, H., *The Shaping of South African Society, 1600-1850,* London 1983.

Fage, J. D., *A History of West Africa,* Cambridge 1969.

Fieldhouse, D.K. (ed.), *The Theory of Capitalist Imperialism*, London 1967.

Fieldhouse, D.K., *The Colonial Empires*, London 1982.

Fitzgerald, C.P., *A Concise History of East Asia*, London 1974.

Flaphan, S., *Zionism and the Palestinians*, London 1979.

Gallagher, J.A., *The Decline, Revival and Fall of the British Empire*, Cambridge 1982.

Gollwitzer, H., *Europe in the Age of Imperialism, 1880-1914*, London 1969.

Graham, G., *British Policy and Canada, 1774-1791*, London 1930.

Groom, A.J.R., and Taylor, P., *The Commonwealth in the 1980s*, London 1984.

Hodson, H.V., *The Great Divide*, London 1969.

Hyam, R. and Martin, G., *Reappraisals in British Imperial History*, London 1975.

Hyam, R., *Britain's Imperial Century, 1815-1914*, London 1976.

Ingram, E., *Commitment to Empire. Prophecies of the Great Game in Asia*, Oxford 1981.

Ingram, E., *In Defence of British India. Great Britain in the Middle East, 1775-1842*, London 1984.

Judd, D. and Slinn, P., *The Evolution of the Modern Commonwealth, 1902-80*, London 1982.

Judd, D., *The Victorian Empire: a Pictorial History, 1837-1901*, London 1970.

Kemp, T., *Theories of Imperialism*, London 1967.

Kennedy, P., *The Rise and Decline of Great Powers*, London 1988.

Kiernan, V.G., *The Lords of Human Kind: European Attitudes to the Outside World in the Imperial Age*, London 1969.

Koebner, R. and Schmidt, H.D., *Imperialism: the Story and Significance of a Political Word*, Cambridge 1964.

Koebner, R., *Empire*, Cambridge 1961.

Lacoutre, J. and S., *Egypt in Transition*, London 1958.

Lapping, B., *The End of Empire*, London 1985.

Louis, W. R., *The British Empire in the Middle East, 1945-1951: Arab Nationalism, the United States, and Postwar Imperialism*, Oxford 1984.

Louis, W.R., *Imperialism at Bay, 1941-1945*, Oxford 1977.

Lowe, C.J., *The Reluctant Imperialists*, 2 vols, London 1967.

MacIntyre, W. D., *Colonies into Commonwealth*, London 1966.

Madden, F.W. (with Fieldhouse, D.K.), *Imperial Reconstruction, 1763-1840, Select Documents on the Constitutional History of the British Empire and Commonwealth*, iii, New York 1987.

Maltby, R. and Quartermaine, P., *The Commonwealth: A Common Culture?*, Exeter 1989.

Manning, H.T., *The Revolt of French Canada, 1800-1835*, London 1962.

Mansergh, P.N.S., *The Commonwealth Experience*, London 1982.

Mansfield, P., *The British in Egypt*, London 1971.

Marshall, P.J., *East India Fortunes. The British in Bengal in the Eighteenth Century*, Oxford 1976.

Marshall, P.J., *The Impeachment of Warren Hastings*, Oxford 1965.

Mayall, J. and Payne, A., *The Fallacies of Hope: The Post-Colonial Record of the Commonwealth Third World*, Manchester 1991.

Monroe, E., *Britain's Moment in the Middle East*, London 1981.

Moore, R.J., *Escape from Empire: the Attlee Government and the Indian Problem*, Oxford 1983.

Moore, R.J., *Making the New Commonwealth*, Oxford 1987.

Morris, J., *Heavens Command, 1837-1897; Pax Britannica, 1897; Farewell to Trumpets, 1897-1965*, London 1979.

Morton, W.L., *The Kingdom of Canada*, Toronto 1963.

Neatby, H., *Quebec. The Revolutionary Age, 1760-91*, Toronto 1966.

Newham, G., *The Rise of English Nationalism*, London 1987.

Nutting, A, *No End of a Lesson*, London 1967.

Ouellet, F., *Lower Canada, 1792-1841*, Toronto 1976.

Owen, R. and Sutcliffe, B. (eds), *Studies in the Theory of Imperialism*, London 1972.

Owen, R., *The Middle East and the World Economy, 1800-1914*, London 1981.

Perham, M., *Colonial Sequence,* London 1970.

Platt, D.C.M., *Finance, Trade and Politics in British Foreign Policy, 1815-1914,* Oxford 1968.

Porter, B., *The Lion's Share: A Short History of British Imperialism 1850-1983,* London 1984.

Robinson, R.E., and Gallacher, J.A., *Africa and the Victorians,* London 1961.

Robinson, R.E. and Gallacher, J., 'The Imperialism of Free Trade, 1814-1915', *Economic History Review,* 2nd series, vi, 2, 1953.

Seal, A., *The Emergence of Indian Nationalism,* Cambridge 1968.

Short, A., *The Communist Insurrection in Malaya, 1948-1960,* London 1975.

Smith, M.G., *The Plural Society in the British West Indies,* Berkeley 1965.

Spiers, E.M., *The Army and Society,* London 1980.

Stokes, E.T., 'Bureaucracy and Ideology: Britain and India in the Nineteenth Century', *Transactions of the Royal Historical Society,* 5th Series, xxx, 1980.

Thornton, A.P., *The Imperial Idea and its Enemies,* London 1959.

Tomlinson, B.R., *The Political Economy of the Raj, 1914-1947,* London 1979.

Ward, J.M., *Colonial Self-Government. The British Experience, 1759-1856,* London 1976.

Williams, E., *Capitalism and Slavery,* London 1964.

Williams, G. and Marshall P., *The British Atlantic Empire before the American Revolution,* London 1980.

Young, D.M., *The Colonial Office in the Early Nineteenth Century,* London 1962.

A

Chou En-lai, 123
Christianity, 17–18, 20, 32
Chumbi Valley, 45
Church Missionary Society, 19–20
Churchill, Sir Winston, 41, 65, 77–78, 80, 81, 85, 89, 90, 91, 92, 93, 98, 100, 101, 103, 121, 129, 131
Cinnamon, 12
Clive, Robert, 7–9
Cocoa, 53
Cohen, Andrew, 106, 107
Colebrooke, Henry, 19
Collins, Michael, 69
Colombo Plan, 108
Colonial conferences, 50. *See also* Imperial Conferences
Colonial Department, 2
Colonial Development and Welfare Act, 72
Colonial Development and Welfare Fund, 89
Colonial Development Corporation, 108
Colonial Office, 143
Colonial service, 19, 22, 29–30, 59, 67, 76
Colonies, administration, 2–3
Committee of Imperial Defence, 50–51
Commonwealth Fund for Technical Co-operation (CFTC), 144, 150, 157, 158
Commonwealth Information Division, 149
Commonwealth Legal Bureau, 148
Commonwealth Legal Education Association, 148
Commonwealth Magistrates' Association 148–49

Commonwealth of Learning, 151
Commonwealth preference, 157
Commonwealth Relations Office, 104, 143
Commonwealth Scholarship and Fellowship Plan, 151
Commonwealth Secretariat, 143, 144–45, 148–49, 159–60
Commonwealth Youth Plan, 151
Commonwealth, and the status of women, 151–52
Commonwealth, Economic Affairs Division, 149
Commonwealth, Export Market Development Division, 158
Commonwealth, General Technical Assistance Division, 150–51
Commonwealth, Group of Eminent Persons, 155–56
Commonwealth, Heads of Government Meetings, 143–45, 152–56, 158, 170
Commonwealth, Legal Division, 148–49
Communism, 101, 169
Communists, 109–11, 127, 130, 139
Commonwealth, International Affairs Division, 149
Company of Merchants Trading into Africa, 16
Congo, 47, 55
Congress Party (India), 44, 52–53, 63, 79–82, 85, 89–90, 115–16
Constantine, Learie, 73
Convention's People's Party, 107, 108, 131–32
Cook, Captain James, 5
Copper, 54, 72, 101, 164
Corfield, Sir Conrad, 119

Organization of American States (OAS), 159
Organization of East Caribbean States, 173
Orissa, 46
Ormsby-Gore, William, 72
Ottawa Agreements, 78
Ottoman Empire, 17, 125, 128
Oudh, wazir of, 10, 11
Overseas Food Corporation, 108

P

Pacific, Commonwealth in the, 167, 169
Paice, Mervyn, 112
Pakistan, 91, 108, 115, 117, 118, 119, 120–21, 122, 145, 169, 175
Palestine Liberation Organization (PLO), 127
Palestine, 64, 65, 66, 73, 84, 85, 98–100, 111–13, 128. See also Israel
Palm oil, 53, 55
Pan-Arabism, 126–28
Papineau, Louis-Joseph, 25
Papua New Guinea, 167
Park, Mungo, 16
Parker, John, 105
Patel, Vithalbhai, 115, 117, 120, 121
Pearce, Lord, 138
Pearl Harbor, 85, 86
Pearls, 12,
Penal colonies, 12
Penang, 12
Persia, 45, 52, 66, 70. *See also* Iran
Persian Gulf States, 66, 70
Pethick-Lawrence, F. W., 115
Philippines, 158
Pindling, Lynden, 156

Pitt, William, the elder, 5
Pitt, William, the younger, 10, 18
Plantation colonies, 1–2, 28, 33
Plassey, Battle of, 8
Plowden Committee, 143
Poland, 84
Port Said, 124
Portuguese, 20, 21, 39, 40, 137, 138
Potsdam Conference, 103
Prasad, Rajendra, 121
Prisoners of war, 95
Profumo scandal, 137
Punjab, 91, 92, 117, 118–19, 120–21

Q

Québec, 4, 5–6, 13,
Québec Act, 13. *See also* Lower Canada

R

Racism, 20, 21, 24, 31, 32, 57, 101, 105–6, 133, 143, 144, 145, 146, 149, 159
Radcliffe, Sir Cyril, 119
Raffles, Thomas Stamford, 12
Rahmen Tunku Abdul, 111
Ramphal, Shridath S., 145, 153–54, 160, 170, 172, 173, 174, 175
Rangoon, 85
Rawlings, Jerry, 168
Reagan, Ronald, 164
Rebellions of 1837, 25, 26
Receprocity, 50
Reform Bill, 24
Responsible government, 14, 24, 25, 27–28, 35. *See also* Self-government

X

Xhosa, 22, 23

Y

Yemen, 126–28
Young, Edward Hilton, 71–72
Young, G. A., 14
Younghusband, Sir Francis, 45

Z

Zambia, 137, 138, 164
Zanzibar, 47
Zimbabwe African National Union,
    138, 139
Zimbabwe African People's Union,
    138
Zimbabwe, 140, 168. *See also*
    Southern Rhodesia
Zionism, 72–73
Zionist Organization, 99
Zionists, 65, 98–99, 111–12
Zulu War, 37
Zulus, 36, 37, 56